AN ANTHROPOLOGY OF ETHICS

Through an ambitious and critical revision of Michel Foucault's investigation of ethics, James D. Faubion develops an original program of empirical inquiry into the ethical domain. From an anthropological perspective, Faubion argues that Foucault's specification of the analytical parameters of this domain is the most productive point of departure in conceptualizing its distinctive features. He further argues that Foucault's framework is in need of substantial revision to be of genuinely anthropological scope. In making this revision, Faubion illustrates his program with two extended case studies: one of a Portuguese marquis and the other of a dual subject made up of the author and a millenarian prophetess. The result is a conceptual apparatus that is able to accommodate ethical pluralism and yield an account of the limits of ethical variation, providing a novel resolution of the problem of relativism that has haunted anthropological inquiry into ethics since its inception.

James D. Faubion is Professor of Anthropology and Director of Graduate Studies at Rice University. In addition to ethics, his interests include epistemic authority, kinship, social and cultural theory, aesthetics, heterodoxy and radicalism. He has published widely on research interests, including *The Shadows and Lights of Waco: Millennialism Today* (2001), and two edited volumes of *Essential Works of Michel Foucault* (1998 and 2000).

NEW DEPARTURES IN ANTHROPOLOGY

New Departures in Anthropology is a book series that focuses on emerging themes in social and cultural anthropology. With original perspectives and syntheses, authors introduce new areas of inquiry in anthropology, explore developments that cross disciplinary boundaries, and weigh in on current debates. Every book illustrates theoretical issues with ethnographic material drawn from current research or classic studies, as well as from literature, memoirs, and other genres of reportage. The aim of the series is to produce books that are accessible enough to be used by college students and instructors, but will also stimulate, provoke, and inform anthropologists at all stages of their careers. Written clearly and concisely, books in the series are designed equally for advanced students and a broader range of readers, inside and outside academic anthropology, who want to be brought up to date on the most exciting developments in the discipline.

Series Editorial Board

An Anthropology of Ethics

JAMES D. FAUBION
Rice University

CAMBRIDGE
UNIVERSITY PRESS

University Printing House, Cambridge CB2 8BS, United Kingdom

Published in the United States of America by Cambridge University Press, New York

Cambridge University Press is part of the University of Cambridge.

It furthers the University's mission by disseminating knowledge in the pursuit of education, learning and research at the highest international levels of excellence.

www.cambridge.org
Information on this title: www.cambridge.org/9780521181952

© James D. Faubion 2011

This publication is in copyright. Subject to statutory exception and to the provisions of relevant collective licensing agreements, no reproduction of any part may take place without the written permission of Cambridge University Press.

First published 2011

A catalogue record for this publication is available from the British Library

Library of Congress Cataloguing in Publication data

Faubion, James D. (James Daniel), 1957– , author.
  An Anthropology of Ethics / James D. Faubion.
    p.   cm. – (New Departures in Anthropology)
    ISBN 978-1-107-00494-8 (Hardback) – ISBN 978-0-521-18195-2 (Paperback)
  1. Foucault, Michel, 1926–1984.   2. Ethics.   I. Title.
  B2430.F724.F38 2011
  170.92–dc22

                                                            2010044489

ISBN 978-1-107-00494-8 Hardback
ISBN 978-0-521-18195-2 Paperback

Cambridge University Press has no responsibility for the persistence or accuracy of URLs for external or third-party internet websites referred to in this publication, and does not guarantee that any content on such websites is, or will remain, accurate or appropriate.

To Shirley Faubion Saunders, with love

Contents

Acknowledgments

Whether through intellectual or other efforts, several students, colleagues and supporters have done their part in seeing this project to a close – some without knowing it. Thanks are much in order to Michael Adair-Kriz, Ala Allazeh, Gaymon Bennett, Joanne Carpenter, Richard Fisher, Stephen Foster, Eugenia Georges, Ann Gleig, Sarah Graham, Hután Hejazi, Andrea Jain, Jeffrey Kripal, Michael Lambek, Daniel Levine, George Marcus, Elise McCarthy, Fernando Mascarenhas, Elinor Ochs, Valerie Olson, Susan Ossman, Stacey Pereira, Lyn Ragsdale, Lucy Rhymer, Amo Paul Bishop Roden, Alan Rumsey, Suzanne Shanahan, Jonathan Spencer, Carole Speranza, Anthony Stavrianakis, Helen Tartar and Cary Wolfe.

I have an enormous, unredeemable debt of gratitude to James Laidlaw, whose acute, meticulous, supportive and lengthy engagement with an earlier version of what follows has left me astonished ever since.

Special thanks go to Mary Murrell; she knows why.

Special thanks as always to Paul Rabinow and to William Düll, who will find an apology enclosed, should he care to look for it.

Some material used in *An Anthropology of Ethics* has previously appeared in my chapter "From the ethical to the themitical (and back): Groundwork for an anthropology of ethics," pp. 84–101, in *Ordinary Ethics: Anthropology, Language, and Action*, ed. Michael Lambek, New York: Fordham University Press, 2010, and is reproduced here with kind permission of Fordham University Press.

PART I

An anthropology of ethics

ONE

Precedents, parameters, potentials

The anthropology of ethics that I seek to develop has many precedents. Those that are theological, those that are grounded in an aprioristic rather than an empirical and thus unresolved concept of human nature and those that pursue the reduction of ethics to or its dissolution into alleged psychological or biological interests or instincts or needs are of little relevance. Or to be more precise: it does not follow but instead diverges from them. Its central precedent resides in the second and third volumes of Michel Foucault's *History of Sexuality* and in several of the interviews that Foucault saw published while he was engaging in the thinking and the research that resulted in those volumes.

Framing Foucault's work of that period are several versions of the concept of governmentality, a concept ranging over not merely such formal and often directly coercive apparatuses of intervention as state administrations and their police but also the great variety of more informal incitements and incentives that ask or invite human actors to govern themselves. Among such incitements and incentives are those that ask or invite actors to make themselves into subjects of esteemed qualities or kinds. Actors who take up such requests and invitations freely and self-reflexively are ethical actors, and their distinctive domain is the ethical domain, of which Foucault identifies four basic parameters. One of these he calls "ethical substance." It refers to that stuff – carnal pleasures, the soul, or what have you – which demands attention and fashioning if a given actor is to realize himself or herself as the subject he or she would be. The second parameter he calls the "mode of subjectivation." It refers to the manner in which a given actor evaluates and engages the criteria that determine what counts as living up to being a subject of one or another quality or kind. The third parameter is that of "askêsis," from the Greek for "training" or "exercise." It refers to the particular work that a given subject has to perform on his or her ethical substance in order to become a subject of a certain quality or kind. The fourth parameter is that of the "telos." It refers precisely to the subject that is the end of any given actor's striving.

Foucault more precisely thinks of the actor as striving toward the occupancy of a "subject position," and does so for at least two good reasons. First, actors are never born ethical subjects. The matter is not merely one of wearing the shoe that fits but also – and crucially – the converse: actors must always also adapt themselves to fit the styles and sizes available to them. Second, indefinitely many actors might strive toward the same telos; indefinitely many of them might thus end up being the same subject, if with idiosyncratic variations from one case to the next. That they thus end up as occupants of the same "position" does not, however, imply that they are prisoners of that position as it stands. Subject positions are malleable, if some more than others. Their legitimacy – or illegitimacy – is susceptible to contestation. As a consequence, they are susceptible to alteration, to coming and going. Positions available at any one point of time may accordingly not be available at another. They are subject to replacement, but also to displacement. Nor is the universe of such positions static. Invention is possible – and as Foucault himself demonstrates, it actually occurs.

Another virtue of Foucault's approach is its analytical and methodological parsimony. It conforms assiduously to the principle that one should not presume any more of the domain under one's investigation than is absolutely necessary; it is an exquisite exercise in the application of Occam's razor. Just such an exercise is all the more obligatory when the domain at issue is that of human action and human affairs. Parsimony does not, however, result in poverty. Foucault's approach is not identical to but still compatible with a systems-theoretic framework grounded in the distinction between an organized process capable of reproducing or rearticulating its organization in something longer than the shortest of short runs and the environment or environments in which it does so (Faubion 2001c: 98–100; cf. Luhmann 1990: 8–9). Any such process is more or less systematic, but as a consequence of those of its features and processes that enable its maintenance through time, it is also "autopoietic" and capable of "autopoiesis" – these latter two terms deriving from the Greek for "self" and "making" or "creation."

Autopoiesis is central to Niklas Luhmann's theoretical enterprise, as – under a somewhat different definition – it is to mine. Luhmann for his part distinguishes three general kinds of autopoietic systems: living, psychic or experiential, and social. Plants exemplify the first but not the remaining kinds. Human beings are not the only but for Luhmann as for me an especially relevant example of the second kind. Human beings constitute the central (but not the sufficient) condition of the existence of the social system. The environment of the autopoietic system may for its part provide not merely resources but also any number of what Luhmann refers to as "irritants" (Luhmann 1998: 62), other autopoietic systems perhaps among them.

It is doubtful that Foucault had ever even heard of Luhmann. Yet he was deeply familiar with at least one version of a systems-theoretic framework through the tutelage of his mentor, the historian of biology Georges Canguilhem. The history of biology is less mechanistic and more vitalistic for Canguilhem than for the classic Darwinist (Rabinow 1994). It is a history not merely of the adaptive match between an organism and its niche, but first and foremost of the maladaptive mismatch between the demands of the organism and the demands of its environments. Summarily, but in what also appears to be something of an endorsement, Foucault himself thus characterizes Canguilhem's view of the history of life as the history of "that which is capable of error" (Foucault 1998: 476; cf. Canguilhem 1989).

A commitment to vitalism might worry us. Yet Foucault asserts that Canguilhem's vitalism is merely "methodological" and what he seems to mean is that, Occamist in its own right, it resists relying on the presumption that vital structures and their dynamics are in all cases simple enough to be susceptible to the structural-functional resolutions that have dominated biological analysis from Aristotle to the neo-Darwinist evolutionary psychology of the present day. Whatever other biologists might think, investigators of human action and human affairs should thus be able to appreciate a systems-theoretical framework that is less teleological, less mechanistic, and less in danger of presuming the very conclusions that it purports to prove than the sort of (quasi-Darwinist) frameworks that they might find in A. R. Radcliffe-Brown, Talcott Parsons or – at least in the most abstract of his typically abstract turns of mind – even Luhmann himself.

I follow Luhmann in distinguishing human beings from the social. The former, again, are psychic or experiential systems (cf. Luhmann 1990: 67). The latter emerges from the communicative and practical interaction of psychic systems (1990: 167). The systematicity of the social has two strata. One is structural. It comprises institutions, statuses, roles and communicative codes. It is systemically open; institutions differentiate; statuses and roles are lost and acquired; codes display historicity, Derridian play, dissolution and reformation. Above that stratum, however, is yet another, which Luhmann terms organizational. It is cybernetically closed – above all, closed off from anything but mediated interaction with its environment, self-monitoring and self-referential. Whatever else, a social system remains a social system – for as long, at least, as it remains capable of autopoiesis and so is not the victim of its environment. Luhmann thus characterizes the social system as such as the "recursively closed organization of an open system" and so can insist that systems theory as he proffers it transcends the common presumption of the opposition between closed and open systems (1990: 12).

The result has its model-theoretical rationale; not least, it insulates the theory itself from the paradoxes that can arise when self-reference has no limit. That virtue, however, comes with a cost that I am unwilling to accept. Its cost is all the more clear in considering Humberto Maturana and Francisco Varela's development of a theory of the recursively closed organization of an open system, to which Luhmann himself is greatly indebted. The theory at issue has cognition as its primary object (Maturana and Varela 1980, 1992). Maturana and Varela treat cognition as an emergent phenomenon and the precondition of its emergence the brain itself. Its cybernetic closure off from its environment has its putative guarantee in the mediatory buffer of the perceptual apparatus. Such closure is, however, disputable even in the case of cognition. It is all the more disputable in the case of the social system. As I shall argue at length in the chapters that follow, Luhmann's rationale for the organizational closure of the social system is neither analytically nor empirically compelling enough to sustain. Among other things, it is insufficiently Occamist.

Even if opened up all the way, the theory of the social system as a communicative system is not the source of the logic of ethics. It is the source instead of the structural and processual hallmarks of ethics as a distinctive orientation of action. Whether or not Foucault might have cared to endorse it, such a framework – once rendered resolutely open and thus a framework in which neither the autopoietic system nor its environment can be conceived as closed (or, more technically, as definable) – will fill a good portion of what will literally appear as the fine print of the chapters that follow. I will also cast in fine print a variety of other technical and scholarly considerations that readers whose inclinations are as pedantic as my own will likely find of interest, but that readers of the educated lay sort (of which, I admit, there may be few) will likely care to ignore. What is indispensable about the framework at issue is its raising the question of the ethical – ontologically and epistemologically – to the level of the collective from the level of the individual (or "subjective"), at which, as Habermas especially has recognized, the very intelligibility of the ethical dissolves in the end into nothing but the unintelligibilty of what is typically put forward as personal opinion.

At no point will readers find me attempting to derive from the facts of autopoietic systems and their environments or, for that matter, from any other facts, any axioms or imperatives of a properly ethical order. The naturalistic fallacy that G. E. Moore (1903: 9–15) and many others would accuse me of committing were I to do so probably is a fallacy, though whether this is so remains something of a matter of philosophical dispute (e.g. Hare 1967; Searle 1967). If to commit it is indeed to err, then doing so is broadly and widely human and certainly doesn't exclude the commissioner from the ethical domain. (The Greek cynics were enthusiasts of it, though not in so many words; cf. Foucault 2009: 234). Yet Occamist rigor once again advises against embracing an inferential license that is neither essential nor uncontroversial. Hence, in accord with Foucault's precedent in *The History of Sexuality*, my project here is not "normative." In other words, I neither begin nor conclude with some collection of directives of judgment and conduct that would constitute what is usually called an "ethics" or a "moral philosophy."

If of necessity I exercise introspection throughout this project, and if the ethical system that I have internalized – that is, my own, recognizably Western – is as good an example of an ethical system as any other, I nevertheless do not rest with introspection alone and do not take what I might find through introspection as the irrevocable conceptual bedrock on which anything cognizable as ethics must be built. This is the primary methodological respect in which an anthropology of ethics as I understand it departs from the typical moral philosophy. As will become apparent, it does not preclude but nevertheless qualifies my appeal to philosophical precedent. Moral and ethical philosophers count as much among my natives as they count among my advisors. My project – like many other anthropological projects – deploys the data of introspection and the data of empirical investigation dialectically, in the sense that the former guide and must guide the formulation of my working postulates of what constitutes the ethical domain just as the latter must correct, enlarge and enrich what intuitively I presume the ethical domain to be. It is, in short, a project of interpretation – with one important qualification. It belongs to the *Geisteswissenschaften*, but always under the control of what is ultimately a cybernetic or more broadly information-theoretic metric, a metric both corrective and having explanatory force and function.

As a project of thus qualified interpretation, it addresses among other things ethical discourses, and addresses them as distinctive semiotic fields that invite such treatment as the philosophical analyst of concepts as well as the anthropological analyst of symbols might offer. If possible at all, ethical inference is possible only intra-discursively, unless precise semantic equivalences can be established across discourses. Short of that, the casuistic drawing of analogies remains possible, but as with any casuistic procedure, always liable to dispute. An anthropology of ethics that left matters just at that, however, would risk substituting a "discursive relativism" for an older "cultural relativism" that itself fell short of generating an explanation of anything at all, even when it was still possible to believe that cultures were integrated wholes of insular specificity as veritably and irreducibly individual as any of the individuals whose cultures they were. A systems-theoretical framework is one of the devices to which I resort in aspiring not to beg many of the questions that a discursively relativistic framework would continue to beg as much as a culturally relativistic framework did before it or does still. Such questions include those that arise in noting the striking similarities among persons of similar class and status everywhere. They include those that arise in noting that, for all its variety, the ethical imagination seems not to vary endlessly and that its basic schematics are considerably fewer than the relativist allows. They include the question of what ethical discourse distinctively communicates and what ethical action distinctively effects. They include the most fundamental of questions: Why ethics? Why is there this thing that we call "ethics" at all? It is difficult to see how either the discursive or the cultural relativist could even begin effectively to pose such questions, much less avoid triviality in answering them.

Jointly and severally, these questions point to precedents beyond that of Foucault alone. Nietzsche's *Genealogy of Morals* (1956) is an inescapable if troubled one. The sociology of religion after Nietzsche remains a particularly plentiful source. The most imposing of its precedents lies with Max Weber's exploration of the "elective affinities" (or lack of affinities) between various religiously sanctioned directives of conduct and the structural-functional imperatives of various means and modes of economic production, with special reference to industrial capitalism. His exploration yields not merely the diagnosis of Calvinist discipline secularized to serve the god of profit that is the centerpiece of *The Protestant Ethic and the Spirit of Capitalism* (1958a). It also yields a diagnosis of the existential core of the world religions, the grand dichotomy between mysticism and asceticism, and the norm of calculability as the regulative principle of a technically rationalist modernity (1958a: 24). Among its successors are Robert Bellah's analysis in *Tokugawa Religion* of Ishida Baigan's eclectic recalibration of Confucian, Daoist and Shinto doctrines in order to allow them to accommodate the legitimacy of the merchant's life and practices (Bellah 1957). A notable parallel is Jacques Le Goff's analysis of the gradual theological accommodation of the charging and collection of interest in medieval Christian Europe (1980). Peter Brown has pursued an array of Weberian themes in his many contributions to the social and cultural history of late antiquity and early Christianity (Brown 1980, 1982, 1988, 1995,

2003). Luc Boltanski and Eve Chiapello (2005) and Nikolas Rose (2006) have sought to update Weber's original argument; Ulrich Beck and Anthony Giddens have also contributed to doing so along the way (Beck, Giddens and Lash 1994; Giddens 1991).

In anthropology, Clifford Geertz treads some of the territory that Weber did not reach in his research into the correlates of class, status and religious sensibilities in Java, elsewhere in Indonesia and in Morocco (Geertz 1960, 1963, 1968). As James Laidlaw (2002), Joel Robbins (2004) and Jarrett Zigon (2007) have all argued, Durkheim's effective reduction of morality to social norms has done as much to foreclose as to stimulate an anthropology of ethics. Yet it has not foreclosed it as thoroughly as they jointly suggest. Philosopher Alexander Macbeath draws on Durkheimian anthropology in his *Experiments in Living* (1952) though – perhaps not as self-consciously as Durkheim before him – may well commit the naturalistic fallacy along his way. Mary Douglas' discernment of the correlations between modalities of social organization and modalities of cosmology in *Natural Symbols* is hardly less large than Macbeath's in its reach, but it is logically more cautious, as is her later work on class standing, the perception of risk and danger and the assignation of blame (Douglas 1970; Douglas and Wildavsky 1982). A large number of American anthropologists in both the Boasian and the psychoanalytic traditions have contributed to the ethnographic documentation of ethical variation, though rarely with the theoretical direction that the Weberian and Durkheimian programs both provide in their way (see Graeber 2001: 3–5).

The ethical domain is also very much a part of contemporary anthropological horizons, and not merely because anthropologists continue to worry over their own professional ethics or because a number of them suffuse their own research and writing with the ethical position that they personally hold most dear. Unsurprisingly, the best of recent contributions to an anthropology of ethics tend to acknowledge Foucault as at least one forerunner. Talal Asad's *Genealogies of Religion*

(1993) is among these, as are Heather Paxson's exploration of reproduction and mothering in Greece (2004), Joel Robbins' investigation of Christian sectarians in Papua New Guinea (2004), Saba Mahmood's study of a women's pietistic movement in Egypt (2005), Elizabeth Davis' study of the relations between psychologists and their patients at an outpost in Greek Thrace (forthcoming) and certain of the essays that Michael Fischer includes in his *Emergent Forms of Life and the Anthropological Voice* (2003; see also Howell 1997; Humphrey 1997; and Lambek 2003). I have made three previous forays of my own. The first juxtaposed Foucault, Aristotle and Luhmann in considering the principles and possibilities of a general program in the anthropology of ethics (Faubion 2001c). The second, more empirically grounded, made up part of the investigation of the works and days of a Branch Davidian claimant to prophetic authority (Faubion 2001b: 115–159; much more below). The third addressed the claims, the duties and the existential hallmarks of kinship (Faubion 2001a; cf. Faubion and Hamilton 2007).

Some (perhaps many) readers may find the first part of what follows all too reminiscent of a nineteenth-century quest for sweeping taxonomies and universal-historical schemata. I am reluctant to affirm the resemblance, but do admit that these chapters are generalist in their design and thus stand in contrast to the prevailing particularisms of so much of current sociocultural research. I approve of most such particularisms. I think that many of them in many instances admit of no responsible alternative. I also think that generalities are sometimes in order. They are in order when they serve to clarify and facilitate the analysis of both the limits and the variations of those domains of human ideation and practice that press toward being collective necessities and thus toward (near-)universal collective distribution, as the ethical domain does. In any event, such is my argument.

Contrary to many of my nineteenth-century predecessors, however, I do not put that argument forward with any presumption that it might or should stand forever – or even briefly – as the only, the consummate, the definitive anthropology of ethics. I presume that the anthropology of ethics consists of an array of diagnostics and theoretical models, of which the one I construct is precisely that – one. Hence the title of the book: not "the anthropology of ethics" but "an (I repeat: an) anthropology of ethics." I would insist only that any anthropologically worthy version of a diagnostics of the ethical domain must address most if not all of the matters of methodological design, thematic parsimony and analytical scale that I myself feel obliged to consider. I offer my results as additions to the anthropological toolkit and each tool labeled with a simple and what to my mind is a quite contemporary instruction: use as needed.

Less ambiguously timely is my effort to clarify the parameters of the ethical domain at a period when I am far from alone in observing that talk of ethics is not often very clear but very often in the air, within anthropology and, as I have already noted, just as much outside of it. In the course of that effort, I also develop tools with which to sharpen conceptually a term that is a contemporary commonplace – within anthropology and outside of it – and perhaps because a commonplace, all too often taken semantically and analytically for granted. The commonplace is that of identity. I confess to having had almost enough of ethnographic inquiries into and too often uncritically essentialist valorizations of this, that or the next identity. In what follows, however, I do not seek to overthrow a commonplace that even in having become something of an idol of the anthropological tribe still has a genuine conceptual function. As a concept, identity needs some demystifying, but once demystified proves to denote a dimension of practice and the organization of practice that no other term, no other concept we currently have, appears to register as precisely. It proves specifically to be irreducible to the more classic sociological concepts of status and role. Even anthropologists need the occasional idol, after all.

An anthropology of ethics

Even more timely, I submit, is my broader effort to develop a diagnostics and a theoretical model capable of a clear-sighted approach to and an elucidation of the consequences of what I will call (at the risk of resorting to another anthropological commonplace) ethical "complexity." Such complexity arises in its simplest form if and when one ethical subject (more technically, the occupant of one or another ethically marked subject position) finds himself or herself or itself to be yet a second ethical subject. Complexity thus realized is hardly only a present-day affair, but it is among the cardinal stimuli both of present-day ethical uncertainties and present-day ethical preoccupations. It merits attending. For reasons – often perfectly good and understandable reasons – that I will educe at length in the first part of the book, Foucault's own diagnostics of the ethical field is weak in its address of complexity and so in need of particular adjustments in two respects. First, it does not formally provide a place for the individual subject of two or more ethical commissions. This is not to say that ethical dyads (or triads, or . . .) have no Foucauldian place. On the contrary. When Foucault pronounces that "the freedom of the subject and its relation to others" is "the very stuff of ethics," he means it (Foucault 1997a: 300). Yet, second, his diagnostic treatment of the complexity of the relations and the dynamics of the relations between ethical subjects and their ethical and extra-ethical others is largely limited to their parrhêsiastic dimensions. His last lectures at the Collège de France suggest that he was seeking the governmental conditions of the existence of and the technologies of the formation and practice of a parrhêsiastic ethics – the reflexive practice of freely and directly speaking the truth (Foucault 2008, 2009.) Such adjustments as I will make to Foucauldian diagnostics respect that quest at the same time that they distance themselves from its specificity. They may not be as elegant as possible, but I hope that they amount to more than mere cosmetic repairs.

If generalist in its propositions, the first part of this book is not indifferent to matters of the applicability of its diagnostics to particular cases. I am not a trained classicist and not thus a philologist, but I have a long-standing and reasonably educated interest in Greek and Roman antiquity, can read much of the Greek that was recorded from the later archaic period forward and have often indulged it in my work to date. Anthropologists had a more regular interest in antiquity in (once again) the nineteenth and early twentieth centuries, when they could depend with some confidence on the great majority of their readership having been tutored in the classics and having at least a passing familiarity with the gods, goddesses and myths that could be found in them. Contrary to my predecessors, I have no concern with pronouncing whether the ancient Greeks were primitive (as such armchair practitioners as Edward Burnett Tylor and, even more emphatically, James Frazer held them to be) or modern (as the roving Louis Henry Morgan held them to be – just for the record). I am well aware that most readers now are likely to find the denizens of classical Athens as foreign and unfamiliar as the denizens of Yap or interior Amazonia, but I return to them here because the ancient and philosophically inclined are, after all, the very denizens that inspire Foucault's own development of a diagnostics of the ethical domain. Like the philosophically inclined ever since, they have their particularities and so their anthropological limits. In revisiting those particularities and those limits, I often find the sources of the particularities and the limits of Foucault's diagnostics itself. In the process, I make use of the ancient corpus but also of a considerable body of classical scholarship. Occasionally, I can't resist passing judgment on one or another anthropologically tempted classicist's ethical presumptuousness or too facile appeal to one or another well-worn piece of outdated anthropological wisdom. Philosophers and classicists are likely to pass judgment on the facile anthropologist as well, which is entirely their prerogative.

In the second part of this project I turn more exclusively to applications and so to fieldwork in ethics proper, which methodologically need not be but here largely is the pursuit and sociocultural contextualization of life histories. Some of the fieldwork is entirely my own. Hence, I pay a retrospective visit to the primary subject of my *Shadows and Lights of Waco*, Amo Paul Bishop Roden. I do so not to repeat the portrait of Ms. Roden's ethics that constitutes the third chapter of that book, however much I will keep it in mind. I do so instead to illustrate and confirm the possibility that the ethical subject can be a composite subject of an indefinite number of players and places. In the case at hand that number is precisely two and subsists in the anthropologist and his primary subject as a pair, Ms. Roden and me. If I may say so, we make quite the pair.

Some of the fieldwork is only partly my own. Hence, in my rendering of the works and days and thoughts of Fernando Mascarenhas, the current holder of the title (among many others) of Marquis of the Portuguese houses of Fronteira and Alorna, I rely on the extensive record of written exchanges and face-to-face meetings that transpired between Fernando (as he has insisted I call him) and George Marcus, which have come into print as *Ocasião: The Marquis and the Anthropologist, A Collaboration* (Marcus and Mascarenhas 2005). Marcus and Fernando first made their acquaintance during a conference on the anthropology of elites that Fernando hosted at his palace on the outskirts of Lisbon. Several months later, the project that led to *Ocasião* began to gather steam, much of it at first over email. Not long after that, Marcus and I began discussing Fernando, matters of European nobility, the sociocultural significance of the noble house and so on, and continued to do so even as *Ocasião* was in its final stages. In the interim, I accompanied Marcus twice to Lisbon: first, to participate in a series of interviews with Fernando and some dozen other members of the Portuguese nobility; second, to attend a conference that gathered together some forty members of the same nobility, held once again at Fernando's palace. I subsequently returned alone to Lisbon to conduct a series of interviews with him concerning matters of his biography and his ethical development that did not find clear, or found only partial, articulation in his collaboration with Marcus. Fernando also read a roughly final draft of the chapter that appears here. He corrected my factual errors and offered occasional editorial comments, which appear in the chapter within brackets. As will be seen, for reasons both personal and sociocultural, Fernando is an unusually self-aware ethical actor and thinker. His "Sermon to [his] Successor," which I translated into English with him and which appears as an appendix to *Ocasião*, is a brief but genuine ethical treatise. His is a special but still illustrative case of contemporary ethical complexity. He is a marquis, but is so in a state that no longer officially recognizes noble privilege. He is thus also a common man, though a commoner of considerable material and social means. The two do not always quite coincide. In just this sense, Fernando might be regarded as a composite ethical subject whose occupant is a single mindful body. It is a matter of research how many others among us are of the same legion – but many of us may turn out to have more in common with a Portuguese marquis than at first we might think we do.

My third and final subject belongs to the past and so demands historical fieldwork, if not of nearly as much depth as fieldwork in classical Athens. As with fieldwork in Athens, it owes much to previous scholarship. The subject is once again Greek – or as he preferred, a "Hellene," so distinguishing himself from those Greeks residing in and taking part in the affairs of the Greek state – and reflects my long-term interest in Greeks both modern and ancient. He further reflects a similarly enduring interest in the anthropology of literature. Constantine Cavafy (such is the anglicized transcription – of which the subject himself approved – of Konstantinos Kavafês) was a polyglot member of the Greek diaspora, born in Alexandria in the later part of the nineteenth century and dying there near the end of the first third of the twentieth century. He wrote essays in English and in Greek, but wrote almost all of the poems for which he is now renowned in the slightly idiomatic Greek of a prominent diasporic community that declined to ever fewer numbers from the time of Egyptian independence forward. To many minds, Cavafy is the greatest of modern Greek poets, of higher achievement than the leading "national" poet, lyricist of the Greek national anthem, Dionusios Solômos, greater even than Lenin Prize winner Yiannis Ritsos or Nobelists George Seferis and Odysseas Elytis.

Hellenophones and Hellenographs will note that, throughout, my transliterations of both ancient and modern Greek names show the same frustrated inconsistencies that confront anyone who deals with other than Roman systems of writing and with figures sometimes well known and sometimes little known or unknown in Roman script. I follow established anglicized transliterations in my use of names that I judge to be already sufficiently familiar to readers of English or in place in established English translation. The former include Seferis, Elytis, Socrates, Plato and Aristotle. The latter include Aischines and (sometimes) Cavafy. I follow current classicist transcriptional practice in bringing into English names and terms that I judge insufficiently known or subject to inconsistencies of established translation or in need of precise identification for technical purposes. I do so with two exceptions. Classicists would prefer macrons where I resort to circumflexes – hence ê for the Greek eta (as opposed to e for epsilon) and ô for omega (as opposed to o for omicron). In modern Greek, beta is not pronounced as the English /b/, but rather as /v/. Hence, in my transliterations of modern Greek names and terms, I have beta appearing as v – Konstantinos Kavafês, for example, rather than the unbearable Konstantinos Kabafês. Not everyone will share my judgment of which mode of transliteration is the more warranted from one instance to another. I sympathize.

During his own lifetime, Cavafy won important literary admirers, some national Greeks and others from the literary metropoles, E. M. Forster and Lawrence Durrell prominent among them. He was, however, far from the heights of the modern Greek canon and the slightly veiled – though not as far as Forster or Durrell were concerned – homoeroticism of his later poems likely to provoke disgust as much as praise. Cavafy was above all a resident of closets – from the colonial to the declassed to the homoerotic closet – and a skillful negotiator of all of them. More laboriously, he also succeeded – in any event, in his own eyes, and with a sense of only partial success – in negotiating a synthesis of aestheticism and ethics that such aestheticist decadents as Charles Baudelaire or Paul Verlaine themselves rejected. Cavafy was ethically too haunted – and too much the man of appearances – to follow their lead. In his last lectures, Foucault points to the modern artist as one of the heirs to ancient cynicism and especially to the cynical commitment to the unadorned, uninhibited and uncompromised telling of the truth – to parrhêsia. That artist materializes under the aegis of a cardinal idea:

that art itself, whether it is a matter of literature, of painting, of music, must establish with the real a relation that is no longer of the order of ornamentation, of the order of imitation, but which is of the order of posing in the nude, of scouring, of excavation, of violent reduction to the elementals of existence. (2009: 173, my translation)

Foucault notes that a parrhêsiastic art unfolds even more markedly from the middle of the nineteenth century forward. His examples are all French. Cavafy is thus not among them. He is among them in fact. As man, he cultivated his share of evasions. As poet, in content and in style, he was Foucault's artist-cynic par excellence.

In the interest of conserving paper (and limiting costs), I have refrained from including my treatment of Cavafy in the book proper. It can be found instead at my personal website: http://anthropology. rice.edu/Content.aspx?id=50.

Cavafy's residence in Alexandria does not allow me to pretend that I am anything more than a Euro-Americanist – should anyone care to insist on the point. I have my limits. I do not, however, think that those limits are the source of an intrinsically Euro-American myopia.

For one thing, Euro-Americans have more ethically in common than they think – and than many anthropologists think – with many of the peoples that have long been the subjects (or objects) of the anthropological gaze, as such recent researchers as Lambek and Robbins have compellingly established. In order to underscore the point and by way of conclusion, I consider again the rationale for a programmatic approach to the anthropology of ethics and with the variety of subjects it is bound to encounter – or yet to encounter. I thus underscore that the anthropology of ethics has both a past and a future.

Coinage should be avoided, but I have resorted to it in one instance. I thus make a distinction between the ethical domain as a totality, and what is "themitical" within it. What I seek to register with that distinction is an important and related series of cognitive, affective, semiotic, pragmatic and structural differences between the more ecological and dynamic and the more homeostatic and reproductive aspects of ethical autopoiesis – the becoming and maintenance of the ethical subject. My fashioning of it has certain elements in common with Jarrett Zigon's recently circulating intuition that ethics is peculiarly visible in moments of "moral breakdown" (Zigon 2007), but ultimately differs from his own distinction between the ethical and the moral both semantically and diagnostically. Above all and counter to what Zigon suggests, I resist both semantically and diagnostically any construal of the dynamic and the homeostatic dimensions of the ethical field as mutually contradictory. I also resist any presumption that the ethics of everyday, ordinary life is without reflection or self-reflexivity. My own distinction is more closely related but still not equivalent to the distinction that has reemerged in the Anglo-American analytical tradition of philosophy in the past couple of decades between an "ethics" centered on the concept of virtue and the rest of "moral philosophy" (see e.g. MacIntyre 1984; Nussbaum 1992). I develop it at length in the third of my chapters.

Recent philosophical usage is a partial echo of Hegel's earlier distinction between *Sittlichkeit* and *Moralität*. The distinction is often translated into English as that between "ethics" or "ethical substance" or "ethical life" and "morality" (Hegel 1952). Within Hegel's philosophy of right, it functions to mark the contrast between the embodiment, the taking into one's flesh and bones, of the only valid corpus of principles of proper conduct and that corpus itself. It is in its own right a partial echo of a tradition extending back to antiquity that distinguishes the exercise of practical reason and decision-making from the corpus of precepts or principles to which that exercise would have to conform in order to "be right" or "for the good." Hegel's distinction for its part still presumes that the domain of rectitude and goodness must include some perfectly general set of principles of conduct – categorical imperatives or commandments – that establish its bylaws. It is thus a distinction of insufficient anthropological generality, since it excludes traditions that engage or respond to questions of rectitude and goodness by appeal either to analogous situational precedents or to more timelessly conceived exemplars. The former traditions include that of casuistry, now denigrated but still alive and more or less well in case law. The latter traditions are widespread, the precise stuff of legend the world over. Though Plato was a great critic of it (see Robb 1994), pedagogical appeal to exemplars remained an important part of the formulation of practical judgment and codification throughout antiquity. Homer's *Iliad* (1951) and Plutarch's *Lives of the Noble Greeks and Romans* (2001) are among other things guidebooks of the heroic way, as is the New Testament for those devoted – in antiquity and much after it – to the ethics of the *imitatio Christi*. More in the fashion of the Old Testament, the Greek and Latin historians, comedians and satirists offer more complex collections, in which bad examples often grab the stage from their nobler counterparts.

It must be admitted and is worth noting in any case that, however it might substantively be made, the distinction between "ethics" and "morals" or "ethics" and "morality" at the sheer level of terminology has little etymological warrant. "Ethics" derives from the Greek *êthika* (neuter plural of the adjectival *êthikos*), a term for an inquiry into or treatise concerning *êthos*, which means "custom" or "usage" but also "disposition" or "character" (also a "customary place"). Êthos is a synonym of the Latin

Hence, politikê might rest largely in the order of the homeostatic, or more simply, in being. In this precise respect, it is on a par with the themitical – and also with what I would myself formerly have designated as "morality." Discussion and commentary at a workshop on ordinary ethics of which Michael Lambek graciously invited me to Toronto in 2008 to be part has convinced me, however, that yet another stipulative foray into the semantics of "ethics" versus those of "morality" is likely to become entangled – and sooner rather than later – in the thick and inconsistent morass of the forays that have preceded it. I see no other alternative as a consequence than neologism. Hence, "themitical" – after the Greek *themitos*, "allowed by the laws of the gods and of men, righteous," as Liddell and Scott's venerable *English–Greek Lexicon* has it. The themitical dimension of the ethical field is hardly without its own dynamics, but they belong largely to the order of the reproduction of what at any particular place and point in time constitutes the regnant normative order, though in its normativity an order that may include values, ideals and exemplars as well as imperatives. Such at least is the meaning I assign to "normativity" here and throughout.

The broader ethical field to which the themitical is internal must always also have one foot at least in the dynamics of production, of becoming, indeed of self-becoming. This is Foucault's particular illumination of that field, but it comes in some measure at the expense of doing full justice to the themitical itself. I have already sought to defend Foucault's approach to the ethical domain against critiques that construe it as aestheticist or individualistic (Faubion 2001c). I accordingly visit the issue only occasionally. I am not in any event aiming to add further commentary, whether laudatory or deprecatory, to the corpus that Foucault's approach has already inspired. I do not aim to fashion either a Foucauldian or an anti-Foucauldian anthropology of ethics. In the two chapters that follow, I am instead a shameless revisionist.

TWO

Foucault in Athens

From flesh to virtue

Sojourner in Sidi Bou Said, Uppsala, Warsaw, San Francisco, Michel Foucault to my knowledge never visited Athens even for a day. Nor is there anything in the first volume of *The History of Sexuality* (Foucault 1978) that anticipated so long a stay as he passed in the ancient world in the last years of his life. In Foucault's initial conception of it, the genealogy of the ethico-medical and biopolitical inscription of sexual desire as and at the heart of our modern being was not historically deep. It was instead a largely nineteenth-century affair. It involved the secularization and psychiatrization of the confessional, the pathologization of masturbation and other putatively wasteful and enervating sexual practices, the development of the diagnostics and theory of female hysteria, the elaboration of a constellation of perversions and, informing it all, the gradual elaboration of an apologia discrediting the "peculiarity" of aristocratic blood in favor of the vitality and fecundity of an ascendant bourgeoisie (1978: 126). The second (1985) and the third (1986) volumes of *The History* are testaments to Foucault's recognition that certain strands of the genealogical fabric of sexuality were in fact historically woven at much greater length than he had at first considered. Even in its earliest establishment, the confession establishes that talk of sex which the *scientia sexualis* of the nineteenth century will codify into genera, species and sub-species of healthy and unhealthy, normal and abnormal pleasures and their correlative types of character. Well prior to that, in classical Athens, a philosophical elite already embarks on the problematization of sexual and other carnal pleasures that will ultimately yield a heteronormativity which, once divested of the most overt of its Christian trappings, the scientia sexualis will be ready fully to endorse.

Sensing among other things a mollification of the rhetorical acidity that is a hallmark of so much of Foucault's earlier work, many readers have been tempted to construe the second volume of *The History* as a change of direction, an abandonment of genealogical inquiry in favor of something more familiarly and palatably philosophical. They have their point. The lectures that Foucault offered at the Collège de France from 1981 through 1983 and many of his essays and interviews that appeared from 1981 forward testify to an increasing and increasingly urgent preoccupation with what the second volume of *The History* first identified as the ethics of *le souci de soi*, the care of or concern for the self. They testify further to a triangulation of focus: on the relation between the ethics of the care of the self as a mode of self-governance and the stewardship, the governance, of others; on the relation between the governance of others and the philosophical practice of parrhêsia, of a particular mode of truth-telling; and on the relation between parrhêsia and the ethics of the care of the self (Foucault 2005, 2008, 2009). Matters of sex and sexuality are nevertheless what bring Foucault to his philosophical triangle, which he himself neatly summarizes by resort to a triad of Greek terms: *alêtheia* (truth), *politeia* (polity), *êthos* (character, habitus, habitat). They remain central to the thematics of *The Care of the Self* – still cast, after all, as the third volume of *The History of Sexuality* (Foucault 1986). Closets and their evasions, more-over, haunt Foucault's fascination with cynical parrhêsia, especially in the last of his lectures at the Collège – notably entitled *Le courage de la vérité*, "The Courage of the Truth." Though I will never be, Foucault will one day have his psychoanalytic biographer (and, in rather crude and definitely partial form, has already had one: see Davidson 2007), for whom the last lectures will provide rich fodder.

In any event, only against the double background of a genealogical inquiry into the emergence of the concept of sexuality and an increasingly philosophical preoccupation with the triangulation of self-governance, the governance of others and speaking the truth does the selectivity at once of Foucault's attention to classical ethical discourse and of the questions that he poses to it in the second volume come fully to the fore. Only against that background can we begin to make proper sense of his very contention that the ancients had no conception of sexuality and so of either heterosexuality or homosexuality as we know them, much less of where that contention does – and does not – take him. Though he has been, Foucault should not be misunderstood to be contending that the ancients lacked any conception of something like "sexual orientation," even of an orientation defined in accord with whether it is directed to an object of the same or of the opposite sex (cf. Cohen 1991: 171–172). Having read Kenneth Dover's *Greek Homosexuality* (1978) and incorporating it thoroughly into his scholarly apparatus, Foucault is aware that there are several loci in the ancient corpus that strongly suggest that such a conception was available. The archaic poet Anacreon's lament, presumed to have Sappho as its subject, is one:

Once again golden-haired Eros strikes me with his porphyry ball and summons me to play together with the girl in the fancy sandals; but she's one of those of Lesbos, and finds fault with my hair, for it is white, and is gaping rather at some girl. (1988: 57 [Anac. 13.599c]; translation slightly modified)

However much it might be deployed for comic effect, the theory of erotic half-souls questing for union that Plato puts into the mouth of Aristophanes in his *Symposium* is another (1961: 542–543 [189c3–193d]) and Foucault addresses it straightforwardly (1985: 232–233). Aischines' insinuations about the consequences of the pederastic relationship gone awry in denouncing his opponent Timarchus is yet another:

[The legislator] regulates the festivals of the Muses in the schoolrooms, and of Hermes in the wrestling schools. Finally, he regulates the companionships that the boys may form at school, and their cyclic dances. He prescribes, namely, that the choragus, a man who is going to spend money for your entertainment, shall be a man of more than forty years of age when he performs this service, in order that he may have reached the most temperate (*sôfrônestatê*) time of life before he comes into contact with your children.

These laws, then, shall be read to you to prove that the lawgiver believed that it is the boy who has been well brought up that will be a useful citizen when he becomes a man. But when a boy's natural disposition (*phusis*) is subjected at the very outset to vicious (*ponêran*) training, the product of such wrong nurture will be, as he believed, a citizen like this man Timarchus. (1919: 10–13 [Aes. 10.6–11.12])

No "gay gene" at issue here. Nor are Timarchus' alleged failings merely sexual. Among them, however, is voluntary self-prostitution beyond his boyhood and taking up extended residence in the lodgings of the men who would pay him for "the thing" he "wanted to do" and to which he "willingly submitted" (37 [41–42]). Similarly submissive and wanton men – younger or older – might thus earn the degrading epithet of *kinaidos* (plural *kinaidoi*). Liddell and Scott gloss the term as "catamite," but its range extends beyond the sexual to include social deviance, social ineptitude, social disgrace (Winkler 1990).

The evaluation of women's sexual conduct – at least free-born women's sexual conduct – revolved primarily around whether or not it constituted *moikheia*, "adultery" or "fornication" or, even more gravely, *porneia*, "prostitution," and thus of matters fundamentally more adverbial than adjectival. A woman's sexual liaison with another man outside marriage was typically denounced as moikheia, though in the classical period at least, the term *moikhos*, (male) "adulterer," has its only attested feminine counterpart in Aristophanes' declamation in *The Symposium* (191e). The sanction of liaisons between women, however, is deeply unclear. Anacreon stands alone in complaining – or at least fussing – about Sappho's alleged "orientation" and might well have complained more about her well-documented husband, who would likely have sought to thwart his interests. As Dover points out, several of the vase paintings depict women in what appears to be mutual sexual play (1978: 173) – though this is hardly evidence that such play was positively regarded. The classical corpus leaves us instead with little evidence but that female homosexual practices won only scant notice, much less anything that would suggest worried scrutiny.

That these and other sexual practices appear in other words to have been semiotically unmarked was certainly not because the Greeks understood women to be either asexual or uninterested in sexual pleasure. Multiple genres of the ancient corpus, from medical and biological writings to the comedies, amply record the opposite. It seems instead to reflect the widespread doxa that what women do sexually – so long as it does not constitute moikheia or porneia – simply makes no difference. Nor can it make any difference: women, by prevailing ancient definition, are naturally equipped only to be sexually "passive," and so can only ever occupy a single place, a single register, in the ancient sexual economy. One can discover a woman in flagrante delicto and, if one is her husband or brother or father, may not hesitate to beat her for being so discovered. Yet it is probably anachronistic – or at least not doxic – to cast her as someone who "commits" adultery. This would attribute to her an *energeia*, an "agency" in the satisfaction of her desire of which Greek men at least did not seem to believe her capable. Ancient women from Helen forward could be and were blamed for their sexual errancies, but they were always also the victims, often the tragic victims, of lusts and passions and appetites that remained beyond their ability to control. Greek men could thus assume the role of being their *kurioi*, "lords" or "stewards" (cf. Hunter 1994: 9–11), as not merely a matter of preference but what doxically was a matter of necessity. Greek men alone were thought to be equipped with the instrument of proper sexual agency and enough *logos* or "powers of reason" to be master of it.

An anthropology of ethics

The stability and subliminality of doxa as what is "taken for granted" have their direct correlates in the stability "of objective structures" and their reproduction "in agents' dispositions" (Bourdieu 1977: 165–166). Social complexity, of which class and status stratification are fundamental constituents in ancient Greece as elsewhere, tends to unsettle doxa just to the extent – an often notable extent – to which it is also an index of competition and conflict. If we can trust Hesiod's *Works and Days* to offer us a rare if still oblique document of something approaching – perhaps through *déclassement* (Adkins 1972: 23–35) – a middle-class, perhaps an even lower than middle-class, perspective, the suspicion of women's capacity for self-control and moral probity seems to have been all the more adamantly doxic the farther one stood from the elite. As Hesiod put it, "You trust a thief when you trust a woman" (1983: 76 [w&D 375]). Leslie Kurke's treatment of what appear to be class-indexed regimes of representation in the corpus of vase painting further suggests what anthropological observation widely confirms: that the semiotic antitheses between gender roles increase as class and status decrease (Kurke 1999). Among elite authors, Aristotle and Xenophon preserve the division between the genders in a thoroughgoing way, but for neither is it marked by the antagonism and mistrust that it is in Hesiod. Against them, the often heterodox Plato found no reason to debar appropriately gifted women from the class of the guardians of his utopic Kallipolis (1992: 129–130 [Rep. 455e–456b]). On a more practical plane, Diogenes Laertius asserts that among the "disciples" at Plato's academy were two women, "Lastheneia of Mantinea and Axiothea of Philus, who is reported by Dicaearchus to have worn men's clothes" (1972: 317 [Dio. III.46]). On the authority of Aristoxenus, Diogenes also attributes most of Pythagoras' "moral training" to a woman, the Delphic priestess Themistoklea (1931: 327, 339 [Dio VIII.8.1–2; VIII.21.1–2]). Memory also preserved a certain Theanô (a very common name for a female cultic specialist) either as Protagoras' wife or as his disciple or as both (1931: 359 [Dio VIII.1–3]). No less heterodox but more common, especially in Athens, were the *hetairai*, female "companions" who collected money or gifts for their services, but were also cultivated paramours sought out for far more than their sexual favors alone. The formidable Aspasia, who came to Athens from Miletus and in due time found herself consort of and strategic advisor to Pericles and the mistress of an extraordinary intellectual and artistic salon, is the object of praise in several of Plato's Socratic dialogues, though more typically that of insult in the comedies. That Greek women suffered semiotic and practical violence and constraint is undeniable. Yet the portrait of a woman bound by the heavy chains of a phallocentric regime (Keuls 1985) is surely a distortion. Scholarship of the past decade and a half has increasingly addressed and sought to resolve the paradox of a Greek woman locked away yet regularly making an appearance at everything from the Assembly (Cohen 1991) to the theater (Sourvino-Inwood 2003: 177–184) to one or another of the public religious rituals or festivals that marked just slightly less than half the days of any given city-state's years (Connelly 2007: 10). Joan Breton Connelly argues that in her role as cult officiant, the Greek woman did not merely find her way regularly out of the confines of home and domestic labor, but – in a society in which the religious and the political were not institutionally distinct and in which religious law and religious office were at least equal in status to civil law and civil office – also might find herself with powers and a social station to rival that of even the highest-ranking man (Connelly 2007). Nor should one overlook the military leadership reputed of such women as Telesilla of Argos, Artemisia of Caria, or Archidamia and Chelidonis of Sparta. In ancient Greece as elsewhere, the stubborn dichotomies of doxic stereotypy allowed of a great deal of practical play.

The idealization – or at least the tolerance – of pederastic relationships among the classical elite is well known. Aischines gives every indication that common Greek citizen opinion in the fourth century BCE had it that the tyrannicides Harmodius and Aristogeiton and the Homeric heroes Achilles and Patroclus (actually a family slave, but also Achilles' comrade-in-arms at Troy) were lovers (1919: 107–109 [Aes. 133]). Henri Marrou plainly has these relationships in mind when asserting that "in Greek thought, there was a strong link uniting pederasty with national honour and the love of independence and liberty" (Marrou 1956: 29). It is likely that most men and women took the tales of the homoerotics of Spartan and Cretan militarism as fact, though these prove difficult to corroborate directly (cf. Dover 1978: 193–194; Halperin 1990: 56). Homosexual acts, including apparent acts of anal penetration, among men of at least roughly the same age is an occasional theme of vase painters – which, once again, may or may not have a direct correlate in actual practice.

As Dover himself argues, the ethical evaluation of sexual conduct did not rest per se on the appropriateness or inappropriateness of the object to which it was directed, but rather on the manner in which it was expressed and consummated (1978: 40–109). Nor does ancient medicine leave us with any reason to presume that the orientation of sexual conduct as such was conceived as belonging to pathology. Like Dover and many others before him, Foucault further recognizes that the praise or blame that a Greek man might garner for his sexual practices does not, again, fundamentally hinge on what we would understand as his orientation – and it is this precisely that is the linchpin of Foucault's judgment that the ancients did not conceive of sexuality as we now know it (1985: 187–189). It is likely that every free-born citizen male was expected ceteris paribus to marry and produce children, but such august exceptions as Plato are enough to underscore that even that expectation fell short of being a hard and fast rule. As it was for women, the fulcrum of the evaluation of a man's sexual conduct in any event rests with adverbial rather than substantive criteria. Not a few Victorians (and post-Victorians) suffering the pangs of the love that dared not speak its name imagined ancient Greece to have been a homosexual Shangri-la. Dover demonstrates that it was not. Many homosexual practices were permissible and many others that were not permissible probably went unpersecuted and unprosecuted if pursued with suitable discretion. Yet quite a lot of what thus might be pursued was not in fact regarded as being permissible and nothing was regarded as permissible in which a citizen man indulged passively. Moreover, no such indulgence was more reprehensible than and none such an icon of the reprehensible as that of what we still refer to as the "passive" participant in anal intercourse (cf. Dover 1978: 188). Energeia was tolerable at least and often even laudable in informing the expression of "manly" comportment. Its negation in (homo)sexual prostitution was a crime by Athenian statute and threatened the loss of many of the privileges of citizenship of the man convicted of it. Aischines invokes a particularly telling statute early on in his (successful) case against Timarchus:

If any Athenian shall have prostituted his person, he shall not be permitted to become one of the nine archons, nor to discharge the office of priest (*mêd' hierôsunên hierosasthai*), nor to act as an advocate for the state, nor shall he hold any office whatsoever, at home or abroad, whether filled by lot or by election; he shall not take part in debate, nor be present at the public sacrifices; when the citizens are wearing garlands, he shall wear none; and he shall not enter within the limits of the place that has been purified for the assembling of the people. (1919: 21 [Ais 21])

The statute could hardly be more clear in its implication that self-prostitution was regarded no less as a political than as a religious crime, deeply and even permanently polluting, rendering the person who committed it spiritually unfit for life in the sacred community that the polis always also was.

This themitically durable and apparently serviceable regime, which remains familiar throughout but is not restricted to the Mediterranean, seems in many places still to be holding its own against the ethico-hygienics of sexualities as we now know them. Or if not against, it is at least quite different from the ethico-hygienics of sexualities as we now know them. Foucault follows Dover in identifying the divide between active and passive as an ethical master-dichotomy (Foucault 1985: 47). Contrary to what James Davidson asserts, nothing in Foucault's writings licenses the inference that Foucault himself conceived that dichotomy – which ranges after all over male–female as well as male–male sexual relations – to have its fons et origo in "buggery" (Davidson 2007: 161), though he most certainly conceived of the grounds of the classical problematization of the self to lie with male pederasty.

In any event, in reviewing the problematization of pleasures more generally, Foucault further discerns an enduring ethical schematic of which that dichotomy is only a part rather than the whole. The schematic links the carnal asceticism of Plato's Socrates with the wisdom of Ischomachus, the exemplar of Xenophon's *Oeconomicus* (1923), whose estate runs quite so smoothly because, after properly training his wife in the arts of domestic management, he allows himself to become her *theraponta*, her "servant" (1923: 429 [Oec. VII.42.3]). Contrastively, it links the degenerate kinaidoi whose sexual vices are barely mentionable even in unmixed company to all the men whose cravings or whose wives are beyond their control. A schematic precisely of characterological control, of right proportion, the active–passive dichotomy determines the divide between the good man and all of those disordered and disorderly men and women, Athenian and (especially) non-Athenian and barbarian, who populate the comedies and provide the butts of their most merciless jokes. Yet the same schematic also determines the division between the Homeric warrior, the Achilles "raging" in his tent or even more bestially or divinely on the battlefield, and the far more affectively disciplined soldier of the city-state, trained to be able to hold his place in a phalanx formation without letting either his rage or his fear get the better of him.

The stigma of the lack of self-control might be the flaw of the tragic hero, but is especially the flaw of the tragic heroine, of Helen or Medea or Clytemnestra or Phaedra, whose hyperbolic and unrestrainable passion hurtles her toward the carrying out of fateful and accursed transgressions. It is perhaps the stigma even of the more ordinary ancient woman, whose putatively greater natural susceptibility to passion and appetite Aristotle registers as a deficiency of *boulêsis*, the faculty of deliberation or the rational consideration of alternatives. In the *Politics*, he grants that women have such a faculty, but declares it *akuron*, "non-governing" (1944: 62–63 [Pol. 1s60a13]; cf. Bradshaw 1991). Summarily put, the schematic at issue distinguishes the person (in Plato's *Republic*, also the collective) actively realizing its capacity to govern itself from the person (or collective) either incapable of or not yet actively realizing its capacity to do so. In the category of those lacking such a capacity, Aristotle puts not only women but anyone who is a slave "by nature" (1944: 22–25 [1255a1–2]). In the category of those not yet fully capable of the self-control to which they still might aspire, the Greeks placed the *pais*, the male child.

Notably, Foucault does not dwell on this well-worn standard-bearer of the civilizing process, carted out in every introductory humanities course but distant from the matter of carnal pleasures as such. He nevertheless has those pleasures guide him to the same object lesson that the humanist also educes. Departing from a consideration of the specific perils and compromises of self that troubled philosophical reflections on the pursuit of and indulgence in fleshly pleasures, he comes to the person the Greeks deemed *sôfrôn* and so in full posses-sion of *sôfrosunê*. Sôfrosunê might be ascribed to either sex (Dover 1974: 66–69), but is the diacritical virtue of the free man (Dover 1974: 116; after Pohlenz 1966: 67–71). It has often been glossed into English as "temperance," but the gloss is misleading in suggesting an unmiti-gated asceticism more typical of the Calvinist than of the ancient (or modern) Athenian. Sôfrosunê is the virtue of a man who can enjoy his sex and his food and his drink, but who knows when to cease indulging in sex and eating and drinking and who can and does cease doing so when he knows he should. It is, moreover, the virtue of the man who need not exercise what one would usually call "self-control" over appetites and passions that call out still to be indulged even after he has already indulged them enough. The sôfrôn or "self-controlling" man is a man whose appetites and passions have already been brought under control, have been so cultivated that they do not linger beyond what his best interests warrant. Foucault is correct to render sôfrosunê the virtue of self-governance and to join many others before him in recognizing it to be at the very core of the ethical imagination of the civic era of ancient Greece, the virtue that complements and completes all others and with which all others synergistically make a Greek man *agathos*, "good."

Ethics under analysis

The analytical trajectory of *The Use of Pleasure* thus does not unfold in mid-air. If I have revisited its substance at some length, I have done so only better to clear the way to a more full consideration of the analytical apparatus that motivates and supports it. Grounding that apparatus is a conception of the ethical domain that can be characterized in Foucauldian terms in two different phrasings. One: it is a domain of the development of one or another competent and conscious exercise of the practice of freedom. Another: it is a domain of the development of the potential occupant into the actual occupant of a subject position in and from which the conscious practice of freedom is exercised. Not an unlimited but still an indefinite multitude of subject positions, which usually function to provide those who occupy them with social identities, might be ethical subject positions or belong to the ethical domain as Foucault conceives it. The subject position – or subject, more briefly put – is always socially, culturally and historically specific. It is thus far removed even from the presumptively teleologically ideal subject of Aristotle's ethics, however much Aristotle's "good man" looks and can only look to us now as peculiarly like an ancient Greek aristocrat. It is far more concrete and without any pretension to the universality of the subject of Kant's Second Critique (2002) and of the idealist philosophical tradition in general.

In glossing Foucault's characterization of ethical practice as the "conscious" practice of freedom, I am departing from the translational standard and from translational propriety. The French term in question is *réfléchi(e)*. I have previously followed the standard in bringing that term into English as "considered" or "reflexive." Such a gloss is appropriate to Foucault's frequent focus on philosophical discourse. It is appropriate to his focus on such techniques or technologies of ethical askêsis as the collecting of exemplary quotations and aphorisms or the exchange of personal letters or the imagination of ethically marked situations in which the imaginer might find himself or self-inquiry into the perhaps dirty underbelly of his conscience (Foucault 2000b). It is appropriate to Foucault's focus on ethical problematization, ethical becoming and rebecoming and largely appropriate to his privileged consideration of the ethics of the care of the self. It is, however, anthropologically too limited a qualification for at least two related reasons. First, it only obliquely registers all those elements of ethical practices – ethical gestures, ethical acts – that actors manifest very much in their wits but more or less "without thinking," as we would say. Second, it only obliquely registers that ethical practices once acquired, ethical subject positions once securely occupied, are always and of necessity embodied – which Foucault himself wants to underscore. They become dispositional. They belong to the habitus. They are capacities that enable productive and creative interventions into the habitus and its environment, but they are also structurally and functionally reproductive and especially in their reproductive aspect are often realized more or less spontaneously. "Conscious" thus seems better suited than either "considered" or "reflexive" to encompass ethical practices in their totality. *Tradutore traditore.*

The subject is, by analytical fiat, "free." At this juncture at least, Foucault retains and sustains an intuition that is integral not merely to the philosophical treatment of ethics but to our common opinion. Though freedom – needless to say – is not a sufficient condition of ethical action, it operates in the Foucauldian apparatus as a necessary condition. If a subject is incapable of anything that could be identified as the exercise of his or her or its work or activity or agency or responsibility (a notion variable from one discursive-practical context and one "semiotic ideology" to another [cf. Keane 2007]), then it falls – again by analytical fiat – outside of the ethical domain. Foucault thus declares that "the slave" – ideal-typically conceived as a subject whose substantive agency is wholly determined by his or her or its master – "has no ethics"

(1997a: 286). The declaration implies appropriately enough that freedom is an insufficient ground for an ethics. It recalls furthermore the close cognatic relationship between both êthos and ethos and the verbs ethô, "to be accustomed," "to be wont," ethizô, "to accustom," and ethelô or thelô, "to be willing," "to wish," "to intend." I see no escape from their implications. With James Laidlaw (2002), I can only treat those implications instead as one axis of the basic facts or, in any event, cognitive schematics of ethics as such. If the most radical of sociological and biological and physical determinists are correct, then our schematic is that of nothing more than a chimera.

A more thorough examination of the four parameters of the ethical domain that Foucault specifies best begins with ethical substance. In French and (as I have mentioned in fine print in my first chapter) in English, the term is a familiar translation of Sittlichkeit as it appears in Hegel's *Philosophy of Right* (1952). Foucault's conceptualization of ethical substance is clearly linked to Hegel's treatment of Sittlichkeit, not least in its emphasis on embodiment.

Unlike Hegel and all the more unlike Foucault, Kant avoids and must avoid the issue of embodiment entirely. This is because of his radical distinction between a noumenal realm where the exercise of an undetermined, autonomous will is possible and the phenomenal realm, the realm of the world of our experience, in which all events, human actions included, are strictly determined. No anthropology of ethics can afford to follow Kant in embracing such a distinction, over the mysteries of which Kantians have long labored. The world of our experience is all that the anthropologist has at hand. If it is a world mechanically determined in every respect, then once again any anthropology of ethics is restricted to recording the variety of ways and means through which actors tilt at windmills. Strongly deontologically biased ethics need, however, only scant room for virtues beyond the singular virtue of some version of rationality or at the very least the capacity to obey or conform to imperative principles.

John Rawls' identification of rationality with "goodness" in *A Theory of Justice* is a case in point (Rawls 1971). It is a case as well of the deontological tendency since the early contractarians and Kant to favor the cognitive over the affective. The coupling of cognitivism, moreover, with the presumption that ethical practice permits of analytical distillation into discrete choices or discrete acts often leaves such dispositional things as virtues with no philosophical place at all to call their own. Among many examples that might be brought forward, the ethics that Jürgen Habermas grounds in his theorization of communicative rationality and the formal pragmatics of communicative action is especially worth noting, at once for its influence and for the distinct echo of Kant's three Critiques in the three universal conditions of validity that it purports to govern every communicative act oriented toward the organization of action and so toward mutual understanding (Habermas 1984).

The link is not, however, one of equivalence. First, for Foucault, ethical substance is whatever stuff – cognitive, emotional, physical or what-not – is the object at once of conscious consideration and of those labors required to realize an ethical end, which is to say the being of a subject of a certain qualitative kind. Any ethical substance is ethically neutral or, better put, conceived neither as irredeemably evil nor as always already and incorruptibly good – here Hegel's treatment is left definitely behind. In the typical case, it is some dimension of what is understood to be constitutive of or a part or aspect of the very being of the subject to whose ethical realization it might serve as resource or roadblock or both. The ethical substance that Foucault deems of par-ticular relevance in pursuing the Greek beginnings of his genealogy of sexuality is – again – carnal pleasures (*ta afrodisia* in the ancient language, a term that – in a marvelous instance of semantic and ethically substantive drift – now denotes venereal diseases in modern Greek), of which sexual pleasure is one. Such pleasures are not the only substance of Greek ethical reflection and labor. *Thumos*, "spirit" or "zeal" or "full-heartedness," has even greater prominence in the philosophical corpus than carnal pleasures themselves, not least because of its association with the heroic warrior and the unruly, potentially counter-civic repercussions of his bellicose rage. Hence, the ethical substance of the Greek sôfrôn is not one but at least two things, and that Foucault leaves aside thumos is not a failing per se but another indication of the specificity of the questions he brings to his inquiry.

Thumos is for Plato to be distinguished from reason and from *epithumia*, "appetite" (including sexual appetite), as a third part of the *psukhê* or "soul." It is further an "ally of reason" against any epithumia indulgence of which runs counter to the dictates of reason (1992: 115–117 [Rep. 439d–441b]). Already fully manifest, however, in children not yet in command of their powers of reason and even in such animals as dogs (117 [Rep. 441b]), thumos fundamentally differs from reason. Those whose souls it dominates, if in the best of circumstances distinguished for their courage, are fit to serve as the warrior-defenders of the ideal polis but not as its rulers (1992: 117–118 [Rep. 441c–442c]). Aristotle is consistent with Plato in designating both epithumia and thumos *aloga pathê*, "unreasoned" or "irrational passions" that may be the source of voluntary actions but not of *proairesis*, "choice" (Aristotle 1934: 128–129 [NE 111a26–1111b4]).

The elevation of the "quiet" and "cooperative" virtues befitting the classical citizen, above all the virtue of justness, against the "competitive" virtues of the Homeric householder-warrior is the subject of Arthur Adkins' *Merit and Responsibility: A Study in Greek Values* (Adkins 1960) and with certain modulations of his *Moral Values and Political Behaviour in Ancient Greece* (Adkins 1972). Adkins' procedures tend more in the direction of moral philosophy than of anthropology, though they are clearly informed by the functionalist and organismic presumption that collective values tend to support the structure and reproduction of the society whose collective values they are (1960: 55). Though Adkins plausibly treats urbanization as among the provocations of a "moral crisis" in the fifth century, he exaggerates the scope and intensity of the crisis in three related respects. First, especially in *Merit and Responsibility*, he

treats the prevailing values of Homeric society as uniformly
consequentialist and having their proof entirely in
competitive success and largely unqualified by any overarching normative
constraints on the means of achieving it. Conversely, "the feeling of
shame" in the "shame culture" that Homeric society putatively is
confuses in practice the distinction between moral error and failure, a
symptom of a moral system whose existence thus demands no explanation
because "it springs from what is primitive and primary" (1960: 49).
Second, Adkins treats Socrates and such members of his inner circle as
Plato as bellwethers of the broader moral climate. Third, he diagnoses the
Athens of the fifth and fourth centuries BCE as having abandoned any
collective conviction, if not in the gods tout court then at least in their
punitive and retributive agency. There is no doubt that ancient moral
philosophy is strongly – though not exclusively – consequentialist and the
reach of its normative principles far less than "categorical" (see Adkins
1960: 253). Ancient moral practice probably followed suit. Yet in insisting
on so great a divide between Homeric values and those suited to the quiet
life of the peaceful polis, Adkins must be dismissing the force of Moses
Finley's analysis of the weight of the norms of reciprocity in the
Homeric corpus (Finley 1954), in spite of his declaration that his own
treatment of Homeric society has Finley's treatment as its "essential
background" (1960: 23, n.3). He is equally dismissive of the significance
of the bonds of kinship and descent and the obligations and privileges that
in ancient Greece as elsewhere they channel. At the very least, he is
unduly hasty in dismissing the obligations that the ancients articulate
in the language of descent, filiation and friendship as far "weaker" than the
skills and qualities of character they praise in the language of the virtues.
Among the ancient obligations and privileges that flow through ties of
kinship and other modalities of social belonging are those that structure
religious devotion and religious practice. As Fustel de Coulanges first
argued (1980) and as Connelly has recently and powerfully underscored
(2007), the polis is always a religious as well as a political institution and
these two of its facets so densely intertwined as barely to permit of
distinction. This is as true of Athens as of other ancient city-states, the
apparent impieties and atheisms of the callow and ambitious upstarts that
a heterodox but still pious Plato reviles in his dialogues notwithstanding.

Second, Foucault's treatment of ethical substance as an aspect of the subject that must be put under ethical review and targeted for ethical labor contrasts sharply with Hegel's Sittlichkeit as a condition of ethical completion, for which whatever review and labor were necessary in bringing it into being are things of the past. Foucault's concept of ethical substance encourages the diagnostic highlighting of such review and such labor in a manner that Hegel's concept of Sittlichkeit does not. His fourfold apparatus does not, however, neglect the concept of Sittlichkeit as it operates in Hegel's philosophy. One can, I think, fairly speak of Foucault's appropriation of the concept – but in high historicizing spirits.

A concept of something that is at once particular and the same in each case becomes in Foucault liable to an indefinite variation in both form and substance. A unitary concept of embodiment arguably becomes in Foucault a concept divided in two. On the one hand, it appears as ethical substance in what might be thought of as its initial state, its crude givenness. On the other hand, it appears as another of Foucault's basic parameters of the ethical field: the telos of the ethical subject (1985: 27–28). In the Greek case, that telos was sôfrosunê and the other cardinal virtues and thus a straightforward instance of the full embodiment and realization of what in Greek philosophical discourse was among the teleological ultimates, the cardinals, of virtue. Whether the telos of the Foucauldian apparatus must be understood in general as the consummation of a "project," which a scholiastic cottage industry of Heideggerian bent seems to take entirely for granted, will not detain me here. Anthropologically, there is little harm in understanding it just so in many cases, and not merely those of the existentialist West. Yet the concept of the project does not belong to the ethical domain with anything approaching the insistence of the concept of freedom itself. The concept of commitment, for example, is not its equivalent – my thanks to Marcus Michelson and Razvan Amironesei for bringing me to this point. Good Occamist style and anthropological caution thus both recommend resisting the reduction of the realization of an ethical telos to that of the consummation of a project.

Foucault sometimes refers to his analytical or diagnostic apparatus as an "analytic." In philosophical discourse, an analytic or analytics is a procedure of demonstration, of logical proof. Its locus classicus is once again one of Aristotle's editors. Aristotle's (probably misnamed) *Prior Analytics* and *Posterior Analytics* treat mathematical and scientific reasoning and more generally the relationship between the knowledge presumed in the premise of an argument and the knowledge educed in its conclusion. In his First Critique (1933), Kant refers to his methodology of the determination of the intellectual categories that order our experience as a "transcendental analytic" (1933: 102). It is part of a methodology specifically designed to identify the necessary conditions of any possible experience (1933: 126). Put in other words, it is designed to identify what must be presumed a priori or without appeal to fact in order to account for what Kant technically defines as experience. More generally, an analytic in its Kantian formulation is any methodology that yields the identification of the necessary conditions of any possible X, for whatever X is in question. Heidegger later titles an "analytic" his effort to elucidate the fundamental ontology of Dasein (1962: 67–77).

In *The Order of Things*, Foucault alludes to Kant and likely also to Heidegger when he characterizes as the "analytic of finitude" an array of methodologies for determining what human beings might aspire to know even though their powers of comprehension and being in the world fall far short of the infinite (1970: 312–318). Yet he also relativizes the very concept of an analytic in bringing it to a historically specific array of methodologies exercised in inquiring into a non-existent object – "Man" (1970: 308). He elsewhere characterizes it as the means of determining the "historical a priori" of a given discourse (1972: 127). His redeployment of the term in the course of his research into ethics often hangs somewhere between philosophical precedent and his own historicization of that precedent. Perhaps this is just where it should remain, for if the empirical investigator, again, cannot do without categories already defined, he or she must also be prepared to adjust such categories to such facts as demand accommodation once they are available. Foucault's actual procedures, however, do not seem appropriately construed as pursuing the necessary conditions that make ancient philosophical discourse on the carnal pleasures possible, much less the necessary conditions of any possible practice or discourse that could be called ethics. I thus refrain from labeling his procedures an analytic, and emphasize the difference between moral philosophy, for which an analytic is standard equipment, and an anthropology of ethics, whose definitional apparatus must always be treated as provisional.

Between the ethical substance and the telos of any given subject lie the two parameters of Foucault's fourfold that give his diagnostics its specific difference, its distinctively Foucauldian twist. One especially – that of ethical askêsis – has also borne notable analytical fruit. Foucault borrows askêsis directly from the Greek, and whatever his precise intention may have been in doing so, it achieves a double citational and rhetorical effect. One, and likely the more intentional such effect, is that at once of evoking and demurring from the critical regard not merely of Nietzsche's *Genealogy of Morals* (1956) but of Nietzsche's broader insinuation that the flesh-denying Christianity that he so despised was the ultimate issue of the ugly Socrates' cruel rationalism (Nietzsche 1954: 473–479). Foucault does not explicitly reject the family tree that Nietzsche sketches. Indeed, in his last lectures, he largely affirms it. Yet he takes considerable pains to demonstrate that Greek sôfrosunê was not in its realization an asceticism of the sort that, in what could be thought of as a democratization of the practices of the spiritual virtuosi that the Catholic church regarded as saints, Calvinist and many denominations of post-Calvinist Protestantism imposed on every believer. The sôfrôn was far from a flesh-denying subject and sôfrosunê the basis not of an ascetics that rejected pleasures carnal or intellectual but of a strategics that put them to best use. (Consequentialism reigns.) The Greek "askêsis" neither denotes nor connotes what its linguistic derivatives do. Nietzsche's satire of the triumph of the ascetic *ressentiment* of the slave and the commoner over the robust self-affirmation of the ancient aristocracy (1956: 170–173) fades in Foucault into a more balanced assessment of a civic aristocracy's own pursuit of disciplined *asujettissement* – not "subjugation," as the term is usually glossed, but instead "subjectivation," a condition that, precisely because it falls short of actual enslavement, falls within the ethical domain.

It is anthropologically imperative and in good accord with Foucault's precedent not to conceive of the subject position within a mechanical model whose variables are finite and definite and whose systematic transformations are strictly determinable. It is imperative, in short, not to conceive of subject positions (and so of subjectivation) as a "social structure" in Claude Lévi-Strauss' sense of that term (Lévi-Strauss 1973). Though subjectivation is a process of the formation of a habitus (among other things), it is not and should not be enclosed within the broader theoretical problematic and theoretical apparatus within which Bourdieu encloses the habitus in *The Outline of a Theory of Practice* (and, with only the briefest of qualifications, in *The Logic of Practice* as well [see Bourdieu 1977, 1990]). The Bourdieusian problematic is one of social-structural reproduction, with special emphasis on the reproduction of domination. Strictly speaking – and by Bourdieu's own account – its attendant apparatus is not a mechanical but instead a "statistical" model, whose field of variables remains indefinite and whose referential relation to the actual world is thus indefinite as well. Even so, the habitus in its Bourdieusian conception is a structuring structure of structured dispositions that fills the theoretical function not merely of translating structure into action (and vice versa) but also of reproducing structures extant in the particulars of action and so of reiterating just those structures within the structural present and projecting them into the structural future. The habitus is thus the primary locus of structural reproduction – but not change. The problematic from which Bourdieu proceeds – precisely that of reproduction – in fact allows no model-theoretic room for structural change, which by definition must be exogenous, must arrive from without. Foucault's own approach to practice – which is as close as Foucault ever comes to proffering a "theory" of his own – is different from the outset. His problematic – in the volumes of the history of sexuality, but at many other junctures as well – is not that of reproduction alone, and not of reproduction primarily. It rather gives a privileged place to change, and especially to change generated through processes of problematization, of putting into question the taken for granted, including what the subject might unreflectively take for granted about itself. Precisely so, it provides analytical space for attention to the subject's capacity to change itself – and since every subject in Foucault's approach to practice is a subject position, attention to the alteration of such positions as well as to the shift from one position to another. Were the subject position enclosed within a mechanical model, every alteration of it would constitute a shift to another position. Such a model is of only partial anthropological utility at best; it encompasses neither coding nor the practical manifestation of alterations of subject positions that do not amount to one subject becoming another but instead to such familiar phenomena as a subject "developing" itself or "becoming more deeply" itself or acquiring or discarding one or another dimension of itself – but without becoming someone or something else in the process. It encompasses neither Foucault's understanding of the relation between ethical substance and ethical telos nor his understanding of the specific dynamics of ethical askêsis. No prevailing problematic of structural reproduction; no mechanization of the ethical subject position: thus, with Foucault, an anthropology of ethics must proceed. For a rhetorically oriented approach to the dynamics of self-formation and reformation deeply sensitive to the limitations of the problematic of reproduction and rich in rendering concrete an alternative to that problematic, the contributors to Debbora Battaglia's *Rhetorics of Self-making* are exemplary – not the least of them, the editor herself (Battaglia 1995).

A second and less likely intentional effect of Foucault's borrowing askêsis from Greek is the evocation and the establishment of a certain rapport with Weber's *Protestant Ethic* (1958a). Weber is also well aware that he is writing in the aftermath of *The Genealogy of Morals* and *Beyond Good and Evil* (Nietzsche 2002). He explicitly evokes Nietzsche when he later and more generally addresses "the motives that have determined the different forms of ethical 'rationalization' of life conduct" (1946c: 270). Yet the evocation is delivered in a skeptical voice: "great caution," he writes, "is necessary in estimating [the] bearing" of

Nietzsche's diagnosis "for social ethics" (270). From *The Protestant Ethic* forward into his investigations of the world religions, Weber's diagnoses comprise an ever more expansive critique of Nietzsche's ethology. Contra Nietzsche, their central conclusion could not be more pointed. Not even the Calvinists can in any coherent sense be held responsible, even causally responsible, for the ascendance and the ubiquity of the asceticism that, in the pursuit of worldly evidence of their transcendent election, they could nevertheless be said to have been the formulators. This is not merely because the relation between their asceticism and that of the daily routine of industrial capitalism is incoherent, a matter of a secular "translation" wrought only through an institutional decontextualization (1958a: 176–177). It is also because, contra Nietzsche, it was not the slave or the underclass that proved to be the greatest and most ready carrier of an ethics of self-denial but instead a social actor that, if no aristocrat, was still considerably more highly placed in the social cosmos. Nor was religion or the cosmodicy it offered the matrix in which that ethics proved most readily to take on a life of its own. The political economy of industrial capitalism provided it far greater nourishment – a point that Foucault came very close to reiterating in his own early work on the technology of the "docile body" (1977: 135–169; cf. Rabinow 1984: 17–18).

Weber is nevertheless content to conceive of ethics as one or another "code of practical conduct." Foucault is not and his elaboration of the parameter of askêsis begins to indicate why. The epitome of that elaboration comes with the concept of the *technique de soi*, "technique" or "technology of the self" (1997d: 223–251). Such technologies include any number of plans, regimes, methods and devices that subjects might employ, follow or perform in the pursuit of their ethical formation. Foucault notes in particular several tools of the examination of the self that antiquity leaves to posterity: the physical exercises that the Greeks pursued in the interest of sustaining their personal vigor and military skill (1997d: 239–40); the Stoic collection of *hupomnêmata*, "notebooks" or "jottings" through which one might "make one's recollection of the fragmentary logos transmitted through teaching, listening, or reading a means of establishing a relationship of oneself with oneself, a relationship as adequate and accomplished as possible" (1997c: 211); meditative disciplines from the Greek *meletê* to the Stoic *praemeditatio malorum* or "pondering of future ills," intended to prepare the self to face with dispassion any misfortune that might befall it (1997d: 239–240); the interpretation of dreams (1997d: 241–242; 1986: 4–36); the writing and exchange of personal letters (1997c: 218–220); Christian *exomologêsis*, the "recognition of truth" or, as it comes to be known, "confession" (1997d: 243). Though with less generality, Weber had already recognized the importance of technologies of the self in his treatment of both Calvinist and yogic "methodism" (1958a: 117–127; 1958b: 163–165).

Analytically, Foucault's delimitation of technologies of the self as instruments of the self's work on itself, hence as reflexive instruments, and very often as instruments of reflection as well, is entirely of a piece with his characterization of ethics broadly as the reflexive practice of freedom. As I have mentioned in the first chapter, it also amounts to an important corrective of Aristotle's ethics, for which the ethical subject is a practitioner and so cannot be a maker, least of all a maker of himself. Reflection in Aristotle's ethics is a matter of judgment, of judging what to do. In Foucault's apparatus, it might also be a matter of self-intervention, of autopoiesis, of the self's production of itself. In his approach to the Greek case as to later cases, however, Foucault lingers over technologies of the self not merely to bring to light the "poetic" aspect of ethics but at least as much to emphasize what he calls the "practice-oriented" nature of ancient ethics (1985: 30).

Weber's treatment of the Calvinists may well have benefited from a more active concept of technologies of the self, but because Calvinist ethics was quite as ascetic as it was, his conception of ethics as a code of practical conduct was at least roughly commensurate with that of his historical subjects. Ancient askêsis reveals an ethics of considerably greater complexity than one in which the ethical status of any action hinges on its conformity or lack of conformity with a statutory canon of imperatives or laws or commandments more or less insensitive to the particularities of context. What captures Foucault's interest is not primarily that ancient Greece and Rome, well stocked with ritual specialists but lacking doctrinal doctors, had no clear sociocultural topos for a clergy of either the doctrinal or the ethical sort. Nor does his interest rest primarily in the ancient tendency to conceive of what is right as relative to what is good rather than the modern tendency to the contrary. As his lectures on the "hermeneutics of the subject" (2005) suggest all the more forcibly in the at best tenuous consistency of their argument, his interest and fascination rather rest with the distinctive personalism of ancient ethics, a personalism that accommodated general conceptions of virtue but left little fertile ground for the taxonomization of ethical genera and species for which later disciplinary and biopolitical regimes provide such rich nourishment. Nor did ancient personalism press nearly as much toward the substantive standardization of the ethical subject as modern philosophies of right from Hegel forward have done.

In its personalism, ancient ethics preserves a hiatus between prescription (and proscription) and action within which the relation between ethics and reflexivity is not merely analytically available but over the course of several centuries also provides the analyst with a rich sampler of its variations. Foucault renders that hiatus analytically formal not only with askêsis but even more primarily with his remaining parameter of the ethical domain, the mode of subjectivation (1985: 27). He characterizes it as "the way in which an individual establishes his relation to the rule and recognizes himself as obligated to put it into practice" (27). At another juncture, he characterizes it slightly differently as "the way in which people are invited or incited to recognize their moral obligations" (1997b: 264). If, again, the way in question is merely that of brutal imposition, then subjectivation falls into subjection and so falls outside the ethical domain. This at least is clear enough. It is also clear that Foucault intends the parameter of the mode of subjectivation to be an index of the "deontological" – precisely that aspect of the ethical domain which has to do with obligation or duty. Moreover, the ambiguity that arises in shifting from the active voice of the subject who "establishes his relation to the rule" to the passive voice of people who "are invited or incited" to recognize their obligations is tolerable, even instructive. As a self-reflexive practice, ethical practice proceeds after all in the middle voice, actively and passively often at one and the same time (Faubion 2001c: 94; cf. Tyler 1998).

It is worth considering – though also difficult to say – whether Foucault's terminology here is intended to allude to Kant's distinction between "mode" and "method" in the Third Critique:

> there neither is, nor can be, a science of the beautiful, and the judgment of taste is not determinable by principles. For, as to the element of science in every art – a matter which turns upon truth in the presentation of the object of the art – while this is, no doubt, the indispensable condition (*conditio sine qua non*) of fine art, it is not itself fine art. Fine art, therefore, has only got a manner (*modus*), and not a method of teaching (*methodus*). The master must illustrate what the pupil is to achieve and how achievement is to be attained, and the proper function of the universal rules to which he ultimately reduces his treatment is rather that of supplying a convenient text for recalling its chief moments to the pupil's mind, than of prescribing them to him. Yet in all this, due regard must be paid to a certain ideal which art must keep in view, even though complete success ever eludes its happiest efforts. (Kant 1952: 548)

Kant's emphasis on the incorrigible informality of aesthetic practice and aesthetic pursuits is consistent with and suggestive of the informality that Aristotle deems an inescapable dimension of ethical inquiry. It is consistent with and suggestive of the hiatus that Foucault opens up between simple obedience and the complexities of ethical practice with the very parameter of the "mode" of subjectivation. Kant's remarks on the relationship between the aesthetic master, the aesthetic pupil and the aesthetic example also have what seems to be more than a merely coincidental reproduction in Foucault's characterization of the relationship between Marcus Aurelius and Cornelius Fronto, which I will address shortly. The Kantian lineaments of the aesthetic education might accordingly serve as a model for and a clarification of Foucault's own aestheticization of the ethical in such rhetorical turns as the question: "Why can't everyone's life become a work of art?" (1997b: 261). If so, they also serve to clarify the limits of that aestheticization. The positing of an analogy or homology should not be confused with a declaration of equivalence. Foucault is quite clear in his last lectures at the Collège in recognizing the possibility – and the actuality – not of a homology but instead of a conflict between what he calls the "aesthetics of existence" and the ethical life. Concerning the relation of the former to the parrhêsiastic turn of the latter, he underscores:

> how truth-speaking, in this ethical modality that appears with Socrates at the very beginning of Western philosophy, interfered with the principle of existence as a work to be fashioned in all its possible perfection, how the care of the self, which, for a long time, before Socrates and in the Greek tradition, had been guided by the principle of an existence striking and memorable, how this principle was not replaced but taken up again, inflected, modified, reelaborated by that of truth-speaking, with which one must confront oneself courageously, how the objective of a beautiful existence and the task of coming to accounts with oneself in the game of truth are combined. (2009: 150, my translation)

No such interference would be possible were the aesthetics of existence and ethics one and the same.

Besides and beyond the rule

An analytical apparatus of properly anthropological scope cannot hope to exhaust the deontological with simple reference to "the rule," a term which, as Bourdieu has pointed out, is subject to multiple interpretations (1977: 22–30). Such an apparatus must include exemplars and precedents among its deontological possibilities and not merely "rules" – unless the former are somehow presumed to count among the latter. Even more oddly, an apparatus that stipulates that the telos of the ethical domain is generally that of the occupation of a given subject position or the becoming of a certain subject surely must include more within the purview of the mode of subjectivation than the subject's mode of recognizing himself or herself or being recognized to be the subject of one or another moral obligation. There is more to the ethical conditioning of a subject than its relation to duty, to which the ethical relevance of exemplars (known in much contemporary ethical discourse under the pale rubric of the "role model") cannot be reduced (Humphrey 1997). One's duties are one matter; one's values and the ideals to which one might aspire are often quite another. Every free-born Athenian male was likely expected – obligated – to cultivate the virtue of sôfrosunê. Anyone who failed to do so was likely to suffer the slings and arrows of a well-honed lexical arsenal of disapprobation. No free-born Athenian male was obligated to achieve the martial prowess of an Achilles or a Hercules. The occasional citizen might aspire to do so, however, and might well win praise for doing so, so long as he also kept his temper in adequate check.

Something is thus missing from the Foucauldian apparatus, however much Foucault's own achievements in the second and third volumes of *The History of Sexuality* prove its merits. Nor does that apparatus have to be in the hands of someone with Foucault's own prodigious intellectual prowess in order to further the mission, such as it is, of an anthropology of ethics. Foucault's concentration on the personalism of ancient ethics and particularly of its ethics of carnal pleasures may have diverted him from assigning as formal and constitutive a place to what might be thought of as the exemplary function within the ethical domain as the Greeks themselves thought it due. What more likely diverted him was his classification of the exemplary figures celebrated in Homer or Pindar precisely as figures of an "aesthetics of existence" and so distinguishable in principle if perhaps not in fact in the archaic

Greek past from figures stricto sensu of an ethical sort (2009: 149–150). Personalism, the aesthetics of heroic self-formation, but above all his increasingly exclusive concern with the parrhêsiastic ethics of the care of the self further seem to have diverted him from developing as thoroughly as he might have the ethical standing or distinction of a subject position of which the ethical exemplar is an occupant, but far from the only one. The Greeks referred to that subject position much as we would do so today. It is that of the other.

To reiterate: the specific questions that guide Foucault's investigations of ancient ethics are largely responsible for what amounts to an analytical evaluation of the other within the ethical domain that is of less breadth than it might in principle be – an issue to which I will return at greater length in the following chapter. The question of what ethical issue carnal pleasures constituted before their indulgence was divided into a Manichean universe of normality and perversity leads Foucault almost immediately to the Delphic imperative *gnôthi seauton*, "know thyself," and so to the cultivation of technologies of self-examination that it inspires. For all of this, he is well aware that the Delphic demand is not inward-turning. Self-knowledge is, however important, rather only one step toward the cultivation of the *sôfrosunê* that alone licenses the *sôfrôn* to exercise the governance of others. Precisely because the *sôfrôn* is responsible for others does pederasty begin to attract a philosophical anxiety that is present even in Diotima's identification of the boy beloved as the initial portal into the ancient dialectic of enlightenment in *The Symposium* (Plato 1961: 561 [210a–b]). Foucault recognizes that the philosophers' worries arise because the boy whose *leitourgia* or "service" the pederast would win greatest honor (or envy) in securing was no mere ethical other. The most desirable boy beloved was free-born and elite and so a future citizen socially qualified to hold the highest political and religious offices that the polis had to fill. The philosophers' worries were twofold. The more explicit – no doubt because it was not beyond the bounds of publicity, at least among philosophical friends – was that the very practice of the relationship, of which the beloved's acceptance of the lover's gifts was a sign and intercrural (not anal: cf. Dover 1978: 98–100) intercourse the tolerable consummation, demoted the boy in many respects to the position of a subordinate, which was incompatible with his future standing. Their less explicit and indeed barely mentionable worry was that the boy would come to savor his social and sexual subordination and continue to do so into his adulthood (Foucault 1985: 211, 222) as an inveterate kinaidos.

In ancient Greece especially, the pederastic lover was no mere sôfrôn, either – or had better not merely be. The fathers of the boys caught up in the "hunt" and "chase" (as the Greek metaphors had it; Dover 1978: 81–91) of pederastic romance by all accounts policed their doings carefully, and above all spent considerable time and trouble collecting information about the character of their sons' would-be lovers. Pederasty was tolerated as romance. Its legitimacy, however, rested in the lover's assumption of his beloved as a pedagogical charge, not in the narrow sense of tutoring him in letters or the harp but always in the sense of offering him an ethical example, the best of citizen manhood (Marrou 1956: 29–32). Thus incorporated into the broader scenes of instruction of the elite sectors of the polis, pederasty can be understood as the domestication of a relationship that in its first Greek expressions belonged more strictly to the pedagogy of the warrior (cf. Marrou 1956: 36). It highlights in any case that the relationship between the future ethical subject and his pedagogue or pedagogues is not merely a potentially delicate one. It is central to ancient philosophical reflection on ethics from Plato forward.

Foucault is perfectly aware of all of this, though his address of it is consistently enclosed within his triangle of interest (care of the self and governance, governance and parrhêsia, parrhêsia and care of the self; alêtheia, politeia, êthos). Especially in his treatment of the relationship – erotic, pedagogical and epistolary – between the young Marcus Aurelius and Cornelius Fronto, he is at pains to point out that the ethical subject in training does not merely benefit from but demands "a master," a figure of already established ethical authority who is not merely worthy of emulation but also capable of serving at once as existential guide, psychological critic and practical advisor (1997d: 233–234). Even a cursory review of the anthropological record proves such masters to be an ethical standard the world over, past and present – but not always concerned with the care of the self, much less with parrhêsia. They very often preside at rites of passage, divulging secrets, offering support but also acting with great anthropological regularity as the violent midwives of social rebirth. They hold ubiquitous religious office and religious sway. For better or worse, many of them offer their services to us modern Westerners today as "therapists" and "counselors." One of them even has the habit of contributing a column or two to the Sunday *New York Times* magazine.

The problematic of pedagogy is in any event something of a foot-note to Socrates: it consists in one or another positive response to Socrates' questioning whether or not virtue could be taught. As I have noted in the first chapter, Aristotle's response to that questioning is emphatically in the affirmative. Aristotle is often classified as an ethical "naturalist" for regarding ethical development and the achievement of the good life as the development and consummation of human nature. He is, however, very much a nurturist in regarding the realization of the virtues as the result entirely of pedagogy and practice. Though the naturists and the nurturists continue to wage their battles, an anthro-pology of ethics cannot dismiss the Aristotelian position as peculiarly Greek. For one thing, anything that could precisely be called good evidence that anything so specific a virtue as sôfrosunê or humility or a sense of honor or generosity belongs to certain human beings as a matter of natural endowment or, conversely, that certain other human beings are just "born bad" is as yet entirely unavailable. For another, it is not clear how the claim that such virtues as these are natural could be made coherently – at least without committing the naturalistic fallacy. Moreover, whether or not just anyone and everyone is equally capable of realizing any of the particular virtues that are attached to a given subject position, there is little else to account for the vast repertoire of competencies that human beings manage in one or another time and place to realize and to sustain than the tricks, the seductions, the threats, the punishments and rewards, the deceptions, the surprises and the delights that coalesce in the schools into pedagogies proper but are present everywhere less formally as technologies of socialization.

That ethics depends on socialization is a causal claim, not a logical claim; it is not definitional. Together with what substantial evidence we already have of the human penchant for ethical variability – or more carefully, for the variability of êthos – it places ethics squarely in the realm of intersubjective phenomena, of Durkheim's "social facts." As such, it is a phenomenon of collective determination, not individual determination. An anthropology of ethics must thus find itself at odds with a notable current of Western moral philosophy that for one or another reason regards ethics as subjective (e.g. Mackie 1977) or even as entirely meaningless (e.g. Ayer 1946: 102–120) because the obligations and values around which it orbits do not exist "objectively," are not things "of nature." The anthropologist risks being arch who points out that understandings of what constitutes nature are themselves social facts – however true this may be. That what is social is thus not natural is of course contrary to Durkheim's own insistence that society is simply nature at its most complex. An anthropology of ethics does not, however, have to embrace Durkheim's organismic (and naturalistically fallacious) conception of society as its only alternative to falling into subjectivism. Nor does it even have to decide definitively whether "the social" as a plane of qualities and processes that do not (currently) permit of explanation by appeal to phenomena of another order is really real or is simply the consequence of the forms and the shortcomings of the modes of knowing and of explaining that are currently available to us. Though it might one day acquire one, an anthropology of ethics does not have to have an ontology of either the social or the cultural definitively in place in order to proceed. It can consider such an ontology part of its own work in progress. Occamist restraint once again calls for not presuming more than is necessary at the outset. This is another reason for holding Durkheim's (onto)logically very strong conception of society at arm's length.

A counter-Durkheimian Occamist restraint – and a dose of practice-theoretical wisdom – also provides reason enough to resist conforming to the letter of systems theory as Luhmann has formulated it. The anthropologist can hardly be as troubled as some of Luhmann's humanist critics have been by his insistence that the basic unit of a theory of the social system is not the individual but rather communication. This is especially advantageous for an anthropology of ethics, which consequently does not have to rest on or with a human subject housed in or identical to a "self," much less an individual and least of all an individualistic individual. It can treat such an equivalence instead as an empirical issue, and constitution (if any) of the self itself as a matter of empirical research. The same starting point – communication, not the atomic, mindful body – further permits an anthropology of ethics to entertain and pursue the investigation of ethical subjects, not really very rare in the ethnographic corpus once one begins to think about it, that are quite different from what we casually consider a human being to be. Such composites of interacting actors' collectives as lineages, for example, which often and widely operate as singular or integrated subjects, at least for certain purposes, are only one of the candidate subjects for an anthropology of ethics no longer restricted to individualized selves. As noted in the first chapter and to be elaborated further in due course, such candidate subjects include the anthropologist and anthropologized pair or aggregate, Amo Paul Bishop Roden and me.

More troubling, however, is Luhmann's highly abstract understanding of the requisites of communication, which reveals the same enchantment with information theory and cybernetics that infuses much of French social thought from Lévi-Strauss to at least the early Foucault

(1970: 378–387; cf. Faubion 2008b) to the Derrida who proclaimed that "one should be able to formalize the rules" of grammatology (Derrida 1974: 24; cf. 10). In particular, Luhmann's assertion that the functional subsystems of the functionally differentiated communicative and organizational system that is (Luhmannian) modernity not only are but – in order to permit communication – must be grounded in the unity of a semiological distinction that is rigorously binary in every case must give any anthropologist of practice, and so any anthropologist aware of the significant difference between code and practice, more than passing pause. Luhmann himself seems to be troubled by the condition he imposes, or so his struggle to make sense of the contemporary dynamics of an aesthetic domain coded (so he thinks) under the binary opposition between the beautiful and the ugly suggests (Luhmann 2000). As Luhmann himself rightly observes: "The theory of functional system-differentiation is a far-reaching, elegant and economical instrument for explaining the positive and negative aspects of modern society. Whether it is correct is an entirely different question" (1989: 35).

Irony aside, this caveat has special force in the face of a theory of communication that, like Luhmann's, is effectively constrained to the plane of semantics. On that plane – where logic prevails, inference can be judged either valid or invalid, terms mean what they are defined to mean and not any other thing and communication accordingly conforms to Cartesian standards of clarity and distinctness – the analyst is entirely correct to assert that a subsystem such as the economy is closed to any other code than that grounded in the distinction between what is and what is not profitable, or politics closed to any other code than that grounded in the distinction between what is and is not effective (Luhmann 1989: 51–62, 84–93). Such an analyst is entitled to conclude that any communicative system can sustain its communicative functionality only because or insofar as it does not communicate directly with or refer without mediation to what is outside of it, to its environment (1989: 29). The same analyst is entitled further to conclude that communication – such as that of environmentalist protest – that introduces other codes, other distinctions into economic or political or other subsystemic discourses than those through which those discourses are closed is essentially only producing irritations (1989: 30) or making noise.

From a strictly semantic or logical point of view, all of this is correct. The problem is that the point of view at issue is strictly semantic and a point of view for which communication is stricto sensu a computational process. The computer scientist might agree, but the anthropologist has to fashion broader and much less closed and fluid communicative horizons. This is not merely because practice is slippery, context-laden, loose, often particular and particularistic, under-coded and over-coded, eclectic and hybrid. It is also because the Occamist should no longer fall, as so many anthropologists and so many others outside of anthropology have previously fallen, into the only apparently innocent embrace of a semiotics of a specifically Saussurean variety (or an epistemology of a specifically Kantian variety), founded on the putative insulation of meaning and so of its analysis from any and every referential function to which language might be put (see Faubion and Marcus 2007). Avoiding that embrace does not preclude the development of diagnostic procedures and theoretical models that are capable of sustaining the analytical divide between system and environment at the same time that they are capable of being sensitive to breaches of that divide. Nor does it preclude recognizing, with Luhmann, that the semantic plane has normative force and so orients communication and other modes of action in a manner to which exclusive attention to the Latourian quasi-objects and the calculative, ethnomethodological improvisations of everyday life cannot do justice (cf. Latour 1993). Whatever else might be said, systems theory is in this respect the great and crucial corrective of the micro-scalar myopia of actor network theory.

Logically, Luhmann's approach to the theorization not merely of the autopoietic system but also of the semantic domain is strictly consistent with Maturana and Varela's cybernetics, which is a cybernetics of the second order, of the cognition of cognition (Maturana and Varela 1992; cf. Varela, Thompson and Rosch 1993). Maturana and Varela are in turn indebted to Heinz von Foerster's original conception of second-order cybernetics – a cybernetics of cybernetics – as a model-theorization of "observing systems" (Scott 2003; cf. von Foerster 1974) whose environments can never gain entry except in the always already internal mode of "information." Such a conception is undoubtedly the source of the humanist "speciesism" that Cary Wolfe detects in

Maturana and Varela's actual ethical sensibilities in spite of their avowedly post-humanist ambitions (Wolfe 1995: 65). It is the probable source as well of the sociological speciesism of the consistently post-humanist Luhmann himself. Together with Saussurean semiotics, it is a conception that the Occamist anthropologist of ethics should do without. If its rejection requires a systems-theoretic perspective grounded no longer in second-order but in a third-order or an n-order cybernetics that may thus have to worry about playing fast and loose with the classic paradoxes of self-reference, so be it. A systems theory thus opened up to the indeterminacy and the imperfect definability or representability of its organizational parameters should also satisfy the Lyotardian's objections to the modern faith in the ultimate programmatization and digitalization even of thought and consciousness (cf. Lyotard 1988: 8–23; cf. also Dreyfus 1992). At least it should satisfy his or her intellectual concerns. Whether it is aesthetically adequate is another matter. If nothing else, it affirms anthropology's own resolute analytical infinitude.

The mode of the determination of subjectivation

Recruitment and selection

Because the ethical pedagogue is intrinsic to the ethical domain, his or her presence deserves a formally more explicit place apart within Foucault's apparatus than Foucault himself saw fit to give or in any event ever got around to giving it. That presence points first of all to what can be thought of as the mode of the determination of the ethical trainee's subjectivation. That mode has its anthropological poles in the dichotomy that analysts of status and role draw between "ascription" and "achievement." The dichotomy is tidy enough, but most subject positions are in one measure ascribed and in another achieved and the operative metric liable to be very different from one case to the next. That the subject who achieves his or her position typically has a pedagogue to thank is obvious enough. The subject who acquires his or her position ascriptively typically has at least one to thank as well. It is one thing to be born a son or daughter, an aristocrat or a commoner. It is another thing, and something always requiring the services of the pedagogue, to develop the competencies required to be good at being a son or a daughter, an aristocrat or even a commoner as the case may be.

Nietzsche made much of the fact – it is indeed a fact – that Greeks typically referred to their aristocrats as *kaloikagathoi* (in the plural; the singular is *kalokagathos*), a contraction of *kalos*, which glosses as either "good" or "beautiful," the conjunction *kai*, "and," and agathos, "good" or "noble." They typically referred to the lower classes (who seem also to have referred to themselves) as *kakoi* (plural; singular *kakos*), the contradictory of kalos, hence "bad" or "ugly" (Nietzsche 1956: 163–164). One may – but also may not – accept Nietzsche's (in)famous interpretation of the contrast as revealing the ancient identification of high and inherited social standing with goodness and low social standing with the opposite and its conversion into the contrast between "good" and "evil" the result of a "slave revolt." As Laidlaw has observed, such a position invites and reinforces Adkins' ascribing to the yet unconverted ancients a "pre-moral" sensibility (Laidlaw 2002). As Laidlaw is further aware, such an ascription is not independent of the meaning one assigns to "morality" itself. Adkins' ascription has a universalist humanism as its apparent underpinning. Not all ethical positions are universalist and even some of those that are universalist are not humanist. Kant's ethical actor, like Aristotle's, must be in the active possession of the powers of reason – a criterion that could well enlarge the ethical universe beyond the human but also restrict it only to some actual human beings. Ethics that populate the ethical universe with all creatures capable of suffering also reach well beyond the merely human in their scope.

In any case, on the pragmatic plane, the Greek example of the kaloikagathoi and their kakoi counterparts is useful in three respects. First, it reminds us of the need to attend not simply to the difference between ascribed and achieved status but also to the dynamics of self-ascription in its interplay with the ascription of particular moral qualities to others or their actions. Second, it allows us to raise the question of the valence of moral ascription. We would unduly restrict the analysis of processes of subjectivation were we to take as an exclusive guide the presumption that subjectivation can have an ethical dimension only if the occupation of a given subject position is in some respect at least a "positive" affair. We would be short-sighted were we further to presume that the valence – ethical or other – of any given position is fixed. Whether because they are stigmatized or because they come with what are experienced as excessive burdens, subject positions can be insufferable to the subjects who occupy them. This does not preclude their allowing ethical breathing room and objective ethical possibilities, psychic and practical. The stigmatized actor is not automatically a Foucauldian slave. Nor, as analysts from Goffman (1963) forward have shown, is stigma beyond manipulation or contextual retuning. Stigmatized minorities are remarkably adept at turning the terms of their detractors into positive signs of intimate community, even if such linguistic and rhetorical liberty is more compromised than some of those who take it appear to be aware. Foucault himself treats this issue with appropriate complexity under the methodological "rule of the tactical polyvalence of discourse" in the first volume of the *History of Sexuality* (1978: 100–102).

The determination of subjectivation has, moreover, two distinct facets. One of these is already implicit in the dichotomy between the ascribed and the achieved. It is that of the mode of the assignation of a given candidate subject to the subject position for which he or she or it is a candidate. Most broadly, it amounts to the mode of recruitment to and selection of a given subject position – of just one only in the logically and sociologically simplest case. Always some mixture of the ascribed and the achieved – as the case of Fernando Mascarenhas will illustrate with particular vividness – such assignation can occasionally be a simple affair, but it is more often protracted and qualitatively baroque. The future Greek sôfrôn of the classical period, for example, began his induction into the ranks of the self-governing once removed from the primary care of his mother and house servants

(Marrou 1956: 142) and delivered to tutors and teachers, who offered him their instruction almost always for a fee – a condition that Plato is characteristically aristocratic in denouncing as vulgar. The child's principal subjects were *gumnasia* (more inclusive than what we now conceive as "gymnastics") and *mousikê*, which included training at least in the lyre, recitation (of Homer and Hesiod among others) and some time after the first quarter of the fourth century, reading and writing (Marrou 1956: 39–45; Robb 1994).

Eric Havelock inaugurated the investigation of the impact of the introduction and acceptance of alphabetic reading and writing in ancient Greece in such masterworks as *Preface to Plato* (1963). Kevin Robb (1994) has continued to develop and refine Havelock's insights. Havelock argues that Greek (more specifically, Athenian) society did not advance beyond a craft literacy limited to scribes until after 440 BCE – the approximate date at which he suggests that *grammatikê* or "the study of letters" was introduced into Athenian primary schools (cf. Havelock 1982). His dating is still under dispute, but at least one of his motives for it is uncontroversial. The Greek aristocracy at first disdained the technology of alphabetic writing and remained devoted instead to the recitative tradition through which it acquired oral fluency with Homer and the few other "inspired" poets whom it sprinkled into daily conversation. Writing and reading may have been regarded as distasteful for any variety of reasons: because they were tasks and skills antithetical to the askêsis of the military life that the typical aristocrat knew; because, in the face of the dramaturgical intensity of an established pedagogy that intimately linked theater, communality and religious devotion, the mechanics of writing and reading could only seem pale and impoverished; because the alphabet may have had its initial Greek invention among Greek merchants or the inscribers of pottery, whom the aristocrat could only disdain. The Greeks themselves – at least in the surviving archive – have remarkably little to say on the subject. Whatever the case may be, literacy in ancient Greece came to be the competency of precisely that stratum which had initially resisted it together with those who came to be their rivals in wealth. It never approached universality, even among the free-born male population.

(Some vase paintings suggest that the elite boy's sisters studied some of the same general subjects as he studied himself, though probably only in the company of other girls and women and, with the exception of choral and other cultic training [see Connelly 2007: 29–39], largely at home.)

If he left his house to visit one or another school, the citizen boy always went in the company of a *paidagôgos*, literally a "child-leader" and always a trusted family slave who acted as his overseer, guardian and chaperone (Marrou 1956: 143–144). His father among others would instruct him in time in estate management and military discipline. He did not absolutely require the further instruction of a lover, and should never express an active desire to have one, but one can imagine that the boy who was neither sufficiently beautiful nor of sufficiently high status to attract suitors might well have suffered from a certain sense of neglect. Signs of puberty were the harbingers of his transition from pais to *ephêbos*, from child to "youth," which very likely had its consummation in ritual. As an ephêbos, he might from the late fifth century BCE forward acquire further training, perhaps hiring the services of a *sophistês*, a sophist, specializing in mathematics or grammar or most often the art of oratory, indispensable to anyone with ambitions to political power and office. Approaching the age of twenty-one, he would return to the *dêmos* or "township" of which he was genealogically native for a public review of his eligibility to become a *politês*, a vested "citizen." The process was a double testament: on the one hand, to the free birth of his parents and grandparents; on the other, to his ethical probity, or at least to his having done nothing of common knowledge to besmirch either his honor or his ritual purity. Passing review and upon the approval of the civic voting body, he was accorded the privileges of citizenship (Ober 1989: 68–71). The title of sôfrôn, however, was yet to come and if it came at all, it did so only after he survived the substantial scrutiny of his peers and especially of his elders well beyond the casting of his first vote, his marriage and his taking upon himself the management of an oikos of his own.

So long a road to adulthood and its signature subject positions is not the anthropological rule, though it is indicative of a degree of social complexity and differentiation with which an ever increasing number of contemporary human beings are becoming familiar, perhaps in spite of themselves. It is a useful reminder that even in simpler instances, the acquisition of the dispositional competencies and affective and perceptual orientations that are prerequisite to the full occupancy of a typical subject position is not an affair of the short run. As I have already suggested, this is true even of positions of a prima facie ascriptive sort such as those of kin relations, of which the anthropological record consistently logs the difference between merely being a kinsperson and being a good or bad one, and to which the Judeo-Christian parable of the prodigal son also attests. Scholars who concern themselves largely with texts tend to underestimate the degree to which even the most rigidly ascriptive of semiotic markers fall far short of determining social identity. Sartre comes close to falling into such an error in his treatment of the moment at which Jean Genet decides as a matter of existential commitment actively to make a project of being the thief that he has been accused of being (Sartre 1963: 49–51). Louis Althusser may also have fallen into the same error in proffering the example of a policeman's "hailing" or "interpellation" of a likely suspect, "who nine times out of ten turns out actually to be guilty of a crime" (Althusser 1971: 173–174). Many of Althusser's textualist readers have taken the example as iconic of the power of language to imprison the subject within its semiotic cells even without the benefit of any actual officer of the law behind it. The charisma with which "the linguistic turn" in social and cultural analysis left language broadly endowed has not yet faded entirely. It should not mystify the fundamental place of the scene of instruction – a place of repetition and sanction, a place of practice – in the formation of social identity, in which language has its powers only as an element and part of the fabric of practice itself. Identities have a temporality, a historicity completely different from that of the singular event of interpellation. They neither come nor go in the course of a single exhalation.

Scope, structure and priority

The second aspect of the mode of the determination of subjectivation is without empirical exception, but all the more apparent as the number and complexity of subject positions increases. Call it that of the scope, structure and priority of subjectivation, or more precisely of any given subject position in its relation to others that might be available for occupancy. Briefly put, certain subject positions include or can include or permit the nesting within them of certain others. Others might in both principle and practice be mutually incompatible. Certain subject positions might be the necessary or the sufficient condition of certain others to which they are nevertheless not equivalent. Certain subject positions are trans-institutional and others not. The demands of certain subject positions may override the demands of certain others. One might occupy a certain position night and day and another only on occasion. Subject positions are variably expansive. They have variable logical profiles. They bear variable ethical weight – though like that of identity, this notion as well will have to wait until the following chapter to receive the clarification it demands.

The position of the Greek sôfrôn extends in principle at least to every free-born adult Greek male of the classical period. Substantively, at least as Aristotle sees it, its full realization can extend no farther than to the owners of large estates with a sufficient staff of slaves to facilitate a life of ample *skholê* or "leisure," which alone provides the opportunity for undistracted *theôria*, the "contemplation" of the really real, the highest of human goods and the only good that allows the anthrôpos to participate in the divine.

It is unclear how far the pattern of the socialization of the aristocratic boy extends to the commoner. It very likely extends to most if not all of the scions of what Josiah Ober refers to as a "wealth elite," which even in the late archaic period had come to rival if not surpass the hereditary aristocracy as a material force (Ober 1989). Yet it just as likely stops short of encompassing any and every citizen boy, and probably remained, as Marrou puts it, an affair of "gentlemen" (1956: 38). With Solon's reforms of 594 BCE, Athenian citizenship ceased to be exclusively based on membership in one of Attica's putatively autochthonous clans but dependent instead on two other criteria: geographic place of birth; and the ownership of real property. The Solonic statutes establish four census classes, the members of each of which have in common the quantity of their annual agricultural yield, presumably of grain. The four are named the *pentekosiomedimnoi* (those producing five hundred medimnoi – one medimnos amounted to about twenty-five kilograms – per annum); the *hippeis* or "horsemen," producing three hundred medimnoi per annum; the *zeugitai* or "pairsmen" or "yokesmen" (so called because they were able to sustain a pair of oxen), producing two hundred medimnoi per annum; and the *thêtes*, "serfs" or "laborers," producing fewer than two hundred medimnoi per annum. The members of only the first two of these classes were eligible for high political office. That the latter two were protected from debt bondage strongly suggests a condition of means too meager to cover the expenses required for the sort of education that could produce an appropriately cultivated and sôfrôn adult.

Within the station of the sôfrôn, such largely ascriptive positions as that of the father and the son and such quasi-administrative and quasi-professional positions as that of the husband householder nest. It is unclear whether the relation between master and slave belongs within the scope of the master's sôfrosunê or whether its peculiar liberties allow sôfrosunê effectively to hang in suspension. In his prosecution of Timarchus, Aischines cites a statute condemning to death any Athenian who "outrages" a free-born child and also holding guilty anyone who does the same to *oiketika sômata*, "the bodies of domestic servants" (1919: 16–17 [Ais. 16]). He immediately comments that one might well wonder why on earth the statute made any mention at all of slaves, though proceeds to praise its wisdom for doing so. In general, in any event, the domestic sovereignty of the adult politês is qualified, though largely informally. He is technically at liberty to beat his wife and may even win quiet approbation for doing so on occasion and in moderation. Yet his excess in this or in the indulgence of any of his other domestic privileges would certainly not escape the critical notice of his neighbors and, from his neighbors, critical notice was likely to spread. Sôfrosunê was thus supposed to attend his pursuit of liberty and happiness as it was supposed to attend his carrying out of his obligations. For all of this, its social distribution remained rather narrow. Far more inclusive is the amalgam virtue of *andreia*, "manliness" or (synonymously) "bravery," which was in far easier reach than sôfrosunê for most free-born men and could even be attributed – almost always with a positive connotation – to a woman.

Nor is the relationship between ethics and talk of it merely incidental. The ethical scene of instruction is a scene of talk, of communication, and hence of language not *per impossibile* as a "private" but instead once again as an intersubjective and social phenomenon (cf. MacIntyre 1984). As such, its terms require being provisioned with or attached to criteria of their proper and improper use. This Wittgensteinian point (Wittgenstein 1858) is not, I admit, likely to impress the diehard ethical subjectivist, who might counter that the very criteria of what constitutes the proper or improper use of such terms as "good" and "right" are themselves so variable that ethics is subjective for all intents and purposes, even if some people can agree on the usage of at least some of the terms of ethical discourse at least some of the time. The anthropologist of ethics does not, however, have to admit defeat. The question of whether the terms of ethical discourse are quite so criterially unstable should for one thing remain an empirical question directed not to a philosophical tradition that has long been devoted to antithetical one-upmanship but instead to the broader domain of collective human practices. An anthropology of ethics is, moreover, in methodological need of no more than Aristotle's own grounds of ethical inquiry, which beyond logical matters are those of shared human opinion (1934: 36–37 [1.viii.1]). Human opinion – on matters of ethics, for example – tends to vary, to be sure, but ethical discourse of even the most obstreperous lack of consensus and just short of complete collapse must still defer to a matrix of the justification of the use of its terms; otherwise, it would not constitute a discourse of any sort at all. The form and substance of that matrix – which generates the grounds or reasons of ethical judgment – may itself be (and in the Western philosophical tradition certainly has been) in dispute. The themes and variations of its form and substance, the ecology of its stability or instability and, above all, the practices that it sustains and by which it is sustained belong to the domain in which an anthropology of ethics conducts its inquiries. Foucault's synopsis of the strategics of the ancient matrix of the justification of indulging or refraining from indulging in one or another of the carnal pleasures is illustrative at once of what such inquiries might seek and of what they might find.

The mode of ethical judgment

As necessary conditions of anything passing for ethical discourse and as conditions that in turn condition what might persuasively pass as the telos of ethical self-formation or the substance of ethical work, matrices of justification warrant for their own part a more formal and specific place in an analytical apparatus than Foucault provided them. The semiotic differentials of one or another mode of ethical judgment, they determine the specificity of and thus determine with greater specificity the ethical orientation toward code or toward practice that Foucault himself noted, even as he included such matrices within his treatment of the modes of subjectivation. Analytically independent consideration of them promises a double advantage. First, it encourages us not to take "the rule" for granted but instead to undertake its analytical disambiguation. It encourages us at least to presume from one ethical discourse to another neither that the semiotics of the rule is always the same nor that it always unfolds with the same clarity. It allows the anthropologist of ethics to anticipate a semiotic catalogue of norms, guidelines, conditional and categorical imperatives rescued from the abstraction that social theorists brought to the conceptualization of the rule even at the very outset of the theorization of the social.

Second, independent consideration of the mode of ethical judgment should lend further content and concrete intricacy to Foucault's intuition that the semiotic being of any apparatus of ethical justification and the semiotic being of the ethical subject are not independent but instead consubstantial. Whatever the future of any metaphysics of morals might be, the future of any anthropology of ethics will be brighter in leaving behind the increasingly tired debate over the relative causal weight of the biological, the psychological and the social planes of human organization in favor of an ecology in which the normative tissue that defines the organization of the subject and the normative tissue that defines the organization of its social environment must always be of something of the same cloth. Though the point will once again have its full elaboration in the following chapter, just what counts, from one semiotics of the ethical to another, as a potential or actual ethical subject belongs a fortiori to the same ecology. Like the totality of which it is one variation, any such semiotics includes a metrics of ethical subjectivation, some means of measuring, if roughly and readily, who or what an ethical subject might be, what subjects do and what subjects do not have potential or actual ethical standing. Aristotelian anthropism yields one such metric; Kant's transcendental logicism yields another. The tally increases from there, all the way to Fernando Mascarenhas and the anthropologist–anthropologized amalgam, both of whose modes of ethical judgment are, like those of many of their contemporaries, difficult to characterize in philosophically consistent terms.

THREE

Ethical others

Justness and the other

The elaboration of the dimensions of the mode of ethical subjectivation just completed has one of its primary motivations in the recognition that ethical discourse and ethical practice are intersubjective and that both require the services of another, and especially of the other in the specific guise of the agent of socialization, the ethical pedagogue. The other in less qualified guise – the ethical subject tout court – remains in need of further attention. Such an other is the second party, the addressee, of the Greek virtue of *dikaiosunê*, "justness" or "justice."

The term dikaiosunê is an abstraction of the earlier attested *dikê*, whom Hesiod personifies as a much-abused goddess in the *Works and Days*. Translators render the goddess "Justice," but dikê has its core meaning in Homer as custom or manner or a way of life or more specifically as order or what is fitting. Dikê is themitical. After Homer (and still today) it is used most frequently to refer to a legal proceeding, a trial or case, and to the punishment or satisfaction that might be its outcome. Dikaiosunê derives from the attachment of the abstracting suffix *–unê* (compare the English cognate *–ness*) to the adjectival *dikaios*. It is attested in Herodotus and the Theognid corpus (cf. Adkins 1972: 42) before taking center stage in Plato's middle dialogues and especially in the *Republic*.

The Foucault who pronounces that "the freedom of the subject and its relationship to others" is "the very stuff of ethics" (1997a: 300) means, again, what he says. That he nevertheless has little to say about justice in the second volume of *The History of Sexuality* should not be surprising. Though it lingers in the background of the problematization of the pederastic relationship, justness is far from the forefront of what the Greeks considered in evaluating the good use of carnal pleasures. It is not central per se to the care of the self. Perhaps it should have been, but it was not. For all of this, no complete nor even a balanced overview of ancient ethics – not, again, that this was Foucault's aim – can ignore it. As the "other-regarding virtue," it becomes the rival in the civic period of the bravery – also other-regarding in its way – that reigned ethically supreme in the Homeric cosmos. Among the virtues constitutive of or on an ethical par with sôfrosunê, it retains a cardinal position well beyond the classical period. Diogenes Laertius reports that the Hellenistic Stoics continued to rank it together with wisdom, courage and sôfrosunê itself as among the "first" of the virtues (1931: 198–199 [Dio. vii.92]).

The contemporary West is in this respect still somewhat Greek, if not entirely. We have relegated bravery to an ethical second tier, though it still has an important place in male socialization and all the more so in times – and they are frequent enough – of war. Bravery has undergone considerable psychologization even so, and now tends to have less the force of a widely distributed virtue than that of a heroic ideal. Moral philosophy indeed continues to be preoccupied with something like justness. Yet, especially in the liberal tradition of moral philosophy, the concept is no longer that of a virtue, a personal disposition, as much as something very like dikê as "right order." It is a quality of the distribution of goods. The same tradition, which has been dominant since the later eighteenth century, has its other cornerstone in freedom or liberty, but no longer understood as a condition of birth or merely as the opposite of enslavement. It is understood in the light of an ontological condition that Greek philosophers did not entertain and might even have found laughable – autonomy, the capacity of radical self-determination.

If other-regarding, neither bravery nor justness necessarily leads away from the ethics of the care of the self. This is all the more true of philosophical discourse in the classical period, in which all of the virtues that merited the title had to pass the test of serving the good and the best interests of the subject whose virtues they were. The pedagogical other remains prominent in that discourse. Yet the dialogical form of so much of classical philosophical reflection may well have been largely that – a matter of form – perhaps even in such conversational environments as those of the Academy and the Lyceum. One further has to wonder just how many hours of the typical symposium were in fact devoted to anything that closely conformed to the standards of philosophical exchange. Foucault's research reveals a philosophical practice that may well have unfolded often alone and in private, its hours frequently passing in self-attention and self-assessment, the ethical become personal. If the pedagogue was always nearby, the pedagogical dynamic no doubt faded in its intensity as the trainee's virtues became second nature and instead of being cultivated could simply be exercised. Its participants in fact had a great deal in common – far more than what would usually be presumed of persons belonging merely to what would usually be called the same "society" or the same "culture." The Greece of the fifth and fourth centuries BCE was hardly cold in Lévi-Strauss' sense of the term (1966: 233–234). The philosophical hothouse of the Athenian agora and its symposium circuit could, however, witness much of what passed perhaps not with a common temper but at least from a common remove. Requirements of space were not the only impetus for locating the Academy and the Lyceum outside of Athens' city walls.

Any discourse of any sort that sustains even a minimum communicative function presupposes that those participating in it share at least something – a modicum – of what casually passes for the same background. The Greek philosophers are not in danger of misleading us on that front. Their high rationalism was exceptional. So, too, were the transformations that they put into motion. A limit-case if not quite an ideal-typification of Weber's sociology of rationalization (1946b, 1958a), the philosophers did not merely isolate a paradox internal to the body of received opinion, the doxa of their day. They did not merely discover the potential ethical inconsistencies of the boy beloved. They made a problem of it. As Foucault's genealogy has shown, they also began to devise and bring together the pieces of an ethical critique that would ever more indissolubly link the self's attention to the dangers that it might pose to itself and to others to a far broader institutional transformation. The result, though the philosophers could not have anticipated it, was Christianity's radical rejection not merely of pederasty but of pagan sôfrosunê and the equally radical valorization of the anerotic life as among the constituents of the pinnacle of human aspiration.

Yet the Greek thinkers are far from historically unique in being a league of critically and speculatively inclined men of privilege whose cogitations were implicated in semiotic and structural changes that reached far beyond their exclusive precincts. The French Revolution – if it happened – had similar fuel. Nor are they at all unique in being a league of critically and speculatively inclined persons of privilege who spent a good deal of time thinking and, not least, thinking about themselves. Logocentric (and phallocentric) perhaps, such an inclination imbues the philosophical temperament wherever we find it. It is also widespread among the humanistic expanses of the contemporary academy.

The classical philosophers might mislead us only if we confuse their inward and reflexive examination of self with an abandonment or even a significant qualification of what remained throughout the ancient period a fundamentally ecological conception of the ethical domain. Foucault makes the point very well, if within the bounds of his triangle:

The care of the self is ethical in itself; but it implies complex relationships with others insofar as ... [the] êthos of freedom is also a way of caring for others. This is why it is important for a free man who conducts himself as he should to be able to govern his wife, his children, his household; it is also the art of governing. Êthos also implies a relationship with others, insofar as the care of the self enables one to occupy his rightful place, the community, or interpersonal relationships, whether as a magistrate or a friend. And the care of the self also implies a relationship with the other as proper care of the self requires listening to the lessons of a master. One needs a guide, a counselor, a friend, someone who will be truthful with you. Thus, the problem of relationships with others is present throughout the development of the care of the self. (1997a: 287; cf. 2008: 35)

Foucault emphasizes here the askêsis that informs the practice of the care of the self, but also its external expression, its enactment over and with others, who themselves demand care, consideration, acknowledgment, direction perhaps, deference sometimes, across all the domains in which the ethical agent acts and must act as a condition of the full realization of his care of himself. Greek ethics is indeed personal, but unlike an ethics grounded in a metaphysics of autonomy, of a radical and absolute freedom, it places ethical practice in the encompassing web of the house and the polis, both of which are also topoi of friendship (at least for Xenophon and Aristotle). Ethics and its domestic and political environment are thus entirely of a piece.

Though the occasional Hellenist might insist to the contrary, the Greeks do not bequeath to the future that appropriates their precedent anything that could properly be called humanism. Their ethical environment is not coterminous with the *oikoumenê*, what they knew of the "inhabited" or, more to the point, "cultivated earth" (and our "ecumene"). It begins to diminish as it blends into the territories of the *barbaros*, the "barbarian," a term that in its earliest usage refers to any non-Greek or non-Greek-speaking person, but in the aftermath of the Persian Wars refers especially to the Persians and the Medes. It denotes ill-spoken Greek as well as gibberish. It can suggest rusticity, lack of cultivation. Not with exclusive but perhaps with special allusion to the Persians, it implies brutality and violence. It is thus built of two basic and telling dichotomies: one communicative, between what can and what cannot be understood, what permits and what does not permit of dialogue; the other political, between the violence and brutality that are incompatible with civilized life and mark the enemy and the peaceful intercourse that comes to fruition only with the fruition of the polis itself. The barbarian does not permit of any strictly genealogical definition, as the case of the metics or non-citizen free residents of Athens already suggests, even if the typical metic was likely to be Greek. Aristotle's notorious remark in the *Politics*, which I have already mentioned in passing, is more definitive of the barbarian qua barbarian, the barbarian "by nature," a being whose incapacity to make sense and to exercise it suit him only for the life of the *doulos*, the "slave" (1944: 6–7 [Pol. 1252b9]). The barbarian "by nature" is thus the quintessence of the ethically abject. For the tutor of Alexander, in the Athens of the fourth and third centuries BCE, the philosophical divide between the ethical environment and the ethical wilderness could be as simple as that – in principle at least. Extrapolating from Foucault's treatment of the domain of ethical value, the domain in other words of those who are endowed with ethical value, one might alternatively cast that principle as demarcating the divide between the governable (the self-governable included) and the non-governable (those merely to be dominated and subjugated among them). Though the extrapolation requires interpretation, it holds the promise of being the most precise and concise formalization of Greek non-humanism that we as yet have.

The classical philosopher could again mislead us, however, if we presumed that the cool and confident logocentrism of his development at once of an ethics and of the scope and limits of its ecology stood as the fundamental principle of the ethical imagination and not instead as merely one of many possible vectors of its routinization. Both before and after the fourth century BCE, the Greek ethical imagination is less certain. Passing just beyond the liminal phase of the historicization of myth and the concomitant ascent of literacy and coming of age in the aftermath of the Persian Wars, Herodotus does not yet take for granted the barbarism of the Persians or Medes or many of the other peoples dwelling around the borders of the Mediterranean. His presentation of the Egyptians – who gave the Greeks the names of so many of their gods (1987: 153 [Hr. 2.50]), who keep such meticulous records (163 [2.70]), who first told of the immortality of the soul (185 [2.124]) – often runs counter to a chauvinism that deemed Greece the origin of all civilization. As he admits, his curiosity often leads him to stray from his primary purpose (290 [4.30]). That purpose lies in providing an account of how even such a people as the Egyptians could have fallen under the yoke of the Persians (of Cambyses, in 525 BCE) and a people so impoverished, so fractious and so few as the Greeks could have resisted them alone. His answer comes through the mouth of Xerxes' advisor Demaratus: "poverty has always been native to Greece, but the courage they have comes imported, and it is achieved by a compound of wisdom and the strength of their laws" (502 [7.102]). Of the Spartans, in particular, he cautions Xerxes: "fighting singly, they are no worse than other people; together, they are the most gallant men on earth. For they are free – but not altogether so. They have as the despot over them Law, and they fear him much more than your men fear you" (504 [7.104]). This is the first properly ethological diagnosis on Western record and, if incomplete, has much ethologically to recommend it. If it cannot quite be called ethically relativist, this is largely because the category of the ethical does not function independently in Herodotus' *Histories* of the category of sin, of inherited curse and divine blessing, of ethos as simple custom. Yet Herodotus is far from being an ethical absolutist and his ethical regard is wide-ranging, falling into pure fabulism only when he vicariously ventures "furthest to the south," to Arabia (257–59 [3.107–113]).

In the first century CE, Athens was under the dominion of Rome. The cultural center of Greece, home to its bureaucrats and other administrative mandarins, was Alexandria. Apollonius of Tyana was of this world, still an admirer of the classical virtues of dikaiosunê and andreia, still holding the philosopher's good of parrhêsia close enough to heart to insult Nero's singing style and only miraculously avoid prosecution for it (Philostratus 2005a: 412–413 [1.iv.43]). He actually spent time in prison under Domitian's later prosecution, but after finally winning acquittal from the emperor, pronounced himself immortal and mysteriously vanished from the courtroom (2005b: 322–323 [II.viii.5.3–4]). In any event, legend and Apollonius' biographer, Philostratus, have it thus. Apollonius has Herodotus' cosmopolitan curiosity; he has a passion for knowledge and is "interested in what has to do with the foreign" (2005a: 154–155 [1.211.3; translation modified]). All the better, he had command of all human languages (2005a: 76–77 [1.1.19.2]) and could declare that "all the world" belonged to him (2005a: 82–83 [1.1.21]). He was tolerant of practices that diverged from his own (2005a: 146–147 [1.2.7.3]), but as a follower of Pythagoreanism he was a strict vegetarian, refused to shed sacrificial blood and was strictly celibate. Like Pythagoras himself:

he surpassed the famous saying of Sophocles, who claimed that he had escaped from a raging master when he reached old age. Due to his virtue (aretê) and self-mastery (sôfrosunê), Apollonius was not subject to it even as an adolescent, but despite his youth and physical strength he overcame and "mastered" its rage. (2005a: 60–61 [1.1.13.3])

With Apollonius, we are well on our way historically to the monastery.

Apollonius' peripatetics were more ambitious than those of Herodotus and led him much farther east, from the Persian court to the *frontisteria* or "ashrams" of the Brahmans that were his final destination (Philostratus 2005a: 316–317 [1.iii.50.1]). Like Herodotus before him and Marco Polo long after him, he traveled in order to enrich the askêsis of his care of himself and thus sought out healing waters and invigorating delicacies as well as spiritual wisdom. Unlike either Herodotus or Marco, so far as we know, he also deigned, justly, to dispense and disperse the powers and the wisdom already in his possession, as exorcist (2005a: 360–362 [I.iv.20.23]; 372–376 [I.iv.25]) and as prophet (2005a: 370–371 [I.iv.24.3]). By all surviving accounts, his reputation – for better and for worse – often preceded him. Philostratus draws much of the material of his biography from the notebooks of one of Apollonius' disciples, Damis of Nineveh, who is concerned to document against nefarious rumors to the contrary that his master was not a *magos*, a "wise man," connotatively a "wizard," even a "charlatan" (2005a: 34–35 [I.1.2]). He emphasized instead Apollonius' gifts of healing (2005b: 206–209 [II.vi.43.1–2]), the striking spiritual aura that filled so many with wonder and opened so many royal and priestly doors and, always, his remarkable wit, the ironies always on the tip of his tongue and his preternatural readiness to correct or complete the judgments of even the wisest of his interlocutors. Following Damis and others, Philostratus' travelogue remains full of reports of wonders to rival Herodotus' own. Indeed, if still occasionally impressionable, Herodotus is a better-honed skeptic than Philostratus.

Foucault was uneasy with Weber's sociology of rationalization for the solid reason – which Weber recognized – that the history of the modernity dominant in the West was a history of much more and much else besides the march of rationalization and thus amenable to many other metrics besides that of rationalization, even as he seemed to agree with Weber that with the ascendance of capitalism and the state, history indeed evinced a slouching toward the Bethlehem of a rationalism of a strongly instrumentalistic variety (Foucault 2000a: 229–233). Apollonius' life is not sufficient to undermine a teleological conception of the history of the West as the unilinear triumph of reason. It is nevertheless a modest but forceful example of the diffusion of the rationalism of the classical philosophers into a broader social and cultural environment in which the miraculous was (not to put too paradoxical a spin on it) commonplace and in which the "extraordinary" person was likely to win a reputation – not always uniform – in which virtue in its ethical sense fused with and tempered even as it was tempered by powers suggesting the order of the divine. E. R. Dodd's seminal *Greeks and the Irrational* can still serve to remind us how deeply even the polis, even Athens, was infused with the ritual and magical arts and esotericism that always thrived in such therapeutic and oracular sites as Eleusis and Delphi (Dodds 1951).

Apollonius for his part is an avatar of the pre-Socratic sage, "whose specialism," as Jonathon Barnes has put it, "was omniscience" (1979: 20; cf. Vernant 1982: 40) and whose revelatory and often practically and poetically inventive intelligence was most convincingly embodied in the recluse wild and long of hair or the wanderer of austere comportment whose abundant energies could not be countenanced to come from the meager means of his material sustenance alone. His semiotic counterpart is the hero, of whom there were any ancient number, but of whom the none too keen-witted Hercules was most widely adored, at least from the late fourth century BCE until the establishment of Christianity. Yet Hercules belongs to the martial virtues that Apollonius at once sublimates and surpasses in his trek toward wisdom. If his is the greater and more complete ethical example – certainly for Damis of Nineveh – this is because he reveals his bravery not in battle but in his very venturing forth into a world only vaguely known and known often enough to be unwelcoming. He reveals the justness that he cherishes at once in his readiness to have others be his masters and to offer to others his powers and his wisdom, to anyone who might care to have them or to anyone who might be in need of them, discreetly if without apparent discrimination.

The charismatic and the ethical

Antitype of the ancient sage and a foreshadowing of the Christian saint, perhaps one of the biographical models for the writers of the gospels of Jesus of Nazareth, Apollonius invites us to turn even further away from the classical philosophers and, once again, toward Weber. Weber famously distinguishes among three types of "legitim-ate domination" or (as we have it in English) "authority": bureau-cratic, traditional and charismatic. The first two are marked by routine: bureaucratic authority has its legitimacy in rules and regu-lations; traditional authority has it in custom. Charismatic authority has no routine and takes us directly to what serves Weber at various junctures as something of a sociological primal scene, a scene in which among other things rationalization approaches absolute zero and the divide between the anethical and the ethical domains, between the one and the other ecology, has yet to be made. This is precisely its analytical importance to an anthropology of ethics. The scene in question is marked by what in Greek would be called *krisis*, "separating" or "distinguishing," "decision," also an "event" or "issue," also the "interpretation" of a dream or omen and, in a sense that converges with that of dikê, a "dispute" or "suit" or the "judg-ment" that concludes a trial (including that of the *hêmera kriseôs*, the Judgment Day of Matthew's gospel). It is, obviously, the source from which the English "crisis" derives. Weber does not appeal to the Greek, but nevertheless depicts a scene of crisis in introducing what in English is his best-known and methodologically most thorough ideal-typification (stress ideal-typification, not empirical descrip-tion) of charismatic authority. The scene is one in which the typically subliminal themitical normativity of everyday routine is in suspension:

The provisioning of all demands that go beyond those of everyday routine has had, in principle, an entirely heterogeneous, namely, a *charismatic* foundation; the further back we look in history, the more we find this to be the case. This means that the "natural" leaders – in times of psychic, physical, economic, ethical, religious, political distress – have been neither officeholders nor incumbents of an "occupation" in the present sense of the word, that is, men who have acquired expert knowledge and who serve for remuneration. The natural leaders in distress have been the holders of specific gifts of body and spirit; and these gifts have been believed to be supernatural, not accessible to everybody. (Weber 1946d: 245)

The scene of crisis is a scene of the unfamiliar or of disturbance, in which the experience of the disruption or of the failure of the reproduction of the routine is also the impetus of thought and action, perhaps of urgent response.

Weber appropriates the historical sociology of charisma and charismatic authority from the first volume of Rudolph Sohm's *Kirchenrecht* (1892), which departs from Paul's evocation of the *kharisma* or "gift of divine grace" in his first epistle to the Corinthians (12:4) in an analysis of the peculiarly counter-ecclesiastic – counter-institutional, even anti-institutional – authority upon which the Christian movement claimed to stand as it was establishing itself. Weber undertakes a "political" expansion of Sohm's conceptualization of charisma, putting the warlord, the raging Achilles, shoulder-to-shoulder with the prophet, with Jesus himself. These are odd bedfellows, but are for Weber a proper pair for at least three of their ideal-typical characteristics. First, both are – for those who deem them charismatic – literally extraordinary, endowed with powers and capable of actions beyond the abilities of the merely mortal. Second, both are radically indifferent if not positively opposed to the routine demands of any given institutional order, and above all of economic routine. As Weber puts it:

The sharp contrast between charisma and any "patriarchal" structure that rests upon the ordered basis of the "household" lies in [the charismatic] rejection of rational economic conduct. In its "pure" form, charisma is never a source of private gain for its holders in the sense of economic exploitation by the making of a deal. Nor is it a source of income in the form of pecuniary compensation, and just as little does it involve an orderly taxation for the material requirement of its mission. If the mission is one of peace, individual patrons provide the necessary means for charismatic structures ... In the case of charismatic warrior heroes, booty represents one of the ends as well as the material means of the mission ...

In order to do justice to their mission, the holders of charisma, the master as well as his disciples and followers, must stand outside the ties of this world, outside of routine occupations, as well as outside the routine obligations of family life. (1946d: 247–248)

Hence, the sociological hallmark of charismatic authority itself: it is stricto sensu non-normative. It is thus both logically and practically antithetical to any of the themitical regimes – whether traditional or rational-legal – that might transpire through one or another process of routinization. The only criteria of its justification are performative: "The charismatic hero gains and maintains authority solely by proving his strength in life. If he wants to be a prophet, he must work miracles; if he wants to be a warlord, he must perform heroic deeds" (1946d: 249). Charismatic authority stands or falls with the charismatic leader's continuous conjuration of extraordinary effects.

Finally, both the warlord and the prophet are of the same political mind or in any event of the same political êthos. Both are sovereign in refusing to recognize any compromise or sharing of power within the realm they claim as their own. They reject any laws, or at least any laws other than those they themselves decree. Weber is very fond of paraphrasing the central rhetorical device of Jesus' Sermon on the Mount (Matt. 5–7): "It is written ... but I say unto you ... " (1946d: 250). If charismatic authority is "revolutionary" (250), this is precisely because the charismatic leader reveals (for those who follow or revere him or her or it) the inadequacy of the established social and cultural order. As leader, however, the charismatic acknowledges and can acknowledge only the powers with which he or she is invested, whether by a god or in essence. Hence, charismatic leadership entails a relationship with the charismatic following that is entirely homologous to that between master and slave. A relationship there must be, since charismatic authority is a social fact, not a psychological one. Yet charismatic leadership can accommodate the other only in one mode: as follower. Here, subjectivation indeed dissolves into subjection and justness along with it.

We are thus warranted in inferring that in Weberian sociology's primal scene – ideal-typically at least and to the extent that it is ever realized in fact – there is no such thing as ethics. That his "value-free" methodology does not inhibit him from considering whether Mormon prophet Joseph Smith might not simply have accomplished a "hoax" (1946d: 246) strongly suggests that Weber himself would license the same inference: in the primal charismatic scene, there is simply no space or place for ethics. That he also finds and takes the opportunity to fashion the ecstatic warriors retained in Byzantium as the "blond beasts" of a *Genealogy of Morals* of whose argument he is skeptical only reinforces that suggestion (1946d: 246; cf. Nietzsche 1956: 175). The logical and practical agon on the charismatic stage pits sovereignty against ethics, but in a quite specific sense. The sovereign actor is an anethical or sur-ethical actor not merely because he or she is the source of the law, of the always somewhat magical crossing of the divide between ought and is, fact and value. Such a conception of sovereignty is narrower than the conception at work in Weber's analysis. The berserk warrior is not sovereign in so strictly a political-theoretic sense and the prophet who teaches by example rather than by decree resists if he or she does not positively defy classification as an executive or legislator. The contradiction between the sovereign and the ethical is also ontological, but in just this sense: in the sovereign's cosmos, there is no one to serve as an ethical other. Such a cosmos, to repeat, includes others; it is always a social cosmos. Yet it includes them only as hierophants, or if not as hierophants then as instruments or altogether unaccommodatingly as enemies to the death. Hierophants might share in the charisma of their sovereign, but what is absent from the sovereign's cosmos is any other with any recognized chrism of his or her or its own.

Zigon attempts to meld Heidegger's analysis of the difference between being ready-at-hand and being present-to-hand together with Knut Ejler Løgstrup's (1997) and Alain Badiou's (2001) none too mutually consistent categoricalisms in conceptualizing the "ethical moment" or the moment at which "ethics must be performed" (2007: 138) as a moment of the "breakdown" or Foucauldian problematization of a moral code or system of conduct taken more or less unreflectively for granted. Such a moment is surely one of crisis, and appeal to Weber's diagnostics of charisma allows us to redeem Zigon's intuition of its diagnostic importance. Yet the same diagnostics also allows us to see the shortcomings of rendering the "moral" (here close to but not the equivalent of my "themitical") and the ethical so diametrically opposed that all continuity between them is lost. Zigon's fashioning of morality as a system effectively without any link to intention or deliberation, as a habitual system of conduct into which human beings are – à la Heidegger – "thrown" (135), as part of the constituents of unthinking everydayness, and the ethical moment as altogether its opposite, does not merely strain semantics. It also disrupts the logical and pragmatic connection between the ethical gesture and themitical principle, or even more broadly between ethical value and themitical normativity. It further disrupts the fundamental connection between the distinctive grounding of ethical discourse in a common semantic code and the distinctive programming of that discourse through one or another regimen of the justification of ethical evaluation.

Such binarism leads Zigon to declare that the "primary goal of ethics" is "to move back *into* the world," once again to "dwell in the unreflective comfort of the familiar," a turning of Heidegger on his head that regrettably leaves all the solid boundaries of the Heideggerian understanding of tradition entirely intact. It leads him to pronounce that it is only in "the moment of breakdown" that "it can be said that people work on themselves" (2007: 138). Put system-theoretically (as Zigon himself almost puts it), ethics so construed amounts to nothing more than a device for the reduction of complexity. What is lost with that construal is, among other things, any capacity to recognize that routinization itself is a mechanism fundamentally of selection that in its most typical modalities reduces the intensity of complexity across certain registers only to allow and even encourage increasing its intensity across others. Methodologically, Zigon is, moreover, committed to a dialogue with philosophers, but a dialogue that has no other final authority than that of philosophical introspection itself. Hence, he cannot treat philosophical discourse as a field of data in need of diagnosis but instead must treat it as the source alone from which an adequate "theoretical framework" for an anthropology of ethics must derive. Since philosophical discourse – and ethics as one among other matters within it – is jointly inconsistent, Zigon is forced to pick, choose and cobble together his framework from philosophical minds most like his own. In the process, he falls into the sort of position-taking that anyone who passes through the doors of the philosophical sanctum cannot avoid, at least until he or she passes out of it again. This leads to his attributing to what he refers to as "neo-Aristotelian and Foucauldian approaches" in the anthropology of ethics the presumption that "one becomes a moral person *not* by following rules or norms, *but* by training oneself in a certain set of practices" (2007: 133; my emphasis). The contrast is false (as is any claim that the neo-Aristotelian or the Foucauldian would think of ethics as only self-taught). Furthermore, and again contrary to what Zigon's commitments effectively force him to conclude, routinization, self-reference and work on the self are not opposed to one another but are instead mutually reinforcing. Without its repertory of pedagogies of autopoiesis, ethics would indeed be only an affair of the critical moment. Even the most casual observation – self-observation included – is enough to confirm that its temporalities are far more diverse and usually of far greater extension than that.

Whatever its (properly) philosophical or political-theoretic implications may be, Weber's primal scene thus generates a sociological lemma that seems to me as fit as any available to serve as a basic working postulate of an anthropology of ethics. Put in the terms of its Weberian semiotics, it would go something like this: Ethics emerges within the primal scene of charismatic performance at the moment at which the charismatic leader recognizes the chrism of the other. Clarification is in order. First, though the contradiction between the sovereign and the ethical is inherent to the Weberian primal scene, its overcoming in the charismatic's gesture of accommodation is still within its bounds.

In any event, that gesture remains so to the extent that the accommodation of the chrism of the other does not yet constitute an act of routinization, the establishment of normativity, and registers only the divide between the charismatic collective and the unextraordinary others who do not belong to it. The charismatic scene is an anethical scene insofar as the leader recognizes his or her or its charisma as a purely personal quality in which followers may bask. It becomes ethical – in however limited a manner – whenever the leader acknowledges that his or her or its charisma is shared among the following, when charisma is no longer a purely personal but instead a collective affair, an affair of the jointly "elect."

It is unclear whether Weber would agree with this formulation. His stipulation that the charismatic leader's mission must prove itself in bringing about the well-being of its followers (1946d: 249) is compatible with it. Yet just such a pragmatic understanding of charismatic proof leads him to cast such apparent failures of worldly success as Jesus' crucifixion in terms perhaps too close to the letter of those of Matthew's and Mark's Jesus himself – as the deprivation of a chrism and so as the loss of the authority it had conferred (1946d: 248). The semiotics of charismatic authority is more complex and so, too, as a consequence is its pragmatics.

In his most programmatic essay on religion, Bourdieu himself notes that Weber's excessively pragmatic comprehension of charismatic authority prevents him "from grasping the religious message ... and from raising the question of strictly logical and noseological functions of what he considers a quasi-systematic ensemble of responses to existential questions" (1991: 4). Bourdieu is remarkably ready to forgive the lapse, however, for he immediately goes on to commend Weber for having given himself

> a way of linking the contents of mythical discourse (and even its syntax) to the religious interests of those who produce it, diffuse it, and receive it, and more profoundly, of constructing a system of religious

beliefs as practices as the more or less transfigured expression of the strategies of different categories of specialists competing for monopoly over the administration of the goods of salvation and of the different classes interested in their services. (1991: 4).

The claim serves as the point of departure of his own analysis, which can thus construe the ideal-typical charismatic, the prophet, as a "petty independent entrepreneur of salvation" claiming to produce and distribute goods of salvation of a new type and devalue the old ones, in the absence of any initial capital or of any security or guarantee other than his "person" and successful in strict accord with "the ability of his discourse and his practice to mobilize the virtually heretical religious interests of determinate groups and classes of laypersons through the effect of consecration" (1991: 24). Inherently at odds with "the church," the prophet must nevertheless appeal as much as his clerical and establishment adversaries to the "religious habitus" of his potential following, to that repository of specifically "religious capital" that is "the generative basis of all thoughts, perceptions, and actions conforming with the norms of a religious representation of the natural and supernatural world" and "objectively adjusted to the principles of a political vision of the social world – and to them only" (1991: 22).

There is nothing primitive about the Bourdieusian prophet. Explicitly rejecting the Durkheimian quest for elementary forms (Durkheim 1995), Bourdieu turns (somewhat surprisingly, given his argument against it in the *Outline*) to a methodological finalism that accords analytical privilege to the necessarily complex and rigorously compartmentalized society in which religion sustains itself as an autonomous "field." The precedent might seem to be Weber's (cf. Weber 1946b), but the outcome is not. Bourdieu's charismatic retains the aura of the sociologically radical in appealing to the virtual heretics in his midst, but he is a much diminished and distinctly Gallicized reflection of his Weberian counterpart. Bourdieusian charismatics are subject to the demands not merely of a potential following but of the structural conditions in which they are embedded at large – or at least of their "virtual" dimensions. They are, moreover, constrained to act only within those conditions, which within Bourdieu's problematic of structural reproduction and thus for his analytical purposes constitute and must constitute both a structurally and an organizationally closed system. Weber's concepts of charismatic authority and charismatic action are, in contrast, ecological concepts, ranging at once over processes transpiring between a system and its environment and those internal to the system itself. As I have already noted, they both have their fulcrum in crisis, in systemic disruption, at the interface between system and environment, and not in competition, as Bourdieu would have it. Bourdieusian charismatics are wielders of religious capital, which is actually political capital, suitably disguised and directed, and precisely as such objectively adjusted to the principles of a political vision of the social world. If they are thus not always agents of social reproduction, of the perfect repetition of the social past in the social future, they are still obedient to the rules of the social game, players who in spite of their intentions are destined to carry forward the rules of the game of the social past into the social future. In its encounter with its apparent nemesis, with crisis itself, the Bourdieusian theory of religious practice still belongs to the universe of von Neumann and Morgenstern (2004 [1944]) – which is once again a system, not an ecology – whose technical rationalism and (polythetic) economism remain intact. For all that Weber was himself tempted to politicize charismatic authority, he was far less vulnerable than Bourdieu to the logocentric seductions of any theory that reveals politics itself to be exclusively a domain of "rationalist deductions," technically rational norms and economistic interests, material or symbolic (cf. Evans 1999: 19).

In any event, one can make little sense of the charisma of the typical Christian martyr, much less of the enduring charisma of Jesus himself, if one rests with interpreting suffering and the sacrifice of the self only as evidence of having been forsaken by one's god and deprived of one's formerly miraculous powers. On the contrary, the Christian interpretation of the crucifixion is not one of the loss of charisma but instead of its miraculous distribution. The Christ who dies for the sins of the other, for the sins of every other, radically extends the election that was formerly the privilege of his fellow Jews. On the cross, but still entirely enclosed within the extraordinary noise and thunder of the denouement of the charismatic agon, the Christ renounces his sovereignty in favor of ethical universality. Nor, for that matter, is it Achilles the slayer of Hector and conqueror of Troy alone who is the most charismatic of the heroes of the *Iliad*. It is also the Achilles enraged and desperate with grief over the death of his beloved Patroclus and the Achilles who, returned to his senses, finds it in himself to pay honor to Hector's grieving father, Priam, the father of Patroclus' own killer.

Modes of ethical evaluation

In the Western philosophical tradition as elsewhere, the ethical acknowledgment and accommodation of the other exhibits impressive semiotic – or as the philosophers would have it, ontological or metaphysical – variety. The ground of the obligation to pay the other ethical regard may be logocentric in the Western classical circle, but it is not purely that of logos even there. In the background even of a cosmology as logophilic as Aristotle's, the ethical subject that remains under the aegis of the gods still asserts its sacral inviolability. In Greece and widely beyond it, the identification of the ethical subject can also include such concrete or mundane or at least experiential considerations as whether someone lives or pursues his or her own interests or appears capable of suffering among many others. Whether or not a subject counts as an ethical subject can hinge on such heady and transcendental criteria as the possession of dignity, belonging to the kingdom of ends or being an end-in-itself or an end-for-itself or indeed a transcendental other (Levinas 2003; Løgstrup 1997). In contrast to these more inclusive categories and qualities, common ethical regard – in the West and elsewhere – often remains resolutely local, extending effective acknowledgment and accommodation no farther than to kin and friends and perhaps the occasional guest or urchin or foundling. Whatever might be expected of the ideal ethical subject, the ethical everyperson is frankly not striking for his or her ardent logicism in the West or anywhere else. An anthropologist of ethics does well to keep this in mind.

One or another grounding of the demand of ethical regard, one or another specification of the criteria of or postulation of the essence of ethical value is, as I have already suggested, nevertheless constitutive of the ethical domain as an ecological domain. Hence, it needs advancing as yet another formal dimension of a diagnostics and theorization of that domain. Call it the dimension of the mode of ethical valuation. Logically, any such mode is a mode of valuation only within a given ethical semiotics and (as I have also already suggested) stands together with one or another mode of the justification of ethical decisions as a constituent of one or another mode of ethical judgment. The anthropologist of ethics should not slip into a naturalistic fallacy in presuming that such value actually resides any more than the criteria of ethical justification in an objective condition functioning as a criterion of the ethical agent or locus of ethical value. Nor should he or she slip into a metaphysical fallacy, a fallacy of pure reason, in accepting that one or another idealization of ethical value is in fact its real essence, and semiotic alternatives be damned. (Philosophers can do what they will.)

That discursive formations do not provide the anthropologist with inferential passes outside of them does not, however, constrain him or her to the vapid relativism that simply sees a thousand flowers blooming and deems them all equally worthy members of the whole grand bouquet. Diversity isn't everything. As a causal-analytical enterprise, an anthropology of ethics can and should endeavor to account for both the scope – which is impressive – and the sensible limits of ethical valuation. Or to put the same point differently: like ethical justification, ethical value is an irreducibly semiotic phenomenon and so belongs to the realm of the intersubjective, to the realm of Wittgensteinian language games and forms of life (Wittgenstein 1958). But not all language games and forms of life autopoietically work equally well. All the anthropological instruments agree that human beings can elaborate codes at a far remove from the stubborn this-worldly requirements and constraints of sustainable autopoiesis. All the instruments agree that human beings are capable of finding and do often find meaning in the most extravagant of ideas. Anthropological instruments can nevertheless provide a measure of that extravagance, without in any way presuming semiotically to invalidate or logically to reduce to absurdity anything short of patent contradiction – or even that – in doing so. The anthropologist of ethics can accordingly make short work of the ethics of the lachrymose doctrines of Karl Robert Eduard von Hartmann, born in Berlin at the cusp of the bourgeois revolutions and dying in the same city just a few years after the turn of the nineteenth into the twentieth century. He was a prolific writer, but his works sit largely uncelebrated on library shelves for good anthropological reason. He argued broadly (and not altogether unreasonably!) that because human happiness is impossible, either in this or in any other world, the only fully rational course of human action consists in the radical pursuit of non-action, and not least in the non-action of a passive genocide, a refusal to reproduce, that would leave the world free of human striving and human suffering alike in the course of a few generations (Anonymous 1911). Hartmann is not a Zen mystic in gloomy, Teutonic fin-de-siècle bearing. His despairing anti-eudaimonism recommends a far more material and global end to our orbit on the wheel of desire than does the Buddhist advocate of satori. For all this, it is not incoherent. Its problem is rather that it is autopoietically bankrupt.

The sovereign regard of human beings as mere instruments is logically incompatible with their being attributed ethical value. The Hartmannian regard of the ethically appropriate destiny of the human species is causally incompatible with social autopoiesis. Were it adopted as the core normative directive of a social system, it would press human action generally toward an end contrary to that of autopoiesis and thus contrary to one fundamental condition of the sustenance of any social system as such. This point does not belong to evolutionary psychology – among other things, it is not a just-so story – but it is functionalist. The anthropologist of ethics is not and cannot be merely a functionalist, but should not hesitate to be one when functionalist assessment is as inescapable as it is here. This does not, again, deprive Hartmann's existentialism of meaning. Plainly, not merely for Hartmann himself but for the considerable number of his late nineteenth-century reader-ship, such Swinburnian or Schopenhauerian pessimism was all the more existentially revelatory for being so bleak. Nor is it inconceivable that the whole of the human species might have embraced it. That it did not do so and has not done so is nevertheless what one might expect. On the anthropological metric of extravagance, Hartmannian pessimism is moderately extreme but his endorsement of passive genocide is genu-inely "far out."

An anthropology of ethics must ground itself in practices for a number of reasons. First, as we have been aware since Geertz's crucial, Wittgensteinian argument in "Thick Description," the meaning of signs and symbols is available to us empirically precisely because it depends in the first instance on their practical deployment in practical contexts in which publicly available criteria can operate as evidence of their proper or improper use (Geertz 1973: 3–30). In its practical deployment alone – its referential deployment included – can most coding approach pragmatic determinacy. Whatever else the post-structuralist critics of the ahistoricity of the structural and organizational matrix of communication may or may not have taught us, they have taught us that the fixity of the relationship between signifier and signified cannot be taken for granted. Whether or not they were uniformly aware that they were doing so, they have accordingly taught us that we must look first not to *langue* but instead to *parole* in compiling the lexicons of the subjects of our research. Even the Derridian must ultimately be in agreement with this position (though not every Derridian might realize it). Second, practice constitutes the primary dynamic of autopoiesis – of systemic reproduction, as Bourdieu has argued, but *pace* Bourdieu also of systemic production and alteration. Third, as every fieldworker knows in the end, only in and through practice – not merely ethical practice and linguistic practice included – can the capacity to participate be transformed into active competence.

These reasons do not, however, imply that practices and their attendant codings are in mutual accord. Correctly, the Bourdieusian has it that the contrary is typically the case. The same reasons do not imply, either, that codings are derivative of practice, much less that their only raison d'être is the sustenance and support of the autopoiesis of the practices they attend. Not as implication but as presumption, sometimes as dogma, the latter is a hallmark of the classically functionalist construal of the relation between actions on the one hand and "norms and beliefs and values" on the other. The presumption is operative still with Parsons, though begins to fade with his students. Among them and in part on the basis of a less mediated reading of Weber than Parsons' own, Geertz gradually drifts toward a textualism that in several of its later expressions also risks detachment from the practice-centered manifesto of interpretive anthropology that he proclaims in "Thick Description." Luhmann for his part insists from *The Differentiation of Society* forward that "structure" and "semantics" diverge and that the former tends to be simpler and less elaborated than the latter. Just this tendency is manifest in philosophical discourse in the West, particularly so in its recent Anglo-American analytical preserves, in which the often wildly improbable scenarios of one or another putatively heuristic *Gedankenexperiment* can better be set within the alien atmospheres of as yet undetected planets and galaxies than within the humdrum of everyday terrestrial life (cf. Bourdieu 1990: 48). A homologous semiotic condition emerges in the literary field once aesthetics as an institution becomes differentiated from the pedagogical and the religious, its criteria of worth increasingly centered on originality and its mode of signification less referential than allusive. None of this, however, entitles the anthropologist of literature or philosophy or ethics to dismiss the discursively outré as somehow beyond the horizons of legitimate anthropological attention. It entitles him or her only to adopt as a working presumption that the outré is parasitic or (more delicately) dependent on discursive complexes more intimately related to the humdrum of everyday practice. At least this should be so in the ultimate analysis – which, granted, isn't very helpful.

Ethical value

That ethical value remains within the Weberian primal scene and that its semiotics in that scene partakes of the semiotics of the chrism suggests a strategy through which to approach its general characterization. It suggests above all that any attempt at a substantive rendering of ethical value, at pursuing in its auratic and atmospheric mist any particular molecular code, is misguided. The substantive variability of the modulations of ethical value merely within the Western tradition already militates against such an approach. The extraordinary and unroutinized powers of the charismatic – in failure as in success – positively preclude it. Semiotically, the schematic of ethical value like that of charisma can permit of so much substantive variation because it is fundamentally substantively indeterminate. A placeholder for the extraordinary, for that which is not profane, for the Durkheimian "sacred" (Durkheim 1995: 35–39), the schematic of ethical value thus approximates what, after Roman Jakobson and Lévi-Strauss, one could call the "zero-phonemic." In his introduction to Marcel Mauss' collected papers, Lévi-Strauss expands Jakobson's concept of a phoneme that has no distinct differential value (Jakobson and Lotz 1949) into the concept of the "floating signifier," a meaning-bearing unit that nevertheless has no distinct meaning and so is capable of bearing any meaning, operating within any given linguistic system as the very possibility of signification itself (Lévi-Strauss 1950: xlix–l). Lévi-Strauss' example is that of "mana," which generations of anthropologists have struggled to define. In its operation, it is in any event very close to charisma – all the more so now that, as Matthew Tomlinson has shown, it has come to serve contemporary Fijians as an index of success and both human and divine blessedness but also of the power of failure and loss (Tomlinson 2006; cf. Graeber 2001: 170–172).

Any rush to identify ethical value in its schematic indeterminacy with the value of signification itself, however, runs the risk of arriving at semiotic fallacy, at the mistaken inference that from significance in its linguistic sense significance in an ethical sense results. Yet the homology between the semiotics of so many of the signifiers of ethical value – "logos" included – and that of both "charisma" and "mana" cannot diagnostically or theoretically be overlooked. Two features of the floating signifier are worth emphasizing. The first is that, because it lacks any precise semiotic determination, it becomes an all the more effective contrary of any sign of instrumentality or contingency. As semiotic systems around the world attest, the floating signifier is an especially effective carrier of conceptions of the transcendent and the absolute. Second, and as Roy Rappaport and Michael Lambek have also underscored, in lacking determination, the floating signifier also positively conveys an omnipotentiality that remains not merely undifferentiated but also atmospheric, ineffable, beyond articulation (Lambek 2008: 144; Rappaport 1999). The floating signifier is thus made for the mystic – not least for such a mystic as Georges Bataille – as that semiotic abyss that is also a plenitude and thus a topos of the excess that permits only of experiencing, never of pinning down or spelling out.

No mode of ethical valuation of any substantive determinacy whatever is thus quite able to preserve the semiotic limitlessness of the floating signifier. Ethics demands judgment, which demands justification, which demands criteria of the rectitude of both diction and declamation, which demand functional language games, Wittgensteinian forms of life. So perhaps such modern mystics as Agehananda Bharati (cf. Kripal 2001: 207–249) are correct in drawing a sharp divide between mystical experience and ethical practice. Yet in doing so, they are also in danger of obscuring not merely the semiotic but also the experiential aura and atmosphere that surround ethical value and the aura and atmosphere that it also frequently inspires. Nor is this merely the aura of the charismatic, the extraordinary man or woman made for extraordinary times. In one of its anthropologically best-known manifestations, it is also the aura that surrounds the initiate passing into and dwelling within the liminal phase of the rite of passage – a phase that Constantine Cavafy often depicted in his poems and in which he was in several respects constrained to dwell in his actual life. For Victor Turner, the liminal is the contradiction and contraversion of the determinacy and definition of ordinary social life. It is "anti-structural" and in its dissolution of the inevitable divisions and compartments of ordinary social life it is at least a momentary liberation from social constraint and a window into our common humanity. So at least the humanist Turner had it (1969: 105–111; cf. Faubion 2008a). We do not, however, need to follow Turner either in his dialectical or in his specifically humanist interpretation of liminality – which can often be full of the worst unpleasantries, as he certainly knew – in order to recognize rites of passage as technologies of the transformation of the subject, targeting its ethical substance, doing their work to displace the subject from its former position and ready it for its placement into a position that will define some part at least of its themitical future. Here what is often at issue is not a mere development or enlargement or diminishing of a given subject position but a shifting from one subject position to another. We do not have to be Turnerians to recognize in that trans-formative process the subject's immersion in or infusion with the overflowing abyss of a significance that is never merely semiotic, but also always that of the ethical itself.

Ethical value and identity

The chrism that marks an Achilles or a Jesus is hardly interpretable within the semiotic systems to which each belongs as anything other than that of divine essence. The chrism that marks the liminal subject-in-transition is also often explicitly sacralized and is so widely and with long-standing anthropological note in such classic rites of passage as baptism, marriage and the funeral. The sacralized chrism is also a familiar stigma of the ascendant not merely to clerical but also to political office, especially the chief or monarch, who in bearing the stigma also bears the warning that what blesses can – if misvalued, if desecrated, if betrayed – turn into poison. Caste in traditional India and throughout Micronesia comes with a sacralized chrism. Both examples are illustrative of a further feature of charisma well recorded in the anthropological record and typical of hierarchically ordered systems the world over. The ancient Greek regard of the free-born (not even to mention the enslaved) woman within a system not quite hierarchical in character is, however, an equally illustrative example in its way. Most modern philosophers won't like it, but the anthropologist has to say it: charismatic universalism is much more the anthropological exception than the anthropological rule. A philosopher might thus argue – and some do – that most human beings and most human collectivities simply fail to realize anything that could properly be called ethics. From a semantically introspective point of view, such a pronouncement is capable of justification. As interpreter rather than a semanticist, however, the anthropologist is not entitled to make the same pronouncement. To be more precise, he or she is not warranted in doing so; even in graduated and particularistic modalities the chrism retains too close a family resemblance to its universalist cousins to be refused entry into the hermeneutical circle. From the heights of a system-theoretic and second- (or n-)order point of view, one can only observe that the effort required in sustaining any organizational asymmetry and its attendant coding tends in the long run to require a greater expenditure of energy and the necessity of coping with a greater train of irritations than abandoning it does. This said, generalized ethical chrisms come with their own cost – that of contextual indeterminacy, which is an irritant in its own right. From a first-order point of view, one might further point out that many "humanist" ethics fall far short of genuine universalism as well. Utilitarianisms tend to do them one better, as does the expansive ethical vitalism of certain Buddhists or the Jinas (on the latter, see Laidlaw 2007).

The ethical chrism has many other modalities besides its sacred modalities. To consider only a single aggregate of cases, the charisma of pleasure and suffering for the hedonist or the utilitarian tends toward secularity and often arrives there. Nevertheless, the chrism always retains its zero-phonemic link to the sacred and so, following Geertz and Robert Bellah, to the relatively "ultimate" (Bellah 1972; Geertz 1973: 98–108; cf. Pandian 1991). Like the zero-phonemic itself, the "ultimate" is only diacritical. It has no determinate content. What content it takes on is, moreover, code-specific and so, once again, must remain a matter of research. Though very, very costly to sustain, coded and correlatively organized subsystems that reduce the distinction between the ultimate and the merely contingent or mundane subject are also part of the anthropological record (and not just the archival record). Such subsystems are often sacralized to the point of saturation. They are often fiercely bounded. Traditional India's caste system may be the most encompassing among them. More typically, they have the character of enclaves and are of relatively small scale. Mormonism at its origins is one case in point. Hasidic Judaism past and present may be another. The aboriginal bands and "tribes" were once deemed such cases as well, and "classic primitives" as a result were so deemed in general. The judgment now looks to have been less evidential than projective, even mythologizing (Kuper 1988). In any event, the more typical case – and the case within the more or less single organizational system within which each one of us as a more or less porous subsystem lives – is one in which the gap between the ultimate subject position and the merely proximate one can be wide. The Calvinist contrary, however, if originally the habit of an enclave, is now diffused through a great swath of the Euro-American middle classes. For the Calvinist, religious or secular, almost any and seemingly even the most proximate occupation can accrue the dignity and sanctity of a calling and thus merge even to the point of equivalence, even to the point of identity, with the realization of the subject in its ultimate ethical fulfillment of and surrender to a calling (cf. Evans 1999: 21, 24). Of course, the New York waiter who aspires to his redemption on the off-Broadway stage is free to disagree.

The gap between proximate and ultimate facilitates several further distinctions and clarifications. First of all, it at once licenses and imposes the distinction between the competencies that must be cultivated in order to occupy a given subject position and ply a given role and what are usually called in English the "virtues" that render a subject position itself ethical. The subject position of the anthropologist is not unusual in this regard, but it is colorful even so. The anthropologist – one must admit – may well be very good and even at his or her best as an anthropologist qua anthropologist, qua inquirer into human and post-human affairs, when he is snooping about, withholding or disguising his actual interests, lying now and again, treating his subjects as if they were merely the means of the accumulation of knowledge, pretending to embrace or at least accept what he in fact finds repulsive and so on. Most anthropologists (and every Internal Board of Review) are now in agreement that he is not rightly considered virtuous in so doing – though certain qualifications might admit of a hearing. In the critique of Plato's ethics that closely follows the introductory remarks of the *Nicomachean Ethics*, Aristotle himself points out the inescapable plurality of "the good." Once again, the anthropologist of ethics is indebted to his wisdom.

The difference between the good anthropologist qua anthropologist and the good anthropologist qua ethical subject displays further features that support a working hypothesis concerning the general relation between the merely competent and the ethical subject. That hypothesis might be phrased as follows: that relation is in its widest distribution a relation in which the ethical has both normative and organizational priority over the merely competent subject. Thus phrased, the hypothesis is ambiguous, but both of the assertions that it puts forward are of analytical and investigative relevance. Hence, one sense in which the ethical subject typically has priority over its merely competent counterpart lies in its imposing normative strictures on what can pass as permissible competency. (Thus, the competent anthropologist might be an extraordinarily competent artist of deceit or liar, but …) Less straightforward, less likely but still of investigative concern is the possibility that the ethical subject has priority over the merely competent subject because logically or causally or both, some or all of its presumptive virtues are requisite to the realization of competencies of almost any sort at all. This is implausible, but the issue merits inquiry not merely of an introspective but also of an empirical sort as much as its more straightforward and likelier counterpart.

Finally, the relatively ultimate position of the ethical subject may allow us to bring some measure of analytical rigor to the now loose and diffuse usage of "identity" in an anthropology that has been overrun with devotion to it since the 1970s. It invites doing so by way of reviving or at least recalling a doxa and so the usually unarticulated tenet of an older cultural anthropology: that the identity of a cultural actor, the question of who (rather than what) he or she is, has to do with his or her place in the cosmos, however variably that place might be conceived from one "worldview" to another (e.g. Hallowell 1960). Whether it might also serve as a rejoinder to the often quite articulate tendency in social anthropology to reduce what I am calling subject positions to some amalgam of status and role and dispense with the category of identity entirely (see, e.g., Nadel 1951) is moot, since social anthropology is now barely discrete if discrete at all from cultural anthropology. (By the by, the author thinks of himself as a sociocultural anthropologist – whatever anyone else might think of him.) In any event, the intervention is not revolutionary. The linkage between identity and one's place in the cosmos is not unknown in contemporary anthropology (e.g. Greenway 1998). A great many anthropologists who currently make use of the category of identity plainly do not think that it is reducible to status or role or some combination of the two. Many of them are correct in thinking so. At least the case can be made.

The identity that abides with the ethical chrism is in any event not identical to status in any of its standard sociological renderings. Status might be understood as position and a position of any particular status as having its status determined by the measure of prestige it commands relative to other positions, of greater or of lesser prestige. Ethically marked identity is not in general or in principle reducible to status understood as a position of (greater or lesser) prestige because of its zero-phonemic indeterminacy. It might be confused with status thus understood in those cases in which ethical value is assigned on a graduated scale and in which that value is thus in close accord with gradations of prestige. The confusion is nevertheless genuine – a blurring of the general logic of zero-phonemic value with its constriction into a mode of prestige in a particular case. With Weber, status enters the taxonomy of classic social theory as a distillation of the historical institution of the estate. It stands in contrast to Marx's class in being defined not in its relation to the means of production but rather in relation to consumption and so to its expression as and in a "lifestyle" (Weber 1946a). The position of the ethical subject may impose limits (sometimes severe limits) on what constitutes (ethically) appropriate sumptuary preferences but it rarely fully determines them and once again cannot be exhausted in or as lifestyle even if it nears such exhaustion in one or another particular instance.

The identity of the ethical subject might thus seem to be more plausibly reduced to some matrix of roles, but in the end such a reduction is itself analytically impoverished, especially semiotically impoverished. Any anthropology of ethics would best have its point of departure and return in ethical practice, but it can no more affirm Aristotle's injunction that the ethical domain is a domain exclusively of praxis rather than poiesis any more than it can affirm that the ethical domain is a domain of poiesis rather than sheer *einai*, "being." As a matter of practical fact, the ethical subject does and must engage in poiesis even in merely being an ethical subject. Because of its grounding in the zero-phonemic, however, the coding of ethical value does not license the reduction of the ethical subject to its or her or his practice any more than any other semiotic value can be reduced semiotically simply and solely to the circumstances of its use. Code and practice are not anthropologically equal partners. They are partners that are typically far from being identical twins. The reduction of ethically marked or relatively ultimate identity to its realization in a role is accordingly analytically indefensible as a general rule. As a good many New York waiters would insist, the ethical domain is not solely made up of Calvinists.

Far from it: among the anthropologically most salient subjects for the past thirty years have been those whom anthropologists themselves have been promoting as ethical subjects – subjects worthy of ethical regard and subjects worthy of ethical recognition. In that promotion, identity has been a fulcrum. The identity at issue has often been gender-indexed. At least as often it has been ethnically indexed. An anthropology of ethics has no inferential ticket that would allow it to participate directly in such processes of ethical validation and invalidation, all of which occur at a logical and so an analytical order of engagement that avoids the paradoxes arising in its own unfolding only by foreclosing acknowledgment of the contingency of the doxa on which it depends for its own autopoiesis. Anthropologists have nevertheless found their way into the ethical scene of just such processes through a pathway or pathways that the Boasians first forged but that only opened fully in the 1970s. From that point forward, a significant number of anthropologists have themselves assumed and have been professionally validated in assuming the role of a secular and political clergy in anointing their subjects of research worthy of recognition and participation within the only cosmos that they can fully share with their subjects, which is a political cosmos. Sohm could not have brought us to a comprehension of this dynamics. Weber's political expansion of the semiotic and institutional reach of charisma is indispensable for doing so.

All this said or written, nothing more than a working hypothesis is once again available. What one or another actor – in the functionally differentiated organization of the social system in which almost all of us now live and have no choice but in which to live – finds her relation to the norms and virtues of her ethical being and her professional or other competencies to be remains empirically to be seen. Or in short and more programmatically: the relationship between an ethically marked subject position and the locus and focus of what might widely be glossed as "identity" might and even should belong to the anthropologist of ethics' regulative ideas – but only as regulative idea.

From the ethical to the themitical

On the plane of working diagnostic postulates, the intimacy of the homology between the schematic of mana and that of ethical value and the attachment of the latter to the primal scene of charismatic anointment is just what invites the analytical distinction between the ethical and the themitical. Within the diagnostics and theory under development here, ethical practice is ethical in its totality. Its themitical dimensions or features are most apparent when considering the ethical subject's mode of subjectivation to norms and values. System-theoretically, the distinction at issue can be put as follows. In its originary moment, ethics does not belong to the anatomy, the physiology or the psychology of system-maintenance or the autopoietic reproduction of systemic structure or even organization. It belongs instead to and is among the constituents of social system-adjustment or the production of a social system that thenceforth will not be altogether the same, even (pace Luhmann) the same thing, that it formerly was. Its specific difference lies in its generating just that sort of adjustment in which, neither closed off from any engagement with its environment nor encountering it simply as hostile or instrumental, a system moves via the actions of the psychic systems that are its sine qua non toward a better or worse or in any case different ecology and does so in part through establishing themical normativity within that ecology. Anthony Wallace provides the partial anthropological precedent for such a view (Wallace 1956).

The distinction between the ethical and the themical might be thought of as the first taxonomical step beyond the even more basic system-theoretic distinction between system and environment. From the concept of the system, the former distinction inherits the qualitative distinctions between code and behavior or, more accurately and all the more exclusively analytically, between meaning and the structure and organization of action. Precisely and only – and again *pace* Luhmann – as the derivative of the concept of the organizationally open rather than organizationally closed system, it is relieved of the burden of accepting among its provisional axiomatics the axiom of the existence of discrete traditions or cultures or societies. Just so, it leaves the existence and the definition of any and all of these as an empirical and provisional matter, though it is capable of including them. It accordingly avoids falling by axiomatic fiat into discursive or cultural or social relativism as we currently know and have known them (cf. Hatch 1983). Technically speaking, an open-system-theoretic approach to the ethical domain is thus axiomatically and ontologically weaker – it assumes less; it is more parsimonious, more Occamist – than its familiar relativist counterparts, whether anthropological or philosophical. It is free, for example, of the analytical impasses that commitment to a Heideggerian ontology of tradition or historical Being entail. It is also able to leave undecided even the more open-ended ontology of traditions that informs the otherwise congenial and relativistically tempered philosophical programs of such virtue ethicists as MacIntyre, and in particular the ontological requisite that any tradition worthy of the name be of narrative tissue, be storied (MacIntyre 1984). That requirement might plausibly be imposed on the traditions with which MacIntyre is specifically concerned – those of distinctively human beings. Whether it should be imposed on all autopoietic systems capable of occupying ethical subject positions is more dubious – the amalgam that was Amo Paul Bishop Roden and me is a case in point – and, once again, thus best left to be empirically decided.

The very generality of the concept of the open system and its autopoiesis further points toward an account – not a normative justification! – of some at least of the universalistic criteria of ethical judgment that deontologically biased philosophies and theologies and cosmologies have yielded over the centuries. It also points toward an account of why some human actions and human practices meet with disapproval and negative sanctions more or less everywhere we find them. Habermas' formal pragmatics of communicative action looks, for example, to be a rationalization (aka reification) of autopoiesis as a communicative process as such (Habermas 1984), in spite of his skepticism toward systems theory. His three criteria of the validity of any communicative act oriented toward mutual understanding – its truth(-functionality), its normative rectitude and its sincerity or truthfulness – echo Kant, but they belong to this, our phenomenal world, and they are meant to articulate not the necessary conditions of coherent thinking and autonomous action but rather the necessary conditions of the maintenance of ongoing intersubjectively intelligible interaction. As Habermas recognizes clearly, they are purely formal criteria – "syntactic" or procedural, not "semantic" or substantive. Substantively, they remain or are compatible with remaining relativistic, since the means of determining the truth, of determining proper authority and of determining what constitutes and how to assess truthfulness may vary from one communicative (sub)system to another. That such procedural criteria are at least highly advantageous to systemic autopoiesis is plausible. Perhaps they are even necessary. If so, however, they are so only as a rule or in the long run. That they are required of every single instance of action oriented toward mutual understanding is flatly false – and would be extraordinarily inefficient as well. The naturalistic fallacy thus admits of no overcoming here, either.

Of course, actions or practices that run against the grain of the sustenance of communication are also costly. The general features of autopoiesis suggest that arbitrariness might rank among the most universal of autopoietic irritants. They might help us to account for why, across so many socioculturally specific communicative regions, the arbitrary actor is likely to be labeled not merely bad or evil but positively mad (or at once bad and evil and positively mad). Of course, systemic irritants are not autopoietically deleterious without qualification; anthropologists and historians can report that even the mad find the occasional audience (e.g. Foucault 2006). Whether or not arbitrary, acts or practices that disrupt the maintenance of communication abruptly or persistently might also be expected to be met with themitical disapprobation the communicative world over. Murder is plausibly one such act or practice. Lying is another. Even with murder and lying, however, extenuating circumstances are in great supply – and often in the name of the maintenance of autopoiesis rather than because of any systemic laxity or decadence. The requirements of communicative autopoiesis might, finally, go some way in explaining why the non-participant and the freeloader tend with ubiquity to be met with considerable disfavor and disesteem – or at the very least, in explaining why crafting an effective response to the question of why one should participate and shouldn't freeload has been a philosophical obsession in the West ever since the first recorded rationally self-interested actor appeared within philosophical horizons. A system-theoretic approach to autopoiesis can at best advise such an actor that non-participation and freeloading are very likely to increase the complexity of the environment with which he or she or it must accordingly cope and hence are likely to be inefficient and cybernetically costly modes of being in the communicative world. Likelihoods are not, however, guarantees and actors with a taste for risk or the increase of complexity or both have no self-interestedly rational reason to be deterred from pursuing their penchants. The philosophers' work is, it seems, never done.

Luhmann for his part distinguishes between ethics and "morality," though in a manner that seems to have far less motivation in systems theory than in his own antipathy toward moralisms of any sort. When at his most consistent and especially when distinguishing himself from Durkheim, he is fully cognizant that from his or any other social theory, no ethical conclusions, or at least no ethical imperatives, can be drawn (Luhmann 1996: 32). Yet, as William Rasch appropriately notes, Luhmann's sociological characterization of modernity often fades into affirmation and often does so to anti-moralizing ends:

> [Luhmann's] description of modernity as differentiated needs to be read both as an empirical fact – "differentiation exists" – and as an imperative – "differentiation ought to (continue to) exist." That differentiation exists and ought to exist translates, then, into a political injunction: "Thou shalt not dedifferentiate!" This perceived imperative dictates Luhmann's concern with ascribing limits to the applicability of the moral code. (Rasch 2000: 145)

For Luhmann, morality is not the anointed normativity of the system (it is thus not precisely themitical). It is rather a discourse grounded in the binary opposition between esteem and disesteem (1996: 29) that concerns "the whole person as communicative agent" (Moeller 2006: 111) and is governed by the interdiction of self-exemption (Luhmann 1996: 29; the moralist thus cannot escape his or her or its own standards of evaluation). Yet, in contrast, say, to economic or political or legal discourse, morality has no correlative institutional locus. It floats systemically and to Luhmann, its origin is "pathological" precisely because it arises out of circumstances of "uncertainty, disunity and conflict" (1989: 140).

The modern or functionally differentiated social system depends for its ongoing autopoiesis on the capacity of its subsystems to "recognize themselves" in terms of the binary codes that are specific to each of them. The recognition and maintenance of those codes is a necessary condition of the effective functioning of the subsystems jointly and severally. It is incompatible with "the moral integration of society" because, as Luhmann emphatically puts it, it *"excludes the identification of the code values of the function systems* with the positive/negative values" that typically constitute the apparatus of justification or "program" of the moral code (1996: 35). Indeed, the genuinely modern moralist would object on moral grounds to the fusion of the codes of the functional subsystems with that of the moral coding of esteem and disesteem, since such a fusion would render what is economically profitable "good" and unprofitable "bad" in a moral as well as an economic sense; what is worthy of an A+ "good" and worthy of an F "bad" in a moral as well as a pedagogical sense, and so on (Moeller 2006). Shades here, too, of Aristotle (though see shortly below). This indicates to Luhmann that "the moral itself accepts and even postulates" its "loss of sovereignty," its "negative self-restraint as a condition of its autonomy" (1996: 35). Otherwise said – though not as Luhmann but as I would say it – modern "themiticality" (if I may) attests to the anointment of the functional differentiation of a system whose normativity is that of functional differentiation. This is the cardinal systemic source of the distinctive complexity of modern ethical practices. This is not at all to say that I presume that non-modern systems are without differentiation of either institutions or codes. Nor does Luhmann so presume. It is rather to say – to my mind and in my terminology in any case – that the cardinal sources of their own ethical complexity do not lie in their functional or semantic differentiation alone.

The same anointment constitutes the cardinal reason for the emergence in the eighteenth century of what Luhmann understands as "ethics," or in any event as the "reformulation of the meaning of ethics" as a "reflection on the grounds of [distinctively] moral judgment" (1996: 35). Ethics thus construed is, in short, a "reflection theory of morality" (1989: 141) whose two great polar alternatives remain for Luhmann Kantian deontology (of which he surely deems Habermas to be an heir) and Benthamite utilitarianism (1996: 33; cf. Moeller 2006: 111). They are, moreover, alternatives that by their very existence betray each the other's inadequacies. Luhmann thinks there is ample empirical evidence – to be found in the fractious history of moral philosophy from the eighteenth century forward – of the impossibility of a fully adequate, fully comprehensive and self-consistent

ethics. After the fall of theology, the sources of moral semantics
are irreducibly plural (cf. Moeller 2006: 111). Ethical absolutism is thus –
system-theoretically, in any case – out of the question. Inspired perhaps
by the experience of the many forms of exclusion and
disenfranchisement that are themselves products of functional
differentiation, such absolutism is of course everywhere. Wherever it is,
however, what it communicates can only be registered à la Luhmann
as anti-modern (cf. Rasch 2000: 122–123).

No doubt, Luhmann was familiar with Aristotle and Plato. His
regular placement of the dawn of "ethics" in the eighteenth century
strongly suggests that he regards both Aristotle and Plato, not yet living
in a functionally differentiated but instead still in an organizationally
stratified social system, as being inevitably guilty in their own moral
philosophies of the conflation of the moral code with that of the code
regnant in the system in which they lived, namely, the code of the
political, grounded, again, in the difference between the effective and
the ineffective. There are many elements of ancient Greek morality that
indeed appear "political" to modern eyes, Foucault's among them
(1997a: 286) and Nietzsche's before Foucault's. Greek morality was
nevertheless no more exclusively "political" in Luhmann's sense than
the ancient polis was reducible to a state. Whatever might be said about
its popular expression, its philosophical expression did tend even so
toward a partial fusion of the sort that the self-referentially modern
Luhmann must disdain. It is at least plausible to propose that, for
Plato and Aristotle alike, the moral code allows of mapping on to the
semiotic coding of the distinction between truth and falsity and
perhaps also on to the aesthetic coding of the distinction between the
beautiful and the ugly without much residue.

This does not, however, fully justify Luhmann's claim that the very
meaning of "ethics" changes with the displacement of the sovereignty of
the church and the ascendance of functional differentiation. If modern
moral philosophers – and aren't the natives (almost) always right? – count
both Plato and Aristotle as members of their own league, this is surely
because their common enterprise includes a reflection on the grounds
of the moral code. It is extraordinarily arbitrary to characterize the
enterprise of their common precedent, Socrates, in any other way, all the

more so because Socrates' own results are every bit as negative as Luhmann regards the results of Socrates' modern successors ultimately to be. To be sure, Luhmann has a broader theoretical investment in treating ethics qua reflection theory of morality as a distinctly and unprecedentedly modern affair. He is invested in particular in placing the emergence of the second-order observation that yields what is to his mind the quintessentially modern recognition of the contingency of reason itself squarely within the history of the functionally differentiated system and as one of that system's signature effects (Luhmann 1998: 44–57). The anthropologist knows now, however, that the stereotypes of the primitive and the traditional peasant are distortions. Even such Luhmannian primitives as Socrates and Plato and Aristotle prove to have been capable of thinking not only at the first order but at the second order as well; they, too, were capable of observing observers observing. This may not have brought them to the realization that contingency is everything. But their shortcoming, such as it is, may be an indication that something more than second-order observation alone is responsible for that most modern of modern *prises de conscience*. Perhaps it is an indication of a broadly modern if somewhat unreflective investment in the moralization of functional differentiation itself, for as (one of the guilty parties) Luhmann remarks, only the maintenance of the autonomy of the codes of the various subsystems of the functionally differentiated system permits the subsystems to remain operatively distinct "and to reproduce open options, that is contingency *within* [themselves]" (1996: 35). In any case, nothing in the basic distinction between system and environment requires the sort of definition, much less the specific temporalization, of ethics that Luhmann adopts. Nor, to repeat, does it entail the moralized differentiationalism to which Luhmann is susceptible.

What anthropologists used to consider culture as a whole is, *pace* Malinowski (1939), not adequately approached as some vast reper-toire of devices of "adaptation." Ethics cannot be adequately com-prehended either as practice or as discourse through an adaptationist (one version of a functionalist) framework alone – but can be so approached at its limits. On the plane of working postulates, ethical space-time has one of its absolute limits when and where any adjustment to, any accommodation of, the environment is impossible. Then and there, one might well find the charismatic leader at his or her most despotically sovereign. It has the other of its limits when and where the environment, and by no means least the other subjects that in part constitute that environment, are reduced – as hierophants or as tools – to being nothing more than followers, to being forced to accommodate without benefiting from any accommodation in return. There is no need to review here the long, long list of the non-ethical, the barely ethical or the sur-ethical practices of which human beings have proved capable. It is still possible to conclude anthropologically that if ethics did not exist, human beings would surely have had to invent it.

It is finally possible to advance a basic diagnostic distinction between the ethical and the themitical for which the Weberian primal scene once again provides the key. I have alluded to it already in characterizing the rationalism of the classical philosophers as only one vector of the routinization of the ethical. In fact, even Weber's exemplars betray elements of their own routinization, the beginnings of their transformation from exemplars of the anethical-becoming-ethical response to extraordinary circumstances into exemplars of the practices best suited to the themiticality of systems already in place and in need less of adjustment than of ongoing maintenance. The Jesus who works miracles remains charismatically pure. His crucifixion is diagnostically quintessential of the flood of ethical value that the rite of passage might unleash. In his broader life, however, as it is variably recorded in the synoptic gospels, Jesus is well on the way from the system-adjusting interventions of a charismatic-becoming-ethicist to the system-maintaining askêsis of the themitically preoccupied ethicist in two respects. First, especially in his Matthewite portraiture, he is the lineal inheritor of the anointment of David and so at once the successor to and teleological culmination of an already normatively routinized politico-religious regime. Second, in practicing precisely what he preaches and thus routinizing through concrete conduct what Paul of Tarsus will first develop into the code of a fully fledged Christian life, he delivers to posterity the precedent for a themitical normativity no longer proper only to the son of god but incorporable into the structure of the values and the obligations of the merely mortal woman and man.

Achilles' charisma, for its part, is also routinized, if only very weakly, for he has the benefit of being the son of a goddess. Though he elects it, his destiny will remain on the side of the always extraordinary circumstances of the battles of which not just Greek legends are made. Yet, when he participates with his fellow heroes in the victory games as in his treatment of Priam, his conduct is entirely of a piece with the normativity of an ethical system that routinized the apportionment and accommodation of every subject's portion of honor and, in its cosmological warning that the beggar at one's door might be Zeus in disguise, came as close to an ethical humanism as it ever would do (cf. Pitt-Rivers 1977).

Like Jesus at his most purely charismatic, the purely charismatic Achilles is hardly a picture of stability, even dynamic stability. He is anything but methodical. This remains true even when, his rage spent, he comes again to recognize that there are others in his environs with grief to bear and bodies to put to themitically proper burial. In general, one can expect the ethical to exhibit a certain lack of fixity, an indeterminacy echoing that of the semiotics of ethical value itself the more its circumstances are extraordinary and the more pressing the need for ecological adjustment or restructuration or reorganization. Achilles is exemplary of the warrior in the extremes of his virtuosity, though his life belongs largely to the domain of the purely charismatic, often over the edge of the ethical and only episodically engaging the themitical (at least as we know him through the *Iliad*).

The Greeks will thus need other exemplars to instruct them in the more cultivated care of the self and citizenship alike.

The themitical as I am designating it tends in contrast – but not dichotomous contrast – to be less mutable. It partakes of whatever longevity the autopoietic system of whose normativity it is the valorization can boast. Again, the anthropologist of ethics slips into yet another modality of the naturalistic fallacy should he or she mistake the normativity – the structural-functional and dynamic principles of the organization of autopoiesis – for the themitical itself. The diagnostics that Foucault and Weber help us bring to the ethical domain, however, permits of two further working postulates. One of these, as Zigon might also have it (2007: 138), is that ethical value and themitical normativity stand in a weakly dialectical relationship to one another. Autopoietic creation *ex nihilo* belongs beyond the reaches of our actual horizons and so should remain beyond our diagnostic horizons as well. Yet we can postulate that, however inextricable their relationship may be, the ethical retains a certain priority over the themitical (here reversing the Aristotelian relation between êthos and politikê). Just this priority: in the Weberian primal scene, ethical value remains resolutely indefinite. Within its semiotically and practically unroutinized ideal-typical ambit, the signifier of the ethical continues and can only continue to float. Only through routinization of one or another of its possible semiotic qualifications or criteria can ethical value itself be adapted to the temporal requirements of autopoiesis as a process of system maintenance. Hence, ethical value becomes themitical normativity and the ethical encounter of crisis a themitical practice of deliberative decision through a translation that is also a reduction at once of complexity and of the scope of the ethical imagination (however autopoietically productive and however compatible with increases of systemic complexity this may be). Contrary to what Zigon (2007: 138) has suggested, however, such a reduction cannot be conceived as the telos of ethics, but must rather be conceived as its retraction. From the vantage of the ethical at its most ideal-typical, any themitical establishment can only appear valuationally partial. This in itself can and does stimulate the undertaking of adjustments even in the absence of any properly environmental irritation. It thus provides the energies for an increase of ethical complexity against its themitical retraction as an always potential countercurrent. It is itself a part of what gives both ethics and the themitical within it their sociocultural variety. It is part of what gives them their histories.

Coda: the schematic parameters of the ethical domain

A skeletal summary of the diagnostics at which I have arrived seems useful, at once to separate the central from the tangential and by way of setting guideposts for the analyses to follow. The better narrative flow of those analyses further invites a revision of the order in which the central dimensions of that diagnostics has so far proceeded. In summary, then, my narrative-friendly version of the anthropological schematic of the ethical domain:

1　Mode of subjectivation

　　Mode of the determination of subjectivation: the specific param-
　　eters of the trajectory through which an actor becomes an
　　ethical subject of a qualitatively distinguishable sort.

　　Recruitment: the conditions that encourage or compel an actor
　　toward becoming and being an ethical subject of a qualitatively
　　distinguishable sort.

　　Selection: the conditions of the assignation of the subject or the
　　subject's self-assignation to a subject position of a qualitatively
　　distinguishable sort.

2　Mode of judgment

　　Mode of ethical valuation: the specific determination of the ethical
　　chrism and so of its extension; the routinization of who or
　　what is the subject of ethical regard.

Mode of justification: the apparatus of the defense of ethical evaluations and ethically marked decisions.

3 Mode of subjectivation (again)

Scope, structure and priority: the relative environment of any given subject position; its distinctive features and relative simplicity or complexity; its ethical weight or precedence relative to other ethical subject positions occupied or capable of being occupied.

4 Telos: the conditions that mark or define the consummation of any given subject position.

5 Substance: the object of ethical askêsis.

6 Askêsis

Pedagogical: the directed exercises through which the actor is taken or in which the actor is immersed in becoming an ethical subject of a qualitatively distinguishable sort.

Reflexive: the exercises, the technologies that the actor applies to himself or herself or itself in becoming and continuing to be an ethical subject of a qualitatively distinguishable sort.

PART II

Fieldwork in ethics

FOUR

An ethics of composure

To reiterate: neither methodologically nor ontologically does an anthro-pology of ethics have its ground in the individual. The population of its interpretive universe is instead one of subjects in or passing through positions in environments. It is thus a population not of atomic units but of complex relata. Its subjects are for their part already highly complex. They may be individual human beings (though never human beings in their pure individuality). They may be the individualized subjects of the formally egalitarian society; *Homines hierarchici*, the holistic dividuals of the caste-structured social system (Daniel 1984; Dumont 1980, 1986); the relationalist subjects that Robbins and many others have encountered in Melanesia (Robbins 2004: 13). They may be human collectives, or even human and non-human collectives or assemblages of one or another kind. Nothing in principle precludes the possibility of a cyborgic ethics, an ethics of quasi-objects (Latour 1993), an ethics of corporations of an economic or of some other sort. The only proviso is that the subject occupying or passing through its position in an environment be at or beyond the threshold of the complexity requisite of any system capable of autopoiesis, though such a requirement is never the sufficient condition of an ethical subject position, even a potentially ethical one. Individual human beings typ-ically display such complexity, yet do so only after a considerable course of socialization has taken place, only after a considerable dose of the intersubjective has already been incorporated, already become part of the self (and hence are never individuals in their pure individuality). Without such a supplement, they – we – would be little more than what Clifford Geertz aptly termed some time ago "basket cases" (1973: 49). Like the typical human being, the ethical subject, even when only an individual human being, is thus already always of intersubjective, social and cultural tissue. Its parts are never entirely its own. Its self-referential "I" is Rimbaudean. Its I is always also other.

Yet the ethical subject is not an abstraction. In its most familiar human form, its tissues are fleshly and its place in its world particular and concrete. It is in every case its own, and among what belongs to it are not merely the dispositions and schemas of perception – the habitus – that it has more or less in common with other subjects whose class and status and experiential trajectories are similar to its own. It can further lay claim to a host of idiosyncrasies, and idiosyncrasies of two sorts. Some – genetic, congenital, situational, temperamental, circumstantial – come to it as gifts or impositions, as legacies or accidents with which it simply must live. They belong to the domain of the given, which is never vacant, even if less stable and well stocked in our age of cures and engineering than it was in ages past. Other of its idiosyncrasies are of its own devising, the result of askêsis if not always of askêsis of a distinctively ethical cast. An anthropology of ethics cannot ignore such peculiarities, such identifying marks, for at least three reasons. Not least, they are likely to condition the objective possibilities that a subject has available in its particularity as an occupant of a subject position in a certain environment, diminishing or enhancing those possibilities and so diminishing or enhancing the range of ethical possibilities from one case to the next. They are also likely to lend to the subject's experiential and ethical trajectory a specificity – once again positive or negative – that exclusive attention to the habitus could fail to register. Finally, they are likely to serve as the stuff of the individualization of the ethical "personality," all the more so when individuality is itself a matter of either themitical obligation or ambition or ethical commitment or quest.

The anthropology of ethics may not be what Edward Sapir had in mind when imagining an anthropology that, fully mature, would dissolve the only apparent divide between culture and personality (Sapir 1949). It must, however, be methodologically prepared to shuttle back and forth between phenomena of a relatively more collective and phenomena of a relatively more individual order. In classical Athens, the surviving materials that would enable it to do so are not altogether lacking, but biographically of irregular yield. Like the tradition of ancient statuary, Plato's and Xenophon's not quite compatible portraits of Socrates favor the exemplary profile over the intimate study. The declaration of the ancient "rise of the individual" (Snodgrass 1980: 160–192) is hyperbolic. Athens did not lack its "personalities." It rewarded individual service and achievement. Its ethical bias was nevertheless slanted decisively in favor of the reward of individual service and achievement that manifested one or another of the standard virtues or conformed to one or another standard expectation. There is little if anything that survives to suggest that the ancient ethical sensibility accorded any esteem to the sort of individuality with which Rousseau credited himself at the opening of his *Confessions*:

I am like no one in the whole world. I may be no better, but at least I am different. Whether Nature did well or ill in breaking the mould in which she formed me, is a question which can only be resolved after the reading of my book. (1953: 17)

The ripple of such Romanticism is increasingly oceanic – with one difference. What for Rousseau was clearly an emergent value, an ideal, has for the contemporary Western(ized) modern become a themitical commandment. An anthropology of the ethics of such a modern subject must be as sensitive to the general pressure of that commandment as to the many modulations of its reception and its effects.

What has been given

Born in Lisbon on April 17, 1945, Fernando José Mascarenhas is of modest stature. He retains a boyish sweetness of face that, when still a small child, led admirers sometimes to think him a girl. He claims that even in his adulthood his "hermaphroditic look" often leads casual observers to mistake him for a woman (Marcus and Mascarenhas 2005 [hereafter, O]: 216). A congenital hormonal deficiency – panhypopituitarism – is in part to blame for his struggles with his weight. It is to blame for his requiring a daily injection of an anti-inflammatory steroid and a daily dosage of levothyroxine, a hormonal agent directed to the thyroid. It has prevented him from fathering a child, though he admits:

My second analyst thought that I was afraid of the challenge of having children. I do not think so, but who am I to say that I am right? At the very least I am an extremely dubious authority on the subject: we all share each our own large dark areas of which we know little or nothing. Also the truth is that during my first marriage I could have made a test of my eventual fertility and I didn't. (O: 81)

Fernando's erotic proclivities are variable. "From a strictly genital point of view," he tends "to be more attracted to men than to women" (O: 71). He believes that attraction to be a part of his "nature," which is constituted to his mind of his need for father-surrogates, his defensive avoidance of his insecurities, his fear of being able to perform adequately – "with a man," he writes Marcus, "that problem ... does not arise" (O: 71). He nevertheless finds women "more challenging" and thus "more interesting" than men (O: 71). They are also more forgiving: "it is easier with them to compensate [for] the lack of physical beauty whilst male homosexuals are very much obsessed with the fitness of bodies" (O: 72). Under a broader concept of sexuality than currently prevails, he would be "more heterosexual than homosexual" (O: 71). Or putting the matter somewhat differently: "in my body I feel homosexual and in my mind heterosexual" – but Fernando, always ready with qualifications, immediately adds that neither the former nor the latter is "entirely true" (O: 72).

Unhappy in their relationship, Fernando's father and mother separated when he was two or three years old. Perhaps he was two, as Fernando recalls his mother having once told him. "However," he says, "three seems to fit my self-probing better" (O: 31). From his birth and until his parents' separation, he lived in the Palácio Fronteira, located within what are now the western borders of Lisbon in the village of São Domingos de Bemfica (or Benfica), in its seventeenth-century origins a summer retreat that became the primary residence of his ancestors after their much grander home in central Lisbon collapsed in the cataclysmic earthquake of 1755. Through his paternal great-great-aunt's bequest, he was at his birth already the owner of Fronteira – as the palace is more briefly known. His grandfather – stern but a bon vivant and much beloved man of humor and practical jokes – lived at Fronteira until his death. In Fernando's earliest years, his was only one of several closely related families living at the Palácio, all under the benevolent despotism and in the grand style of his grandfather (Marcus and Hill 2005: 376–379). After his parents' divorce, however, and for the next ten years, Fernando lived with his mother and maternal grandparents at a fashionable address in the center of Lisbon. When he was eleven, his father – a man of bravado and flourish – died after failing to navigate a turn in the car that he had been racing. An only child, already the owner of the palace and one of the most substantial agricultural estates in Portugal, the Condado de Torre, Fernando was accordingly left to claim his father's titles. He returned to the Palácio to live some three years later and has made it his regular if not exclusive residence ever since.

Fernando has an extensive roster of noble titles. At his death, he will pass those that he has not already ceded technically to his first cousin, José Maria Pinto Basto, but ultimately to his cousin's son, António Maria. António will thus assume the titles of Marquis of Fronteira,

Alorna and Aracaty; Count of Torre, Coculim and Assumar; Portuguese representation of the title of Count of Oyenhausen-Gravenbourg; genealogical representation of Count of Saint John of Pesqueira, Count of Alvor and Marquis of Távora; honorary title of Sir (i.e. *Dom*) [there is no exact translation of Dom, but "Lord" would be a more suitable translation; the right to the title (or form of address) of Dom was granted to all those who descended through a male line from the holder of a title with "grandeza" and to a very small number of other families (less than a dozen): FM]; Full stucheon of the Mascarenhas; Donator of the Mordomia-Mór of the city of Faro and of Fronteira; Coculim and Verodá; Assumar; Mogadouro, Paredes, Penela, Cevadeira, Ordea, Camudães, Paradela, Távora, Valença and Castanheiro; and representative of the Houses of Fronteira, Alorna and Távora (O: 328).

The given has its contrary in the contingent and the indeterminate, but the distinction between the two does not constitute a binary dichotomy. It admits of degrees, of ambiguities, all the more so because it further admits of both subjective and objective renderings. Correlatively, it sets the limit of two different domains of possibility and impossibility. One of these, of which an actor is conscious, which he or she may embrace or regret, may find inconsequential or the very fulcrum of self-definition, is accordingly subjective, whatever else it may be. The other, of which an actor may be unaware, is a domain of fate and fortune whose axes include those of "native" abilities and incapacities, the psychological and social determinations that are realized as habitus, the store of material and symbolic resources at one's disposal, the measure of both geographical and upward social mobility to which one potentially or in fact can lay claim, the languages of which one does and does not have command, to name only the most obvious. We must follow Bourdieu's insistence that the two domains never be conflated analytically. We need not, however, follow him further in his insistence – plainly indebted to the Marxist tradition and approaching the dogmatic in the *Outline* (Bourdieu 1977), though more tempered in *The Logic of Practice* (Bourdieu 1990) – that the actor's subjective comprehension of both possibilities and impossibilities is always infused with misrecognition, whose opacity only the social scientist is able to penetrate and demystify. In a present in which an ever-increasing number of actors do and even must cultivate at least an educated lay fluency in sociological and culturological diagnosis to sustain successfully the practices in which they engage (Beck, Giddens and Lash 1994; Holmes 2000; Holmes and Marcus 2005, 2006), Bourdieu's dictum that what the actor does always means more than what he knows needs rephrasing. What a good many actors today think and do, they know very well to mean more than merely what they know.

The given for its part has a way of fading into the contingent especially when crossing the divide between present and future. Perhaps Fernando's passing of his titles to António is thus better cast as all but given; it is done in principle but not yet a concrete fait accompli. As I have already suggested, the given admits of other degrees as well, and not merely because of our ever-expanding repertoire of technologies of the self (and of entities other than the self). Fernando's birth at a particular time and in a particular place to particular parents, his entry accordingly into the realm of the creatural and the human – all this is given in the strict sense of the term. As we shall see, Fernando takes all of his endowments altogether seriously as well, as a matter of fact but more importantly as constitutive of an ethical subject position. What has been given to Fernando for the rest has been given him more or less, and some of it with anything but a guarantee of permanence. Toward but not at the semantically stricter pole, one might place his sexual orientation(s), his endocrinic syndrome and most of its consequences. Perhaps his temperament should be placed with them, though many a contemporary clinical psychologist would insist that even apparently congenital temperaments are susceptible to readjustment and their counterparts of being acquired. In any event, more toward the opposite pole one might place some of the more salient circumstances of Fernando's upbringing – his parents' divorce, his subsequent move to his grandparents' home, his father's death. Some of these circumstances might look "predictable." None was inevitable. One might say the same – as he himself does – of the titles he currently possesses. As it turns out, even closer to the pole of contingency and uncertainty lie Fernando's agricultural holdings, his wealth and not at all least Palácio Fronteira. Though it could often confer some ease, being of noble status was perhaps never easy, whatever those of us who have never had the opportunity to be so might resentfully imagine. Fernando joins many of his peers in status in insisting that being noble now is harder than it used to be – and quite a different social fact from the fact it used to be as well. It is less clear whether many of his peers in status would join him further in understanding nobility as an ethically charged subject position. Not likely. Fernando himself looks at once to the past, the present and the future in understanding it precisely to be so. The view is thus eccentric. Fernando is comfortable with his eccentricity.

The given, whether subjective or objective, might be called a metamodal condition of subjectivation, negative and positive, a modality encompassing several others, more specific. It is not alone. Its contrary is also metamodal. It is the condition – though not the only one – of pragmatic modes of engagement with normativity, also of relativistic, libertarian, instrumentalistic, egoistic and some existentialist modes. Class, at least class *für sich*, effectively given to some and mutable for others, is further metamodal. In the current ecumene, citizenship is yet again metamodal, as is its own contrary – neither of the two uniformly given, but as any follower of Hannah Arendt would, and a recent body of fieldwork does, attest, both of them determinative of quite distinct arrays of subject positions and modes of subjectivation, available and unavailable (Arendt 1998; Biehl 2005; Holston 1999, 2008; Petryna 2002). Modernity – in Arendt's but also in many other conceptions – is metamodal of subjectivation. All of the world religions – and a number of others not quite as expansive or inclusive or of variable expression and practice – are similarly metamodal.

Subjectivation: recruitment

"To the manner born": the phrase is multiply ambiguous. It can be read to suggest that noble character and its attendant comportment are a veritable genetic endowment, a simple matter of "blood" or some other equally essential substance. Throughout its history, the European nobility has been fond of such a suggestion, but anthropologists have encountered such fondness widely elsewhere. It often comes with the embellishment that nobility is always also a matter of acts and deeds, so much so that even the person born without title might occasionally achieve noble status. Ernest Gellner declared the suggestion thus embellished incoherent in his admonishment of anthropologists inclined to excesses of interpretive charity (Gellner 1970). It is logically contradictory only when its unembellished version is construed as the proposition that birth to the manner is a necessary and sufficient condition of nobility and the embellishment construed as the proposition that achievements alone are themselves also a sufficient condition of the same status. Asad doesn't quite say so but seems to recognize that, even as a contradiction, such a pair of propositions is hardly incoherent, even if it is self-serving (Asad 1986). The pair does not constitute a contradiction – though it does involve some equivocation – if it is construed as implying merely that birth and achievement are both sufficient conditions of nobility. It is neither contradictory nor equivocal if construed simply as the complex but plausible assertion that being born into nobility offers a special and privileged possibility for the one so born to effect the achievements that might also prove the commoner to be genuinely noble in his or her own right. It is neither contradictory nor equivocal if construed as the equally complex but entirely unimpeachable assertion that birth might endow one with noble status merely, but only achievement with the right to claim that one is a good noble, a noble of characteristically noble virtue, a noble in the ethical sense of the term.

I might add that Gellner is an all too typical Oxonian in presuming that everything that people say makes (or does not make) sense only once it is fashioned as propositional. In any event, I think that I am not guilty of an excess of interpretive charity in attributing to Fernando the double but cogent view that being born into nobility is a condition of privileged possibility but also that between the noble by birth and the good noble there can be every difference in the world. So, to his mind, his fellow title-holders and he are of noble status, but the Kennedy brothers – as he once pronounced to Marcus and me – are among those whom he would offer as exemplary of those noble by achievement and noble precisely in the distinctively noble goodness of their deeds. (The judgment is at least arguable.) Fernando generally refers to the specific privilege that noble birth confers as "status." One of his titled fellows pronounced to me that nobles were a "class," that they thus had as much historical warrant as any other class to engage in a "struggle," if not for supremacy then certainly for their continued "survival." That noble birth comes with a good dose of "status" passes in the vernacular and can pass more scrupulous sociological muster – if with some qualification and at least in the Portuguese present. That nobility by birth confers membership in a class in a Marxist sense, whether in itself or for itself, is a sociological mistake, at least in the Portuguese present and most likely from nineteenth-century or even eighteenth-century Portugal forward as well. In any event, neither ascription advances the distinction between the mere and the good noble to the semantic foreground. Only once that distinction assumes salience does nobility stand clearly as an ethically marked subject position. Just that distinction is Fernando's own.

A historico-sociological excursus: The Portuguese abolished their monarchy in 1910 (Wheeler 2002: xxiv) and the nobility lost its only source of the endowment of formal privileges and immunities at the same time. The research of such leading historians of that nobility as Nuno Gonçalo Monteiro has established at length that well before 1910 and perhaps as early as the later eighteenth century it retained much (if not the pinnacles) of its status but as a totality had already lost the character of anything that with sociological precision could be designated a status group. Not least, this is because it was internally differentiated in both title and habit, all the more pronouncedly with the consolidation of the Bragança dynasty in the middle of the seventeenth century. The nobility emerged as a ranked cadre beginning in the twelfth century, with the original consolidation of the monarchy. The Portuguese kings at once conferred, defined the terms and were the ultimate arbiters of the members of that cadre. No one retains the license of conferral; the Portuguese nobility is thus at a titular standstill. The current pretender to the throne, Dom Duarte, Duke of Bragança, nevertheless presided over the recognition of existing titles with the collaboration of the *Conselho de Nobreza*, the Nobility's Council, his father's creation, until 2002. [The Duke dissolved the Council in 2002. On July 5, 2004, at his request, the *Instituto da Nobreza Portuguesa* (The Institute of the Portuguese Nobility) was established, of which I am one of the five founding members and directors: FM.]

In his remarkably thorough study, Monteiro records the early distinction between the *fidalguia* (roughly a "knighthood") and the much broader category of *nobreza*, "nobility." At a minimum and by the seventeenth century, the latter category had as its markers a family name and a coat of arms (Monteiro 1998: 81; 2000: 139). Within it, the *Grandeza* or "grandeeship" was composed only of counts, marquises and dukes and, under the Bragança dynasty, could by the seventeenth century appropriately be characterized as a "court aristocracy" (Monteiro 1998: 45). A smaller portion of the grandeeship came further to occupy "premier" status at court (Monteiro 1998: 427). Under the Braganças, the grandeeship was, as category if not as community, an unusually stable group and remained so until the First Liberal Revolution of 1832–1834. The royals were disinclined significantly to expand their numbers and were consistent in renewing the titles of those who were already to be counted among them. The grandeeship as a whole was a proper status group during the same period. Until the First Revolution, it was almost always endogamous and homogamous, its members avoiding marriage with the lower nobility but above all with any members of the ascendant bourgeoisie with whom they might nevertheless mix socially (Monteiro 1998: 423, 429). It was also urban. The Braganças established their seat in Lisbon after securing independence from Spain. Monteiro can report astonishingly that by the end of the seventeenth century, the grandees without exception had their primary residences in Lisbon as well (1998: 427). They follow the royals in appearing as the leading figures of urban society and the setting of and partaking in urban fashions (1998: 421). One might come across an occasional defense of noble rusticity (1998: 228), but in striking contrast to their German and especially to their English counterparts, the higher reaches of the Portuguese nobility could in no way be considered a gentry (1998: 232–233). The unusual intimacy of the royals and the grandeeship is due in important part to the terms of the "service" that the former formally expected of the latter – above all but not exclusively service of a military and thus often peripatetic sort (1998: 230). Monteiro reports that after 1750, some 90 percent of the grandees had military careers (1998: 527). Such service was normatively the "principle and the justification of the existence" of the grandeeship as a group (1998: 235). The Braganças rewarded it with a variety of payments and honors – military orders but also court offices and commended properties, many of which became entailments (1998: 471). The grandees alone afforded the sort of services to the court that could and would be so rewarded. The lesser nobility had no such privilege and perhaps accordingly its numbers increasingly grew, so much so that Monteiro writes of its gradual "banalization" (1998: 23). With very few exceptions, the grandees were descendants of the fidalguia and their relative rank commensurate with the rank and antiquity of their ancestors, from whom they took their surnames. By the eighteenth century, however, they could not sustain their standing without first and foremost sustaining the prestige of their *casa*, a "house" – not the Lisbon palace but instead the seat of one or another of the rural properties that they had inherited, preferably the longest standing, though in the end not necessarily literally so (Monteiro 2000: 141). [The casa was much more than a "house," whether urban or rural; it was a house plus an estate plus a family plus servants, etc.: FM.] Again in contrast to at least some of their counterparts elsewhere in Europe, they did so by resort among other things to primogeniture, though titles could pass through both male and female lines (Monteiro 1998: 82). Monteiro is emphatic in arguing that the double obligation to serve the realm and glorify the house – the latter in accord with the "Aristotelian" balance of "liberality" and "prudence" – was the impetus of strict familial discipline and the suppression of individualistic self-indulgence (Monteiro 1998: 95, 229; 2000: 145). Fernando is heir to just this tradition. His individualism – which is considerable – is tempered accordingly.

The first Marquis of Fronteira was valorous and successful on the battlefield, as were many of his direct descendants. Colonial empire, the fruits of which many of the royals kept largely to themselves, saw interdependency fade, or at the very least become less stable, and at times highly antagonistic. The unhappy outcome of Queen Maria I's displeasure with and suspicion of the Marquis de Pombal, whom the Queen's father had endowed with his high title and who gained much glory for overseeing (and recruiting local bourgeois financing for) the rebuilding of Lisbon after the 1755 earthquake, is a famous case in point. The 1832–1834 War of the Brothers or First Liberal Revolution, which pitted the absolutist Miguel I and his (noble and non-noble) supporters against the constitutionalist and ultimately victorious Pedro IV and his league, is another – and one that still casts its schismatic shadow over the noble Portuguese present. Fernando takes some pride in and feels a special affinity with his nineteenth-century ancestors, who supported the "liberal" Pedro. He writes Marcus that he has consciously connected his own leftist politics to their precedent, though adds that "whether they were the inspiration or just a 'legitimization' I can't tell – perhaps the difference doesn't really exist and it comes to the same" (O: 59). (A hermeneutics of suspicion – source of endless qualifications – is one of Fernando's readiest technologies of the self.) At odds with his own convictions, the majority of his titled fellows in the present are of a decidedly conservative political cast.

By the middle of the eighteenth century, the story of the decline of the nobility in Portugal has a more broadly European leitmotif: that of the ascendance, increasing economic dominance and the seductiveness of a merchant bourgeoisie. The higher nobility were unquestionably urbanites from the foundation of the Bragança dynasty and even after the Lisbon earthquake. Like most of their European cousins, however, they were rentier capitalists, attached economically and affectively to their estates and the houses they held and disdainful of the vulgarities of the growing numbers of rich upstarts around them. At least in my limited personal experience, noble disdain of the bourgeoisie also marks the Portuguese present, but it is highly discreet in its expression, and for good reason. From the middle of the eighteenth century, a higher nobility that had previously enforced and had the means to enforce status endogamy increasingly resorted to marriage with wealthy bourgeois and bourgeoises in order to sustain the styles of life that inflation and the other concomitants of market capitalism were putting into peril (Pedroso de Lima 2000; O: 173). In the course of doing so, many of them adapted themselves to bourgeois sensibilities – and vice versa. Fernando is characteristically frank about the motive of such couplings: "money on the one side, status on the other." One can detect disdain [distaste?: FM] when he refers to bourgeois money as "new" (O: 269).

Sociologically and attitudinally, the antagonism that such contrasts – status vs. money; old money vs. new money – suggest is not restricted to the Portuguese nobility nor a fortiori to Fernando himself. It is exemplary of the general antagonism between symbolic and material capital. It is exemplary as well of the agonistic dynamics that Bourdieu has generalized from the results of Norbert Elias' historical investigations of the "civilizing process" in Western Europe (Bourdieu 1984; Elias 2000). It is, in short, a familiar coding of the broadly distributed relationship between a sociocultural aristocracy always striving to remain one distinctive step ahead of an upper middle class that would at once emulate and usurp it and two steps ahead of a petty bourgeoisie that would hold it and the upper middle class along with it in mutual disdain for their inauthenticity, their pretensions, their effeminacy and their decadence. The controversy has its fulcrum in "respectability," which can fuel certain modes of conservative radicalism. The petty bourgeois must cherish respectability as virtually the only symbolic capital available to them – and they are episodically inclined to carry their adoration to radical limits. The nobility, for its part, can and does transgress the norms of respectability precisely in asserting its transcendence of merely common strictures and expectations. As it turns out, Fernando's profile amply attests to his refusal to bow to the standards of conventional respectability (which to Fernando's mind should never be confused with genuine decency). It is further consistent with a penchant manifest in both his more proximate and more distant male forebears as with their colleagues in nobility elsewhere to sample liberally of the common and the vulgar in gaining full command of the polished nonchalance of aristocratic *sprezzatura*. So Shakespeare's young Henry IV (one of Fernando's very distant relations, if I am not mistaken, through a centuries-old ancestral link to the line of the Lancasters) caroused in English taverns with his friend Falstaff. Fernando's father and his companions found entertainment in starting fights in taverns and in the bullfight. His paternal great-grandfather was (literally) a bastard – because his great-great-grandfather sired him and his several siblings without benefit of marriage [true: however, he was legitimized – recognized by his father as his son: FM]. And so on.

There is some accounting for taste, after all, and Fernando's admixture of noble eclecticism has its most overt expression in his tastes in music. On the one hand, he can list with precision a corpus of classical compositions that he holds dear, from certain of Beethoven's symphonies and sonatas to Vivaldi to the operas of Puccini, Wagner and Mozart among others (O: 105). On the other hand, he is attracted to popular singers and musical genres with checkered social pedigrees. Some of the singers are Francophone (Edith Piaf, Charles Aznavour, Barbara, Patachou). [Not untrue, but first and foremost Jacques Brel and La Piaf; the others follow at a distance. I might add also Leonard Cohen, Joan Baez, Pete Seeger and a couple of Sinatra's songs (particularly "My Way" – bet you'll like that): FM.] The genre for which he seems to have the greatest raw affection is much closer to home. In a message reflecting on his attachment to Lisbon, he writes Marcus that he "loves fado" and adds that though it has become a national song tradition it is first of all Lisbon's own (O: 103). [I do love fado, but I don't know if

I love it more than I love Jacques Brel: FM.] Marcus and I became well aware of this one of Fernando's loves during our joint stays in Lisbon. During each of them, Fernando arranged an excursion to a fado house, the first a fashionable expression not merely of the relatively recent revival of the tradition but of its even more recent chic, the second a solid edifice serving locally familiar fare for dinner and tucking its singers and their accompanists into a corner of the dining-room floor. Fernando has never ventured frequently into Lisbon's public and semi-public places. He is, however, a man of note whose appearances on television and in other media lend him something of a high profile. He is recognized. His familiarity at and with the fado houses to which we accompanied him was, however, not due to his presence in the media alone. At both, he was on speaking terms with at least one of the singers (one of whom, a woman, "may" have been a noble). At the first, he found inspiration at a pause in his friend's set to recite an apposite poem. The performance met with applause all around.

Fado translates from the Portuguese as "destiny" or "fate." It thus serves appropriately as the name also of a repertory whose melodies are typically plaintive and melancholic and whose lyrics, though admitting now and again of wry humor, even of joy, typically tell of love lost or unrequited, of the bullfight, of violence, of the perils and loneliness of the seafaring life and of the suffering and hardships of the poor. Like American blues or Argentine tango or Greek *rebetika*, it emerged most likely among the urban underclasses and has left at best a spotty evidentiary trail. Musicologically and sociologically, its history remains under debate.

Music historian Paul Vernon argues that fado's roots are Brazilian, a fusion of such Afro-Brazilian dances as the lundum and the fofa with the modinha, "a song-form with similarities to the popular quatrain" (Vernon 1998). He presumes – with considerable local opinion if by no means universal consensus on his side – that it coalesced in the early nineteenth century in Lisbon's Alfama, Mouraria and Bairro Alto, poor inner-city districts in which Afro-Brazilian immigrants settled after the abolition of slavery in 1761. Kimberly DaCosta Holton offers a review of the history of the debates surrounding the origins of the genre, favoring José Ramos Tinhorão's argument that fado indeed has an Afro-Brazilian heritage (Holton 2002: 113; Tinhorão 1994). In the inner city, the immigrants could ply a meager living, rub shoulders and dance and sing with beggars, street entertainers, prostitutes and other quasi-outcasts whom reputable citizens held in disdain – but were not beyond contacting as need or occasion might arise. The same districts were home as well to a troop of low Bohemians who seem to have dressed in black, let their hair grow long and busied themselves developing and sustaining their reputation as "unsavory and dangerous characters." Known as *Fadistas*, "Fatalists," they have in Vernon's opinion bequeathed their name to the singers male and female of what thus became known as fado (Vernon 1998: 6–7). The genre had its first icon in Maria Severa, prostitute and lover of the rakish Count of Vimioso. Vimioso was no stranger to the codes of the cultivation of aristocratic sprezzatura. Severa died in 1820. The themes and the vocal style of fado – deemed unpretentious and natural, even unrefined – began to appeal to middle-class audiences in the latter part of the nineteenth century (Vernon 1998: 9–10). Fadistas sing to the typical accompaniment of the Spanish guitar (in Portuguese, the *viola*) and the distinctive Portuguese *guitarra*. Several virtuosi of the latter instrument – especially those who have also been composers and lyricists – have enjoyed a good measure of national celebrity in their own right. In the mid-twentieth century, fado found its way into the hands of Lisbon intellectuals. Its songbook subsequently included the quatrains of some of Portugal's greatest poets and writers, including Fernando Pessoa (Vernon 1998: 17). At the turn of the century, an alternative songbook and ultimately a distinct variation of the fado emerged in the university town of Coimbra (1998: 45–54). The bawdier and most obviously politically militant of fado lyrics were banned – from public venues, in any case – during the fifty years of António Oliveira Salazar's dictatorship. At least from the turn of the twentieth century, however, and especially in such masterful (and for the most part decorous) expressions as that of Amália Rodrigues, fado has figured in the minds of many Portuguese and many foreign admirers as a distinctively Portuguese or perhaps "Lusotropical" phenomenon (Vale de

Almeida 2004: 45–64), a cultural hallmark, a part of the national or imperial patrimony. Holton reports with considerable musicological and museological approval on what amounted to its cultural consecration in an extensive multimedia exhibit at the *Museu Nacional de Etnologia*, the National Museum of Ethnology, in 1994, when Lisbon served as the European Capital of Culture (Holton 2002).

What is not in dispute is that, whatever the variety of its lyrics, the emotional substance and emotional centerpiece of fado is that particular feeling, the very signature of the Portuguese or Lusotropical soul, known as *saudade*. Most Lusophones insist that the term has no English translation. "Nostalgia" is a frequent gloss, but it is surely inadequate, since saudade might have its provocation in the imagination of a future out of grasp as well as in the recollection of a lost past. "Longing" is inadequate because it does not per se include regret for what cannot be grasped or for what has been lost. "Homesickness" is inadequate as well; as the range of fado lyrics itself makes clear, one might feel saudade for any number of objects besides one's distant home. One must agree in the end with the Lusophones: hereafter, "saudade" it shall be.

In its very translational recalcitrance, "saudade" does heuristic service. Among other things, it reminds us – and in the face of so many manifestologists of psycho-neurological reductionism these days, we probably do need to remind ourselves – that emotions in and of themselves are communicative ciphers. Their communicability rests entirely with their coding, which is to say, with the objects to which they can be attached, the criteria by which their expression can be determined and by which one of them can be distinguished from another. Accordingly, whatever they "really" are (cf. Griffiths 1997), emotions in their communicability are social facts of neither a psychologically particular nor psychologically universal but instead of a collective order. The very translational recalcitrance of saudade renders the point emphatic. Just as much to the point here, the differentials of the coding of the emotions provide us with one of the most perspicuous means we have of educing the dynamics of normativity and permissibility at play in any structuration of preferences (and vice versa). Such differentials suffered considerable anthropological distortion in the frameworks at play in the culture and personality school. They have fared better in more recent anthropological attention to gender and sexuality (e.g. Abu-Lughod 1986; Boddy 1989; Boellstorff 2005; Brandes 1980; Gutmann 1996; Herzfeld 1985; Lingis 2000; Pandolfo 1997; Rosaldo 1980; Strathern 1988). Only in relatively few cases so far, however, and only as vignettes even in Bourdieu's otherwise precedent-setting *Distinction*, has their investigation unfolded at the level of something approaching the bioethnographic (Bourdieu 1984; Crapanzano 1980; Kirtsoglou 2004; Shostak 1981).

Any concrete actor's tastes and distastes are, stricto sensu, his or her or its own. In their imbricated totality, they may approach being no one else's but the actor's own and his or hers alone. As we must recognize after Bourdieu, however, they are also a tracery of processes of socialization and enculturation that are no more unique to such a person as Fernando Mascarenhas than they are common to the Portuguese citizen at large. In the diagnostics and theoretical model operative here, they testify to askêsis both pedagogical and reflexive and so, in Bourdieusian terms, to various modalities of capital – symbolic and material, inherited and acquired – that render such askêsis at once possible and necessary to the production and reproduction of the subject position whose technologies they are. For the diagnostics and theoretical model operative here, however, concretization is every bit as important as the model-theoretic abstraction that permits us – again, following Bourdieu – to treat the subject of a sociocultural system in which material capital has come to dominate symbolic capital as the practitioner of a "lifestyle" that is the misrecognized manifestation of just that summation of material and symbolic capital that constitutes an actor's "class" (Bourdieu 1984: 169–172). Bourdieu is well aware that his theory of practice, dedicated to elucidating the necessary and sufficient conditions of the reproduction of any given sociocultural system through time, must rest on statistical frequencies and distributions rather than concrete tokens (Bourdieu 1977: 85–86; 1984: 169–170). As I have previously noted, it must also treat the causes of structural change of whatever sort as structurally exogenous. What should be added – and as Michel de Certeau recognized some time ago – is that the Bourdieusian theory of practice is thus restricted to addressing the concrete actor exclusively in his or her or its structural representativity and so incapable of addressing actors or actions that intervene refractively or fractiously into the very constraints and possibilities that define their structural parameters (Certeau 1984: 55–56). As de Certeau also recognized, Foucault's own approach to practice is thus not merely an addendum to Bourdieu's theorization but a correction of it. My approach is meant to perform a similar function, though a correction that clings to Bourdieu's – and also Luhmann's and Foucault's – conviction that structural constraints and structural inertia are in the long run far more likely than not to trump whatever reformist or revolutionary ambitions concrete actors jointly or severally might have. The anthropologist of ethics cannot be saddled with the problematic of reproduction, but he or she cannot be a Pollyanna about the scope of what everyone now seems fond of calling "agency."

Even saudade may be of insufficient breadth to encompass all that Fernando feels in exercising his musical tastes, though it is clearly some of what he feels – and seeks to feel. It points in any event to the countervailing though not mutually inconsistent pull of the "popular" and the academic or refined in Fernando's sensuous and so his ethical cosmos. The contrast is a partial – but only a partial – homologue of Bourdieu's contrast between the "intuitive" sense of aesthetic distinction characteristic of the elite actor whose sentimental education has been largely informal and whose store of symbolic capital has been largely inherited and the studied and intellectualist aesthetic sense of the counterpart actor whose symbolic capital has come largely through formal training and so has not been inherited but instead acquired. Fernando's pedagogy must be plotted nearer the former than the latter of these two poles. It cannot, however, be plotted nearly as far in that direction as the sentimental educations of most other Portuguese heirs to higher titles past, notorious among visitors from abroad for their lack of books and bookishness (cf. Monteiro 1998: 521). Fernando's taste for the popular should in any case not be mistaken for a rusticity at odds with the tastes of the court aristocracy from which he is descended. In this respect at least, he is very much his father's son – if not quite on a par with original fadista Maria Severa's lover, the noble Count Vimioso.

The more general result of the downward drift of both high and lower noble status was a gradual dissolution of any thoroughgoing divide between nobility and bourgeoisie, even if that dissolution was and is far from complete. Hence, a nobility that might have constituted a sociologically proper status group before the War of the Brothers has largely become a hybrid of capital, especially symbolic capital, with no distinct style of life to claim distinctively its own. The nobles who gathered at Palácio de Fronteira during one of my visits did, for the most part, sport common attire – but a gold-buttoned blazer does not a status group make. Some but not many nobles in title retain a connection to agricultural estates; in this respect as in many others, Fernando is slightly unusual. Very, very few nobles retain possession of the most prominent material accoutrement of noble status, at least in actual material form; very, very few retain their familial and historical house. In Portugal as elsewhere, the upkeep of palaces is no small task and in Portugal as elsewhere, if palaces have survived at all, they have done so either through the resources that one or another bourgeois has been willing to devote to them or through their partial or complete nationalization. That Fernando has his familial house is once again most unusual – but his possession of it comes at the cost of modern compromise.

For all its couplings, the nobility of the present is not effectively a bourgeoisie. Some nobles are wealthy capitalists – in (almost?) every case because they are the affines or the descendants of the affines of bourgeois families. Others – and some of the most elaborately titled and highly ranked – are wage-earners, though I did not hear of any who were – and who would bear among most nobles the leprous stigma of being – manual laborers. They are thus not a Marxian class. They are not a socioeconomic class and they are not a class in the sense that Bourdieu has given to that term. Noble status constitutes social capital in contemporary Portugal, though more or less depending on rank. It does not rest in or generate any consistent form of symbolic capital. Fernando's upbringing has provided him with inherited modalities of symbolic capital – of aesthetic but also other modes of judgment – that many of his titled fellows lack. His travels have led to acquisitions of such capital (elevated and not as elevated) that neither match nor radically depart from those fellows. His education is – in contrast and once again as an exception to the rule – more extensive than that of most of his noble contemporaries and more humanistic in its foci. Such a scattering of profiles – of status and of class – has led some scholars to declare that the Portuguese nobility no longer exists. Indeed: it does not exist as a status group, nor as a class, nor even as an effective network. The social capital it possesses is, however, of a highly particular kind and far from being without cultural and social consequence. Whether or not it is of consequence of a sufficiently consistent and visible sort to warrant the sociological conclusion that it has a consistent and identifiable source is not clear. Whether or not, that question should in any event remain an empirical question whose answer should be open to the consideration of more than the most tried and true sociological categories. The gathering of the nobles at the palace – and all that went into gathering them there – suggests at the very least that nobility continues to constitute a point of reference for the titled generally. The latter do not constitute a corporate group in the classic sociological sense of the term, but they might well constitute something like a mutual reference network.

Back to the primary subject: An only and so his parents' eldest male child, Fernando assumed not merely his properties but also his titles without complication shortly after his father's death. So Fernando became the Marquis at age eleven. [Well, you can say so, but when in that first winter I was taken to visit HRH Dom Duarte Nuno (father to the current Dom Duarte) to ask permission to use the family titles, he said I could use the title of Conde de Torre (which is *de juro e herdade* [of law and bequest]) and that about the others *mais tarde se verá* (roughly translated, "I will decide later"): FM.] The event appears to be ascriptive. It is an instance of ascription as far as it goes. It is vague in Fernando's memory. It was hardly a matter of his exercise of will, of his own choosing. He did not become the Marquis so much as the Marquis became him. Metaphysically mysterious perhaps, such an event is an anthropological commonplace. The various subject positions that coalesce in and as kinship and descent usually acquire their occupants in similar fashion. The subject positions constitutive of one or another caste system do so more or less as well. In all of these types of cases, the process of recruiting the subject to occupy the position that will be its own approaches the instantaneous. Instantaneous or not, the process is rarely ethically neutral, even when it consists simply of the assignation of a personal name. System-theoretically, it tidily reduces complexity. Or to be more precise: it reduces the complexity of recruitment of certain social contingencies but usually leaves open, makes possible and can even exacerbate the complexity of certain others. The daughter becomes a particular girl. The girl must still become the daughter. The Marquis becomes Fernando. Fernando must still become the Marquis – at least should he aspire to be someone more than a mere Marquis. As we already know, he does so aspire, though the aspiration did not come to him at the age of eleven. It took some time to gain form and focus and direction.

It would be misleading to identify the moment of Fernando's assumption of his titles as the moment at which the Marquis became him, once and for all. Only much later would he actively seek from Dom Duarte and the Asociação the formal acknowledgment of his titles, some of which came to him through an illegitimate ancestor (the bastard previously mentioned) and so in principle at least were subject to doubt. It would be equally misleading to identify that moment of ascription as the moment from which he began or could begin to become the Marquis that he now is. His recruitment to the higher nobility began well before – perhaps from the moment that he became capable of communicating effectively with those around him. It required that he learn – sometimes with strict attention, sometimes not. It unfolded through and as a process of socialization and of what used to be called enculturation. Following Bourdieu, it unfolded in and as the acquisition of a distinctive habitus. At first, at least, Fernando can hardly have had any forceful hand in it, coming as it did and as all of our habitus initially do in the course of play and lessons, admonishments and rewards, failures and successes, the receiving of gifts and the suffering of deprivations, others' coercion and others' enticement. So goes primary education – formal and informal – everywhere. If thus an acquisition – of schemata of perception and interpretation, bodily hexis, a share meager or ample of symbolic capital – it is an acquisition largely in the mode of an endowment. In just this sense Bourdieu fashions his own category of an aesthetic sense inherited instead of acquired – but such terminology might befuddle more than it clarifies (Bourdieu 1984: 80–85). In any event, what is at issue is not a process of ascription but instead one of absorption. What is at issue is consequently a mode of recruitment that often works subliminally, implicitly, before the subject knows it. The anthropologist may not be able to witness its course. Nor can he or she rely exhaustively on the subject to recount it; precisely because of its subliminality, it often goes without saying. It is nevertheless partially available in memory. It also remains with and in the body and its modes of being and acting in its world in the manner of a first language – though not beyond disguising. If a thing of the past, in short, its marks and traces typically manifest themselves in the subjective present.

Fernando's memory of his upbringing is detailed – and that it is so is already an indication of the mnemonic density of his early as well as his current environs. He tells stories of his playful grandfather. He tells a story of a contestation with his father. Fernando's declaration to his father at the dinner table one day that Fronteira was "my house" was technically correct, but resulted in his being sent to the corner. He said the same when his father asked him whose house Fronteira really was. He persisted. Only once he responded to his father with the pronouncement that the house was "ours" was he allowed out of the corner and back to the table. He recalls his parents arguing, his mother crying. He remarks being provided early on with a tutor in French and somewhat later with a tutor in English – in both cases before he began his first formal lessons in Portuguese. He "loved" French, and is proudly fluent in it. He "hated" English – but he is fluent in it as well. He remarks having been raised a Catholic. [I went to Sunday Catholic "school" to prepare for my first communion, but I studied at the Lycée Français and then the state school near my grandparents' house: FM.] Any piousness he might once have displayed has (once again in contrast to most of his titled fellows) been lost:

[I] went regularly to mass until I was 18, but by then my faith had grown to a point where I felt that a church and the ritual were much too confined a space for finding God, so I stopped going to mass. Eventually ... I lost my faith. It was then that I understood what organized religion and ritual were all about, but by then, apart from the intellectual insight, it was too late. (O: 48)

He suggests that "being raised a Catholic" has nevertheless shaped his character, and favorably so. Above all, he does not suffer from the Protestant obsession with sin or affliction with guilt over his transgressions – such as they are – against himself. [It is true that I do not suffer from the "Protestant obsession with sin," but I did suffer from the milder Catholic variety until I was old enough to get rid of it: FM.]

Fernando's recruiters have in any event been diverse – but not all of them and not only the more important of them human. Actors are at work and at play in Fernando's past, but so are actants. Among the latter, some are more accommodating and inviting than others. The Palácio de Fronteira looms unquestionably as the most imposing of them all.

The anthropology of embodiment is currently more fashionable, but the anthropology of emplacement rivals it in importance and complexity alike. Its roots are those of anthropology itself. The aboriginals of nineteenth-century Australia are its oldest testament – though the missionaries who recorded or reconstructed their elaborate translation of cosmologies and social identities into landscape and the translation of landscape into identities and cosmologies were not yet speaking of "emplacement" as such. Lévi-Strauss does not write of emplacement, either – but appeals to the example of the aboriginals in arguing that a principle of residence is one of the essential constituents of the elementary structures of kinship (Lévi-Strauss 1969). Emplacement remains a central theme in research into aboriginal ontologies, epistemologies and aesthetics even at present – in Australia and elsewhere in Oceania (Rosaldo 1980; Rumsey and Weiner 2000), in Amazonia (Whitehead 2003), North America (Feld and Basso 1996) and North Africa (Rabinow 1975) among others. Marilyn Strathern has suggested that some sense of home or dwelling is crucial to any adequate conception of the anthropological subject (Strathern 2004). Theorists from Alain Touraine to David Harvey have blamed dislocation and displacement for much of the malaise of "post-industrial society" (Touraine 1971) or postmodernity (Harvey 1990). Others have regarded them as at least potentially beneficial (Baumann 1993; Deleuze and Guattari 1983). The larger but by no means total share of the daunting recent corpus of anthropological inquiry into migrants, refugees and others displaced or misplaced favors the former positions over the latter. In our allegedly deterritorialized, transnational, rootless but still ostensibly autopoietic ecumene, it is difficult to conclude that a sense of place is anthropologically essential or pivotal. But then again ...

Anyone might visit Fronteira: several of the rooms of its main floor and its substantial formal gardens are regularly open to the public. Certain of its carriage houses have been converted into a ticket booth and a gift shop. The shop offers periodistic trinkets, examples of such signature local handicrafts as lace-bordered table linens and reproductions of decorative elements found in Fronteira itself, not least its *azulejos*, the blue-painted tiles whose techniques of production derive from China, then Persia, then the Moors, but whose architectural elaborations have become iconic of Portugal itself. The gift shop also offers an official, richly illustrated history of Fronteira and its gardens, available in several European languages. What it highlights is characteristic of the genre. It introduces its subject with a collection of encomia that one or another visitor saw fit to put down on paper in the past. It offers stylistic assessments (Fronteira owes much to Italian architectural and decorative precedents). It provides the dates of the construction of various foundational units (the exterior of Fronteira preserves its original, seventeenth-century realization of ceramic, stucco and brick; several of the interior rooms and spaces drift toward the more baroque tastes of the subsequent century; a few other rooms evoke the more somber elegance of the nineteenth century). It notes costs (building the palace was a very expensive project and approached being an extravagance among a nobility that several visitors noticed to be less inclined to flamboyance and opulence than its relatives to the north). It declares Fronteira a historical and national treasure. It celebrates the aesthetic accomplishments of the many artisans who contributed to its construction. It sketches the biographies of its ancestral owners and residents. Its tone is at once enthusiastic and respectful.

The palace imposed and imposes itself upon Fernando, however, less as an aesthetic and strictly architectural actant than as an insistent themitical presence in all its righteousness, demanding the sort of attention and reverence that one might be expected to pay to an aging parent or grandparent. For Fernando, it exercises an irrevocable ethical force and a force that testifies to a process of recruitment that has left his house belonging to him no more – indeed even less – than he belongs to it. Nothing subliminal here: Fernando himself is altogether aware of and altogether articulate in pronouncing on the house's dominance over him and the debt it continues to extract from him. The value that inheres in Fronteira for Fernando has nothing whatever to do with its being what our realtors like to characterize as an "investment." Its value is as far removed from that of a commodity as it possibly could be. It is instead a precise analogue of the value that Annette Weiner discerned in the Maori textiles that would make their appearance at ceremonials of reciprocal exchange but could never be exchanged themselves (Weiner 1992). Obligatorily keeping them while giving other objects away, they were – and continue to be – the very thread and fabric of a social identity in the present that simultaneously attests that the actor giving or receiving is in the proper position to do so and that the same actor owes that position entirely to his or her figuratively and literally material tie to identities and positions that are in both the temporal and the ethical sense prior to his or her own.

To the gardens then. When Fernando decided not merely to reside in the palace but also to devote himself to it, they were in a condition of disrepair. Much of the rest of the palace, exterior and interior, was in some measure of disrepair as well. Many of the lead and bronze and stone statues that decorate the gardens' byways were bent, some broken. Fernando pointedly chose the statue named *Ocasião* (Opportunity – hence the title of his collaboration with Marcus) as the first whose repair he would oversee. (Yes – the choice is ethically and self-reflexively pregnant.) The child Fernando would regularly have looked out on what the poet manqué might see as an allegory of decline – but Fernando gave neither Marcus nor me any indication that he saw it so, at least not as a child. He would in any case have looked out just as regularly from the southern windows of the palace on to the *Galeria dos Reis*, the Gallery of the Kings, whose high walkway affords a panorama of Fronteira and its Classical Garden all of a piece. Some four meters below it, a rectangular pool (officially the Great Lake), fifty meters long and nineteen wide, spreads out east to west. Aggressive swans were keeping watch over it during my tours. On each side of the pool, curving, tile-adorned staircases lead to two pavilions between which the upper walkway itself stretches. Balustrades protect the visitor from a fall. At water's edge are fourteen tall tile panels, all of them beneath high-relief stone arches. The panels all depict vigorous, handsome knight-warriors with ostrich-festooned helmets, swords aloft and steeds rearing. The author of the official history, José Cassiano Neves, rejects the earlier interpretive position that the twelve central panels represent the Dukes of England and only the two at the side Mascarenhas marquises. From a child's point of view, the debate is moot. What stands out regardless are the dynamism, the courageousness, the dedication and the masculine beauty of well-appointed men of battle.

Climb the western staircase (if the swans permit): one can look down onto the Venus Gardens and, beyond them, a productive vegetable garden, a more cultivated tract within the woods that insulate the palace to the north and to the east, where they meet a lawn and, beyond it, a collection of apartments that house lessees and occasional guests. Continue up the stairs and arrive at the Gallery proper with its twenty-four busts, some affixed to the exterior of the towers sheltering the pavilions but most in niches along the back wall of the walkway. Each honors and holds a bust of one of the kings of Portugal. Chronologically the first is Dom Henrique – not a king, technically, but the Burgundian count who wrested Portuguese independence from Leon of Castile and fathered the first king proper, Afonso Henriques (c.1140–1185) (Wheeler 2002: 85). The last is Dom Pedro II – depicted as the Prince Regent as he was at the time of the execution of his portrait and so not quite yet the King in his own right that he soon became. Opposite the busts, at the center of the Gallery and standing atop the tall, false portico that interrupts the walkway's balustrade presides what, in a photograph included in Fernando's collaboration with Marcus, is explicitly identified as the flowing, full-standing, life-size female nude, Opportunity.

Allegory and mythology – sufficiently recherché to put their didactic function into question – mingle with the crests and crowns of the Mascarenhas marquises throughout the Classical Garden. Allegory and mythology continue into the more informal and intimate garden that borders the steps and patio terrace at the back of the palace, at one side of which stands a small chapel. The entryway into the chapel and the expansive back wall of Fronteira are an elaborate architectural orchestra of classical quotation (largely Roman, as one would expect; the classical Greeks did not return to European fashion until the middle of the nineteenth century), intricately painted tilework, ceramic floral and fruit motifs and shell flourishes. The back wall itself constitutes the Gallery of Art and Promenade of Oratoria. Nine protruding arches enclose slightly larger-than-life statues of Roman gods and goddesses. Venus is here again. So are Apollo and the shepherd Marsyas, the latter holding his skin of which the god stripped him as punishment for having dared pretend himself of divine virtuosity on the flute. Even larger inset arches shelter tile panels of dignified, ample women iconic of the classical *liberes artes* and the senses and faculties essential to their acquisition. Poetry has preeminence in the overarching design – a clear symptom of the incipient Italian Baroque. The message of the terrace is far from subtle, though probably not obvious to a small child, even if one or another of his elders put it into words for him. Probably early on Fernando could, and certainly now he can in any event, readily identify those several of its figures that stand without the benefit of banners or pedestals on which their names would have been inscribed.

No more subtle is the message that confronts anyone who proceeds from the patio to the formal dining room, known and famous as the *Sala das Batalhas*, the Room of the Battles. It is the grandest of the palace's rooms, more than eleven meters long and nine wide and its ceiling more than seven meters high. Painted tile paneling fills the bottom third of its walls. Ceramic reliefs, painted and gilded, cover the top two-thirds of the walls and the ceiling. When Fernando first took me into the room and I began to ask after its details, he began to explain, but then declared that "Cristina would do all that." Cristina was the woman employed as the palace's tour guide. He was perhaps bored at the prospect of having to repeat again a report that he had made a hundred times before. He was, however, also less than secure with some of the more minor details of the iconography around him. Here as elsewhere, small details tend to come as acquired capital. It is the intuitive sense of things that tends to come as bequest.

The sense of the Room of the Battles is in accord with its moniker. The Gallery of the Kings salutes the Portuguese royals first and foremost. The panels of the Room of the Battles salute the valiants responsible for securing Portugal's independence from Spain between 1644 and the Lisbon Treaty of 1688. An unsigned artist or artists filled the panels with decisive scenes from eight battles, the first three featuring the achievements of the Count of Cantanhede and the earliest of the titled knights Mascarenhas. The scene of the fourth battle in chronological order, the legendary Battle of Ameixial, shows the first Marquis of Fronteira in combat with a doomed Castilian general. The panels are very busy and the identities of their personae not always nor always meant to be clear. The Lusoliterate viewer uncertain of the larger picture, however, has immediate aid. The panel scenes have the accompaniment of lengthy descriptions written out in what is still an only slightly archaic Portuguese. The young Fernando may not have visited the room daily and would not at first have been able to decipher its written accounts. Even so, he could not but have found it a repeated and so repeatedly reinforced envelope of his formative experience.

The focal centers of the reliefs of the room, surrounded by garlands and putti, are the titled senhores Mascarenhas in triumphant and august poses. The palace historian deems their portraits "effigies." At the very least, they tend toward individualization, though with conventionalized diacriticals. They tend enough toward individualization that Fernando could not have avoided noticing or having others make note of his resemblance to several of them. Chronologically, they extend back from the fifth Marquis of Fronteira to Dom Fernão Martins Mascarenhas [the first to bear the title of Dom: FM]. The Lusoliterate viewer once again has the service of inscribed eulogistic dedications featuring achievements in battle and in most cases dates of birth and death. The fifth Marquis, responsible for the renovation and enlargement of the palace, modestly rests with the inscription of his title alone. Though decoratively of the Italianate eighteenth century and so manneristically replete with exaggeration, whorls and other frills, the room is masculine and masculinist: mounts and martial regalia; great men and their great battles; history in the making. Putti abound, but women are notable for their pictorial absence. [Granted they are not particularly feminine, but still you have allegories of War, Victory (Minerva) and Peace, all three female: FM.]

Fronteira has many other coded spaces, but before turning and returning to them, one of Fernando's remarks to Marcus merits consideration: "About Fronteira there is something you should know. My love and fascination for it are something that I only acquired with maturity" (O: 49). Fernando visited Fronteira frequently after his parents' divorce and lived in it more or less permanently – though with interruptions – once his father had died. His own explicit account of what he of course does not call "recruitment through emplacement," however, does not concentrate on Fronteira. It concentrates instead on "the farm" (as he refers to it in English – the Portuguese *quinta*) at the Condado de Torre. He spent long summers at the farm, often in the company of the cousins with whom as a small child he had shared the palace itself. [My mother managed the farm from 1956 (my father's death) to 1970 and I managed it from there until 1974; we had three attempts to manage the farm together, but we had very different ideas about it. The first two times, I told my mother to go on managing it by herself; the third time I said that I would manage it myself: FM.] The farm, he writes Marcus, "is where not only my childhood's but, more important, my adolescent's love lay primarily. It was probably there that I acquired my aristocratic bones and blood; it was there that I felt like a feudal (I'm exaggerating a bit!) Lord" (O: 49). The exaggeration is not extreme. He elaborates for Marcus subsequently that "it was my sole source of income, the oldest family asset in my possession." He describes its cultural economy. Of the farm's employees, he writes:

I would wave at them and they were supposed to wave back when I was driving through the farm; they were supposed to take off their hats or caps when they addressed me; we would also shake hands normally when we met. I remember quite well that there was something reminiscent of feudalism, which I became aware of when one of them was showing me the landscape and calling it "ours"... I believe I felt proud when they said "ours," and I thought that to a certain point I was the embodiment, or the crown, of that "ours." (O: 123–124)

The farm is the object of the cathexis of other affects as well:

It was where my sacred places lay and my emotional (material) ties were. There was one special place above all others, which I always related to the big stone where a spring is "born" in Steinbeck's *To a God Unknown*. This was #1 of the magic books of my adolescence, to which I can add the *Grand Meaulnes* by Alain Fourier and *Les Enfants Terribles* by Jean Cocteau. Bli [who would become his first wife and whose full first name is Isabel: JDF] introduced me to all these books.

Inside the house in front of a big fireplace was an L-shaped sofa where, after my mother went to bed, most of the important long nights and fascinating or hilarious conversations with friends took place. (O: 49)

Such observations suggest a far-reaching contrast: between a palace alienating, emotionally aloof and a farm inviting, embracing and intimate; between a palace not quite yet suited to the young Fernando and a farm that fit him readily and comfortably, in and at which he could become the person of the Marquis that would and had become him; between the House of the Father (that was not technically the father's house) and the house and farm that his father, evidently a man of urban tastes, had left under the direction of a foreman, which Fernando would visit in the sole parental company of his mother; between a palace official and officious and a farm informal, light, even magical. Anthropologists know of such contrasts elsewhere. They famously distinguish the relation between the mother's brother and the father among Malinowski's matrilineal Kiriwanians. Matrilineages reveal similar and more elaborate contrasts widely in the ethnographic record. Conversely, they distinguish the relationship between the father and his agnates from that between the mother and her enates in many patrilineal and domestically patriarchical social arrangements of record. They often mark the distinction between successive and disjunctive generations (for example, the parent–child relation vs. the grandparent–grandchild relation). In Turnerian terms, they distinguish the structural from the liminal, societas from communitas. For Fernando, the gendered divide between his parents is correlative of similar dichotomies – if always, always with qualification. Though the Portuguese and aristocratic European succession of titles is broadly bilateral (if with a clear patrilateral bias), the divide between the more distant of his male Mascarenhas ancestors and at least some of his female ancestors more definitely established such dichotomies. Yet in his recruitment stricto sensu into the subject position he would merely occupy from pre-adolescence forward, in his own mind place trumps both filiation and descent.

Here, too, one must note a contrast – if not a polar contrast – between Fernando and all but a few of his noble contemporaries. During the period of its historical coalescence, from the thirteenth and perhaps until the late fifteenth century, the Portuguese nobility had its social and cultural grounding in the *linhagem* – the "descent group" (here as elsewhere in Europe, not the same structural or functional entity as the "lineage" strictly social-anthropologically speaking; cf. Goody 1983). By the eighteenth century, however, the casa, the house, had become the territorial and the coded fulcrum of noble standing. The house thus settled has some similarities with but is not ultimately to be confused with the Portuguese casa of such anthropological studies as João de Pina Cabral's *Sons of Adam, Daughters of Eve* (1986; and Monteiro and Pina Cabral, personal conversation). It melds standing vernacular conceptions with sociological and cultural importations of more northerly and aristocratic provenance, on which Marcus and Hill enlarge in their essay on Fernando's contemporaries (Marcus and Hill 2005). On the one hand, the house is a legacy and a repository of that legacy, to be kept while other properties, other accoutrements of self and standing, are passed into the realm of exchange. On the other, it is – or at least it is to Fernando's mind – the site of an obligatory, if disciplined, individuation, of the householder's duty to leave his or her own mark, in deference to but also in distinction from his or her ancestors (Marcus and Hill 2005: 352–363). American individualism, as de Tocqueville conceived it, this definitely is not. Marcus and Hill argue forcibly that traces of such a conception remain among the majority of the contemporary nobility as "the enduring center to the field of diffuse opportunity that constitutes the space of nobility" (Marcus and Hill 2005: 358). Yet it is a conception that, to a great many nobles' enormous regret, remains a thing of traces only, of memories and stories, of necessity faced and necessity victorious. In order to meet their obligations as householders, their ancestors may have married into the monied bourgeoisie – but only at the cost of seeing the distinctive nobility of their house irreversibly diluted. Having lost the means to fulfill what was expected of them (and what most also expected of themselves), their ancestors were compelled to put their houses on the market. Those members of the bourgeoisie with sufficient means were often eager buyers – and a further tainting of the noble aura of the house was the result of the sale. Other noble houses fell into disrepair and gradual decay. Though precise numbers are elusive, few noble houses in Portugal remain in the hands of their titled legatees today. With their loss, the descent group seems to have recovered something of the collective saliency that it had in the distant past. So, in any case, Fernando's own intuitions have it.

Mode of Subjectivation: Selection

Gallant or gentry: the Fernando whom Marcus and I visited at Fronteira was indeed the former, though hardly in the manner of his warrior ancestors. He was never the latter. Life at the farm has marked him deeply and at length; it was his primary residence for some four years. He moved on, however, to other occupations and preoccupations after his career as manager came abruptly to an end. The alternative paths of self-formation that he pursued opened themselves to him in the course of the conscious practice of freedom, to be sure. His way upon them also had the help – sometimes critical help – of those who continued to serve him as teachers and guides well into his mature adulthood. It also had the help of place – and not just the farm. The palace is a paean to the martial virtues – among other things. It nevertheless offers other, alternative codings of taste and temper. It offers alternative codings of virtue and achievement. It gives alternative subjects their own share of honor, of pride enough of place. It pays revisiting (if inevitably a selective revisiting).

For example: the visitor can (and typically will) climb the marble steps of the front approach to the palace and enter it through its principal door. In the foyer, beneath a marble arch, in a deep, benched recess, surrounded by intricately painted azulejos, stands a fountain basin topped with marine motifs. Take the stairs to the left. Proceed upward to encounter a remarkable trompe-l'oeil rendering of half-open paned windows and veined marble. Reach a hall that displays the portrait of the seventh Marchioness of Fronteira, Maria Constança da Câmara, posed at her desk with an open book and an unrolled vellum scroll. A portrait of her husband also hangs there.

Move on to the *Torrinha Sul*, the Little South Tower. The room is boxy and lofty. Once again, the prevailing iconography is mythological, but its themes those of the rhythms of the seasons, of hibernation and bloom. (Similar themes are repeated on the same floor in the *Sala das Quatro Estações*, Room of the Four Seasons, also known as the Smoking Room.) At the center of its ceiling is a high-relief emblematization of what Neves is likely correct in reading as Demeter, goddess of the wild, cloud-borne, a putto with leash in hand and dog or lion in his trust loyally or in any event obediently in tow. Cherubs or babes sit plumply in the corners below. Neoclassical landscape paintings depict the passage of the seasons between them. With unabashed consistency, the design and its effect are purely rococo.

At the palace's south, a formerly open-air gallery overlooking the Classical Garden now holds the palace library. A marble bust of Dom José Trazimundo Mascarenhas Barreto, the seventh Marquis of Fronteira, is among its decorations. Here, this devotee of Fronteira wears no martial regalia. His presence – or so one of Fernando and his second wife's emendations of Neves suggests – belongs in the room in commemoration of his authoring a five-volume memoir (Neves 1995: 48). [They are a major source of nineteenth-century Portuguese history studies: FM.] Trazimundo sits among large standing globes – one terrestrial and the other celestial, produced in a London atelier in the eighteenth century. They share space with a painted screen, Chippendale chairs, a nineteenth-century French harp and piano, and photographs of the family and the last of the Portuguese kings. The inner walls of the library are shelved and hold what Neves estimated during his investigation to be some five thousand books. The older titles fall somewhere between the Portuguese Renaissance and the Portuguese Enlightenment. They include histories (predictably including military histories), treatments of astronomy and other natural sciences, Greek and Latin standards, and biographies of the illustrious, saints among them (Neves 1995: 50). Only a few of the titles that I myself saw were of recent publication. The great bulk were obviously old and probably rare. They were also in need of repair. The afternoon sun that flowed through the library's French windows can lend the room an ethereal beauty, but it had wreaked damage on the books' leather bindings. They are on Fernando's long list of possessions still in need of tending.

Once again on the main floor of the palace, looking out on the front courtyard, are the *Sala de Juno* (Juno's Room, for the goddess floating within high relief at the peak of the ceiling) or the *Sala Império* (Empire Room). Putti, trompe-l'oeil floral and arabesque motifs, Louis XV chests of drawers, a small table reputed to have been Marie Antionette's gift to the fourth Marchioness of Alorna, an inlaid miniature writing desk, tilework, ornate clocks and candelabra, a dark wooden floor, handsome antique couches and rugs, family portraits. Nearby, the portrait-hung and well-furnished *Sala dos Paneis*, Room of the Panels, serves as a formal dining room. Juno's Room, however, captures more thoroughly than any other in Fronteira the full resonance of the Mascarenhas way with old money. Pre-Romanticism is hegemonic, though not without competition. It exudes comfort, the familiar and the familial. Over its fireplace mantel hangs an early nineteenth-century portrait of Trazimundo – but here as a child of perhaps nine or ten years old, and in the company of his brother Dom Carlos and his sister Dona Leonor.

In Fernando's self-formation, Trazimundo cannot be overlooked. Another of the emendations that Fernando and his second wife insert into Neves's history is nevertheless self-formationally more telling: "Also of importance is a pastel drawing of Alcipe." This drawing hangs in the Room of the Four Elements. An oil painting of her in her old age hangs in the Room of the Panels. Bold, artistic, learned, cultured and influential, Alcipe seems to Fernando's mind to be an ancestral exemplar if he had and has any such exemplar at all – and he is far from alone among his family in his admiration of her (O: 369). Alcipe: thus the fourth Marchioness of Alorna, mother of the sixth Marchioness of

Fronteira, with whose marriage to João José Luis Mascarenhas the houses of Fronteira and Alorna were joined, eighth Countess of Assumar, Countess d'Oyenhausen-Gravenbourg Dona Leonor Almeida Portugal de Lorena e Lencastre was and is economically known. It is not her titles – many now his own – that Fernando emphasizes. It is rather Alcipe's distinction as a writer, whose "six volumes" of poetry, "richly bound in velvet and gold," are shelved not in the library but in the more protective and smaller Room of the Four Elements. The room that was hers during her time at Fronteira is perhaps pointedly known as the *Sala de Eros* or *Sala de Cúpido* (no translation needed; Fernando's mother resided in the palace's master bedroom during my visits and I did not see it personally, but Neves' description suggests that its style is similar to that of the Sala de Eros). [The drawing room, which was my mother's, is in the same rococo style as the Sala de Eros, but it is much more elaborate and includes ten wall paintings and seven ceiling paintings, two of which are quite large: FM.] It is the site of daily, informal meals, where Fernando would be joined by his mother, before her death, and where he might still be joined by his cousin José Maria, the father, again, of Fernando's presumptive heir and long-time manager of the farm, and his dear friend Regina, a Brazilian artist whose works include a striking impressionist rendering of Fernando himself. Alcipe was a woman of considerable note in her day – Marie Antoinette would not offer a table to just anyone. She could only have stood out as one of a rare cadre of women of her day, many of them noble, who had begun to delve into artistic media formerly the preserve of men [true for the recent past but not really for the sixteenth and seventeenth centuries: FM]. So far as I know, however, her poetry has yet to be translated into English. (Fernando may have been seeking such a translator when he showed some of her poetry to my bilingual colleague Hill. Dr. Hill found its syntactically involuted, virtuoso and far from vernacular Portuguese beyond her competence and Fernando, visibly if briefly disgruntled, would be left to look elsewhere.)

Alcipe is not, however, determinative of his emplacement, much less of the techniques of his self-fashioning. She sets into motion a vector of legitimate differentiation that Fernando will join and follow and make his own. Fernando refused to confirm that, like the subjects of Marcus' North American inquiries, he had himself experienced the "dynastic uncanny" (Marcus 1992: 173–187). He had never felt the weird spark of the recognition of an ancestor in his own gesture, his own demeanor or visage, his own embodiment and emplacement in and of the present. [I felt it all right, but never as weird: FM.] Alcipe seems, however, to be iconic for him at once of the continuity of his heritage and the dynamics of individualization within it. With Alcipe, Fernando's difference from the majority of his fellow nobles present and past – he admitted to Marcus that he wouldn't mind thinking of it in characteristically upper-class fashion as eccentricity – is first of all given as an objective possibility within his emplacement. Alcipe's precedent opens up some though hardly all of the objective range of the alternative realizations of the subject that he was being recruited to be ab origo.

Merely as an objective possibility, however, that precedent was in no way guaranteed to function as a regulative figura of the subject in which Fernando would come to see something of himself, the subject that would become him and that he would pursue becoming. Emplacement is not selection. Like the process of the former, the process of selection is not without impingements – those of actors and those of actants alike. It is, however, a process in which actors are less and less likely to have the character of molders and shapers and more and more the character of advisors. It is a process in which actants continue to constrain but more and more can be put into service to facilitate the becoming of the subject and the concretization of subjectivation. It is correlatively a process in which the limitations of and alternatives within the objectively possible are objects of reflection, of the conscious exercise of what measure of liberty the subject-in-becoming has available. Training gives way (in some measure) to the deployment of techniques of subjectivation. Such techniques should never be presumed to be always techniques of individuation. Subjects must carry through the concretization of the positions they occupy; they must make hypostases of themselves. Whether they must or whether they care at all to individuate themselves rather than devote themselves entirely to emulation is an entirely different question and one that does not likely permit of a uniformly positive answer even in the pressure-cooker of themitical individuation of the modernity that now submerges all of us. It can for all of this be answered affirmatively in Fernando's case – though in this case as in (almost?) every other, only with qualification.

Interpellation might sometimes have the fuel of the spark of uncanny self-recognition, but fuel is still in need of a conducive atmosphere. As I have already argued, interpellation cannot in general be treated as having both its onset and its consummation in a single moment of psychoanalytic alchemy. Name-calling is better approached simply as one type of recruitment, and a type of uncertain outcome. Whether or not stigmatic, labels can lead to the ethical nullification of the subject labeled, to his or her or its subjugation, if their naturalization ("it's in my blood," "I was born this way," etc.) proceeds so far as to close off any objective possibility but the sole possibility of obedience to all and only what nature dictates. Labeling theorists from W. E. B. Du Bois forward have documented that such processes are a ubiquitous feature of sociological landscapes. Even when they admit of no contestation ("everybody knows that he's a . . ."), however, they are rarely instantaneous in effecting such nullification. Even when they do so before the subject is capable of taking up actively one or another of the objective possibilities within the social and cultural landscape, they do not necessarily constitute an irremediable *huis clos*, a permanent ethical impasse. Nor is this merely because discourses manifest tactical polyvalence. It is also because autopoietic psychic systems are always – in principle – capable of engaging both their discursive and practical environments creatively, of intervening into or at the very least reexperiencing the terms and the paths imposed upon them. Such systems might meet with considerable negative reinforcement, but the energies required positively to thwart them would typically surpass those powering the technologies of conformity of Orwell's *1984* and so typically aren't worth expending. Hence, even nearing the abyss of ethical nullification, interpellation is better folded into the more general schema of recruitment to and selection of possibilities within a subject position rather than set apart as some terrible talisman of sociological mechanics and alchemy alike. Genet is again worth recalling. The child called a thief and so called to account and put into crisis determines that he will be the thief that he is called, not at all because he aims to please but instead because he hears in the call the invitation to live the life of the thief to its fullest, to savor it, to become its connoisseur. The project (here that term is entirely apt) is arduous, but yields a rich harvest – homoerotic, lyrical, dramatic, and even political, once the thief-become-celebrated-author could take up and lend legitimacy to the Palestinian cause. Ethically, the political Genet is not as interesting as the erotic and lyrical and dramatic Genet and the latter never more interesting than when, in *Our Lady of the Flowers*, he extracts all the aesthetic and ethical complexity from the single adverb qualifying the confession before court by a homosexual criminal, who committed his crime not simply because he was "broke" but because he was "fabulously" broke (2008: 186).

The various dynamics of settling – or with Genet, jumping – ethically into a stigmatic subject position illustrate with particular clarity that the legitimacy of what is ethical in and about any subject position must have at least two facets. The first of these is the legitimacy of one or another subject position as such – which is anything but socially and culturally given in the case of a subject position such as that of thief or homosexual and so must itself be achieved. If Genet's case is misleading – and it is misleading, all the more so when in Sartre's existentialist hands – this is because such an achievement is not ever the achievement of the genius demiurge at work alone in his laboratory. *Pace* Sartre – who is much more sociologically and psychologically convincing if still the existentialist in his endless biography of Gustave Flaubert (Sartre 1981) – neither meaning nor practice has any existence as a purely subjective phenomenon. Neither can emerge or be sustained *incommunicado*. Genet has more help than he admits in his prose works – the help of the French cultural elite of his day in particular – in giving ethical flavor to the homosexual (and the) thief. That he succeeds in some eyes in doing so, however, does not amount to his succeeding at one and the same time in endowing with legitimacy the particular realization of the subject position in question in which he has taken up occupancy – the legitimation of being this sort of homosexual, that sort of thief, one or another sort of homosexual thief. Here, too, the process of legitimation is eminently in need of communicative others to unfold. Here, too, the communication at issue – which includes and must include the not necessarily conscious communication of the subject with itself – has the dynamic form of a feedback loop, or rather of feedback loops, negative and positive, typically at least partially open, of both cognitive and affective charge.

Fernando thus is not nor does he aspire to be the perfect epigone *à la masculine* of his great-great-great-great-grandmother, at least not to the letter. Among other things, he pronounces himself terrible at poetry. He has some ambition to write a novel – as yet unfulfilled. He tried to learn the piano when an adolescent – but "too late," he had to conclude. The aesthetic arena is among the foci of his adult ambitions, though most often in the role of impresario and overseer of programs rather than in that of a performer. He has, however, presented readings of Alcipe's poems at the palace. He also arranged and was among the readers there of several of the cantos of Luís de Camões' *Os Lusiadas, The Lusiad*. Written in the later sixteenth century, Camões' epic had in Fernando's judgment become among the treasures of the national patrimony too taken for granted and too little known. He sought not merely to remind Lisboans of its actual text – a celebration of the voyages of Vasco da Gama aswirl with Greek and Roman deities. He took particular relish in bringing again to public light its ninth canto and, within it, the events on the *Ilha dos Amores*, Isle of Loves, a frank and to his mind still fresh (pun intended) erotic fantasy. The Portuguese shielding of eyes from Camões' eroticism – if shielding there is – may not have a culturally internal origin. In a programmatic overview of what he regards as Portugal's colonization even in its colonial period, Boaventura de Sousa Santos pointedly underscores the English poet Robert Southey's judgment that the penultimate canto of *Os Lusiadas* is emblematic of the "sensuality" that is the signature Portuguese vice (Santos 2002: 23).

Several kriseis, several critical and decisive episodes, have played their part in Fernando's trajectory from the Marquis who became a child to the adult Marquis, senhor Mascarenhas. Fernando recalls the first in the wry tone typical of him. It occurred the year before his father died, after he had finished primary school, at the age of ten:

Then a big problem appeared on the horizon of my life. My father wanted me to go to the military school, at the idea of which I was appalled, as, thank God, were my mother and grandparents. After one of those arguments they had, and being unable to reach an agreement, my mother suggested there should be a sort of family counsel composed of 4 members, 2 chosen by each. "OK," my father said and then asked: "Whom do you choose?" To which my mother replied: "Your mother and your best friend, Fernando's Godfather." At that moment my father understood he was defeated but demanded that at least I should not stay in a private school but go to an ordinary one. (O: 35)

The vignette portrays a boy already certain, if not about the course of life he wished to pursue, then at least about one course of life that he did not wish to pursue. The anthropologist, ever indiscreet, has to assume that his budding awareness of the cognitive and affective dissonance of his specific engenderment with that of the typical cadet (the sexual practices of boys in boarding schools at that life stage are quite another matter) had more than a little to do with his aversion. Some boys may like their soccer – Fernando enjoys watching the game – but are not made to be cadets. Fernando may not have been entirely comfortable with his engenderment – he is not entirely comfortable with it as an adult. If, however, he experienced his being made for other things than the life of the military man as a failure, the account bears no trace of his having done so. No doubt, his supporters provided him with comfort, even though their motive is unclear. Perhaps it was sympathy for what some contemporary psychologists are calling "gender nonconformity." Perhaps it was the anticipation of the approval of the man he might alternatively become. Perhaps it was fear. The year was 1957. Portugal was still solidly under the rule of Salazar, quasi-fascist and authoritarian and complaisant in his imperialism. Colonial empires were beginning to crumble. Troubles in the form of independence parties had emerged in many of the Portuguese colonies in the later 1950s. Full-fledged war was on the horizon: in Angola beginning in 1961 and in Mozambique and Guinea the following year. All of these wars would continue for more than a decade, past Fernando's teenage years and until the overthrow of Salazar's feckless successor's administration. They saw casualties – vast on the side of the resistance, approaching or surpassing ten thousand on the side of Portugal. Cadet Mascarenhas could – just could – have been among them. [You mean my parents and my grandparents? If so, then why is it unclear? I was ten years old, very short for my age, not much inclined to the physical, highly sensitive for my age, extremely attached to my mother; I would clearly have felt miserable in any boarding school, let alone a military school, which I knew from my cousin Fernando had very harsh treatment of freshmen. In the public eye in Portugal, nothing had happened before the first Angolan massacre in 1961, except for Goa in 1960: FM.]

The second crisis was much more extended. By Fernando's retrospective reckoning, it began without his really being aware of it when he was fourteen – a relationship with a certain Manuel. The relationship extended through to his twenty-second year. It was Platonic throughout. In what Fernando identifies as its first phase, it had intensity, but was ostensibly not erotic. That phase came to an end three years later, when "the beginning of the end of innocence started" (O: 129). The year before, his mother remarried – to a "wonderful man" of whom Fernando has many fond memories; Hamlet's crisis never struck Fernando. Next phase of the ongoing crisis: a "Platonic but totally

conscious homosexual love affair – the most intense relationship ever."
Fernando adds parenthetically: "Of course I speak only for myself"
(O: 129). When Fernando was twenty-two, Manuel focused his affections elsewhere. The third phase of the crisis begins: "Devastating
jealousy, but I behaved with total decency, so perhaps jealousy is not
the right word, sense of loss? I wish to make it clear that I verbalised
these feelings" (O: 129). Fernando wants to make it clear to Marcus that
he made it clear – and he is not referring to his feelings of jealousy or
loss alone. He put his feelings into words. He rendered the subjective
intersubjective. He gave the subjective an intersubjective coding, in the
explicit modality of the erotic. If still within an inner circle, he thus
stepped out of the closet.

In contrast to Sartre, the anthropologist is not a psychoanalyst in the
end and so must refrain from undertaking an exegesis of Fernando's
own turn at twenty-two to the Isabel whom he already knew and who
would shortly become his first wife. (Fernando recalls with some
vagueness that he began to see a psychoanalyst at more or less the same
time.) [I began to see a psychoanalyst about a year and a half after my
marriage: FM.] The marriage was brief, lasting only two and a half
years. Its decline coincided with a crisis within crisis that bears prodigious ethical weight in Fernando's narrativization of his maturation. It
was another affair, once again with a man, though a man who cannot be
named. It was, Fernando writes, his "one and only serious homosexual
love affair; only satisfactory homosexual sex relationship for me"
(O: 129). It was also brief, over within a single year. It was disruptive
as long as it lasted. Fernando did not seek to publicize it – but, he wrote
to Marcus and reiterated to me, he "made no effort to hide it, either." At
Fronteira, it was a scandal. He fought about it with his mother. He
recalls with a mixture of pain and disgust the moment during one of
their arguments when his mother disowned him as her son. She was not
alone in insisting that it was entirely inappropriate to his standing and
the duties that standing entailed. Fernando's stepfather was more

understanding, but he seems to have agreed with his mother that the affair simply had to pass. Or simply be kept as a skeleton, back in the closet? Fernando would not suffer any compromise. The relationship may well have been brief, but Fernando spoke of it to Marcus and to me as an emotional pinnacle. "It was," he said to me, "the only thing that I have ever done that I did purely for love." His pride in the purity and singular intensity of the commitment remains unfaded. He writes Marcus that when, in his youth, he would listen to music as when he "was feeling cornered and attacked by nearly everyone [he] loved because of this homosexual affair," he was "living out the hero that there is, or I imagine there is, in me" (O: 119–120) – though he quickly adds (yet another qualification) that he supposes that "the fantasy comes with the aristocratic inheritance (never asked anyone), but I believe it is also a very adolescent thing." When writing previously to Marcus of his musical tastes, he had been more specific. "At the core of my self-image," he inserted parenthetically, "I am an emotional hero" (O: 105).

The would-be, erstwhile emotional hero faced another crisis, a crisis of great material, social and cultural moment – and not for him alone – in 1975, when he was twenty-nine years old and manager of his farm. Its precipitants arose the year before, though they had been brewing for nearly a decade. On April 25, 1974, a cadre of officers in the Portuguese military carried out a coup against the Salazarist regime, the premier of which since 1968 had been Marcelo Caetano. The act was nearly bloodless; civilians joined the officers in the streets of Lisbon and proceeded with them to offer red carnations (of the usual communist connotations) to their armed opponents, who were happy to accept them. Hence, the Carnation Revolution: among its first acts was the cessation of the colonial wars and the dismantling of the empire that remained in Africa and the Indian Ocean. Domestic transformations occurred in tandem. The officers initially at the forefront of the revolution were populist – though the genuineness of their leftist credentials and of the leftist parties in alliance with them, at the time and afterward, has been a matter of debate (cf. Lomax 1983). In any event, they tolerated and indeed sanctioned in policy smallholders' and agricultural employees' seizures of latifundist and minifundist holdings. Most analysts focus on the seizures that occurred in Alentejo, in the formal south of Portugal. Such seizures also occurred in the southern part of the north of the country – and not least at the Condado de Torre. A substantial portion of Fernando's agricultural estate suddenly found itself in the hands of others. His income – and in several respects, his security – collapsed just as suddenly.

Fernando was unable to pinpoint either the date or the particular spark of his having found himself – in great contrast to his titled fellows – a supporter of communism, which later earned him the epithet of the "Red Marquis." Bourdieu has observed briefly that leftist commitments (if not active leftist practices) tend to mark the dominated fractions of the dominant class – those endowed with a high store of symbolic capital but relatively little of its material counterparts (1984: 420–421). In making the observation, he has French academics specifically in mind. Fernando for his part could not ever and cannot now be relegated to the position of a French academic. He does, however, have an advanced education. His grandfather, who held a degree in the law, encouraged his grandson to follow in his footsteps. Fernando initially complied, but soon found that the law was not to his liking. He turned instead toward philosophy and in doing so turned – here, too – away from the more customary noble *Bildung* of even an educated sort. He succeeded in securing the equivalent of a Master's degree. His wealth nevertheless continues to set him well apart from his academic peers. Though with ups and downs in the course of his life (see shortly below), Fernando is not as grandly wealthy as the grandest of the grande bourgeoisie, but he is a wealthy man. If he suffers domination, he does so within the specific economy of gender and sexuality, the Portuguese constellation of which has until recently – if even recently – been no friendlier to the overtly and exclusively homosexual than most of the other countries with borders on the Mediterranean have been (McGovern 2006; *Situacão Portuguesa* 2002; Vale de Almeida 1996). His subjection within the economy of gender and sexuality cannot, however, fully account for his politics. Take his politics together with his other deviations from the standard. The immediate conclusion is that Fernando is a subject of contrasts – if not within himself then from those others who constitute his most obvious reference network. A further conclusion invites airing – that Fernando is not merely a subject of contrasts but also something of a contrarian. At the very least, he is strategically evasive of labels. Consider all those qualifications.

In any event, if quite contrary to his objective material interests, Fernando's support for the communist cause was firm at the time of the revolution. He had no self-consistent alternative but to participate willingly in the cession of the farm to his employees. He remembers the latter still deferring to him even as and after he did so. If comfortable among them, he was nevertheless uncomfortable in the country at the time. Uncomfortable in their own right, many other major landowners went into exile (Lomax 1983: 120). Fernando for his own part went into voluntary exile in Morocco for two and a half months. He returned to Europe in 1975, first to England and then back to Portugal, after a republican and less radical government had been established and acquired a measure of stability. That government began the review of the appropriation of properties of the revolutionary period. It would determine that a substantial proportion of the properties that workers had seized or that were initially signed over to them were appropriated illegally and should be returned to their former owners (Gallagher 1981). It also began to assess damages and calculate restitution for the *frutos pudendos* – the "fruits on the vine" – that such owners had lost with their land. Restitution was not yet complete during my interviews with Fernando; he was himself awaiting restitution that was officially his due. After his return, however, he no longer kept the farm at the center of his attention. Though he was still the owner of what remained of it, he turned over its management just then to José Maria. The latter was the prime mover in the effort to recover through economic transactions the lands of the Condado de Torre that remained in others' hands in the aftermath of the government's assessment of the legality of their seizure. The farm was restored to its former proportions by the later 1980s. Fernando's assignation of its management to José Maria does not in any event mark the clear and distinct beginning of his near-exclusive devotion to the restoration of Fronteira. From the age of thirty-three until the age of forty-one, he resided at the palace but also maintained an apartment in Évora, at whose university he taught courses in history and philosophy. The aftermath of the revolution seems even so to have begun a gradual reorientation of priorities of which the security and flourishing of Fronteira was the culmination.

Mode of judgment: ethical valuation and ethical justification

Emotional hero: a pinnacle, an image of the core of the self. Fernando's ironic qualification of his emotional heroism as an adolescent fantasy nevertheless leads away from positing it as constituting the telos of his ethics, or even the cardinal virtue of that ethics. Like Prince Hal, Fernando had to temper his youthful exuberance and excess in order to befit his titles, to wear them well. He had to do so in the name of what, when asked, he pronounced more than once to be "survival" – not itself the telos, the culmination of the subject he should become, either, but one of its regulative imperatives. As I have already indicated, several of Fernando's titled peers produced the very same term when we solicited from them a summary conception of their common project. For once, Fernando thus sounds just like the noble that he is. Survival functions for him as for other nobles at once as a badge of honor and a badge of concern, of common anxiety, if at a higher pitch in some cases than in others. It has diverse objects, diverse concentrations: landed estate, house, heirlooms, titles as such. Like nobility, it is a term that can be equivocal. It operates equivocally in Fernando's own general usage. He proves capable, however, of distinguishing each of its enfolded senses in turn. In doing so, he also makes manifest the distinctive complexity of the nesting of subject positions, one within another but one also potentially at odds with another as priorities compete, circumstances demand and opportunities warrant.

Fernando thought it time, when his presumptive heir António was eight years old, to compose and deliver publicly to him a lecture treating the imperatives of life, the compromises that any life would have to face, but also the privileges and the burdens of inheritance and in particular of the inheritance of both high title and three-story palace. Fernando wrote it on three weekends over a nine-week period. Its composition takes its intended audience well into account. It is relatively brief; it is supplied with examples whose significance a near-adolescent might easily grasp. It is nevertheless a systematic tract and its approach to the relation between past, present and future indebted in part to R. G. Collingwood, among Fernando's most admired thinkers. Not everyone writes a *Sermão a meu sucessor*, a "Sermon ['address' might be less misleading in English: JDF] to my Successor." That Fernando did so and felt compelled to do so is not without noble precedent (Monteiro 1998: 229). It is in any event an indication of an askêsis of self-reflection that has become integrated into the habitus – and an indication of the privilege of sufficient time and leisure for such an askêsis to have become part of everyday life. It is an indication further of irregular circumstances of the succession itself. António is not his son and though he refers to the young man as his *sobrinho*, "nephew," and to himself reciprocally as *tio*, "uncle," António is (in the Portuguese and standard European reckoning) his first cousin once removed. Though they are female, two other members of António's own generation stand in the same relation to Fernando and are in principle candidates for his titles. The public anointment of a successor is thus a bulwark against potential future controversy. Fernando hoped the delivery of the Sermon would be a "big event." It was instead something of a disappointment to him. António's parents feared that such attention and exhortation might overwhelm and disorient their son; Fernando thus delivered the Sermon with his heir in absentia.

Fernando subtitles his Sermon "Toward an Ethics of Survival," but again, survival is a specifically deontological element of his ethical system, not the be all and end all of it. His introduction to the topic is understated, though telling, and his treatment of it characteristically down to earth:

The world is made up of sentient beings. The thought that we believe to be private can surface on our faces and disturb those who love us and know us well or, if only in a small degree, influence our actions. A half-hearted smile can hurt a friend even if he isn't aware of it at the time.

Even our seemingly most irrelevant and banal actions can kill living creatures. We have to consider that other creatures have the same right as we do to be where they are and to live without our interference. *When we pick up a can of insecticide we must learn to consider that perhaps a fly has as much right to live as we do and that the insecticide may kill more than just the fly. We can do it but we have to know what we're doing. And if we could use a fly-swatter or, better still, shoo the fly away, so that it continues its life without upsetting our own, then we should shoo it away without killing it.*

It is true that our own survival requires the destruction of other creatures. Nearly all of our food comes from creatures that were alive, whether animals or plants, before falling into the trap of the food chain. And our mortal remains, our own ashes, come to be part of the nourishment of other creatures, just as our own death is sometimes the result of infectious bacteria or the irregular growth of cells. We don't stop eating because of this, but we should be aware that our life has regrettable consequences for others.

The difference between us and these other beings is that our responsibility is greater. We are not only sentient but conscious beings. We should do what we do knowing what we are doing and not acting tropistically or out of sheer compulsion, or because we see others doing the same, or because someone taught us as a child to do it this or that way, *much less because an old, boring uncle resolves to give a sermon and doesn't find anything better to tell you.* (O: 320)

Fernando's extension of the chrism and mode of ethical valuation is thus expansive, well beyond the usual Kantian universe. Though it has one of its motives in a conception of that which might be vulnerable to harm, it extends even beyond the usual utilitarian universe in conceiving of harm as reaching beyond suffering to the sheer loss of life. On the face of it at least, it stops short of the chrism of the deep ecologists, which reaches even beyond the organic in its anointment of the earth as a whole. It stops well short of cosmicism. Fernando's is a chrism extended in a vitalistic mode, at least to "sentient beings" and even to those living beings to which we have no plausible reason to attribute the capacity to experience pain or pleasure. It seems indeed to reach as far as the ethically anointed universe implied by the most absolutist of the interpretations of the first of the Buddhists' Five Precepts. It is as expansive as the ethical chrism of the Jain saints.

Fernando's conception of who and what are due ethical regard, however, evinces nothing of the sacred. Perhaps it amounts to a secularization of the Buddhist sacralization of life – but if so, it comes with no categorical deontological rider attached. Its attendant right of survival is instead a right with a ceteris paribus clause in train: should circumstances permit of no reasonable alternative, the fly might have to go. It is, however, a conception of much broader reach than that whose attendant imperative is the Biblical imperative not to kill, which is more accurately an imperative not to commit murder, or even more precisely not to murder innocent human beings. Interestingly, Fernando makes no mention of innocence either here or at any other juncture in the Sermon. His ethical regard is not founded upon the dichotomy between the innocent and the guilty, as one might argue the regard of the Commandments to be. It cannot be translated into or reduced to the presumptive granting of innocence to all those who have yet to be proved guilty. It is a regard devoid of legalism. Fernando's chrism nevertheless places the anointed within the domain of something like that of natural law. What lives has, purely in living, a claim on that which also lives – and derivatively, on the inorganic as well. It is not merely at liberty to survive. It has the right to do so, and as much of a right as any other similarly vital being.

Hence, Fernando's ethical domain includes *zoê*, Hannah Arendt's and Giorgio Agamben's bare or naked life (Arendt 1998; Agamben 1998). Not that Arendt or Agamben is his likely inspiration. Fernando never mentioned Arendt – and certainly does not do so in his address to António. He never mentioned and is probably unfamiliar with Agamben's works. His assertion of a right to survive equally distributed across the vital kingdom and, derivatively, his conception of survival are in any event equivocal in their relation to zoê. The bacterium has a right to survival as a matter of the continuation of its naked life – or almost naked, since it is after all a creature of at least one right – because a bacterium can have no other kind of life. At what rung on the ladder of organic complexity Fernando might begin to distinguish naked from some more textured life is not clear. Perhaps it comes with sentience, with the capacity to suffer. Perhaps it comes only with being human. What is clear in any case is that the right to survive that human beings might claim – and the duty to do so, cardinal among their greater responsibilities – is in every case more than a right merely to continue barely, nakedly living. It is never merely a right to zoê. It is always also the right to survive as a distinctly human being, a cultural and social creature, a creature of passions and reasons, a creature of memory and imagination, a creature of need and hopeful anticipation.

Fernando's human beings have a right – every one an equal right – to the survival of their *bios*, their way of life, their preferred manner of living.

Hence, human beings have more rights than merely the right to survive. Three principles are in force in Fernando's exhortations to his nephew. The first is that of distributive equality: "other human beings have exactly the same rights as we do" (O: 320). The second is that of the equal distribution at once of the right and the duty of ethical regard:

To have others respect our rights, two things are of the essence: first, that we respect their rights, and second, that we know how to make our own rights be respected. *If you steal your neighbor's eraser, you can't complain if someone steals your pen, but if you let yourself be bullied without provocation and if you don't know how to indicate that you won't take it, you will never get rid of bullies.* (O: 321)

The third is a historistically driven principle of ethical uncertainty – and its pragmatic resolution:

There are no set rules to define, clearly and forever, what others' rights are, but there is a touchstone that serves in the majority of cases for recognizing others' rights: think of your own rights and project them symmetrically onto others. It doesn't solve everything, but it's an excellent starting point. *Don't step on the cat's tail if you don't want it to scratch you!* (O: 321)

Fernando's emphatic conclusion reveals a frequent inclination of his ethical reasoning: from what looks to be the sort of principlism familiar from the contractarian and Hegelian traditions toward a consequentialism of a roughly utilitarian sort. The turn indicates Fernando's distance from ethical Kantianism. It demonstrates that he is not an obsessive rationalist of any stripe whatever.

The first of the responsibilities that Fernando cares to impress upon his nephew is already clear enough in his recommendation not to follow the advice of a boring uncle's idle pronouncements. It is the responsibility to think and even to cultivate one's feelings critically and independently – and once again, it comes with the correlative right to do so. The exercise of both thinking and the cultivation of feeling is an overt and self-conscious hallmark of Fernando's mode of subjectivation and at the forefront of his own understanding of his approach to his central ethical crises. Both come with their own ceteris paribus clause: give others the benefit of the doubt. "*When your teacher tells you ... that the highest of the mountains of Portugal is the Serra da Estrela, you aren't going to refuse to believe her...*" (O: 316). Even so, one should never take others' assertions entirely for granted:

> *you aren't going to refuse to believe her until you have the occasion ... to survey the summit of the mountains. Give credit to what your teacher tells you, but you must cling to the idea that, when you come across a map of Portugal, you will go ... read the altitudinal measurements of the mountains to see if there is any taller than the Serra da Estrela, which there happens to be on the Azores.* (O: 316)

The principle is also reflexive: one might give oneself the benefit of the doubt, but one must not believe true anything and everything that one believes or think legitimate everything that one feels. Arrogance is Fernando's cardinal epistemic failing (O: 318) and its remedial obligation is that of listening to others, to the wise but also to the simple, to those who flatter but also to critics, to those "who know how to explain" but also "to those who only stammer" (O: 319). Epistemic historicism – which is to say, a conviction in the historicity of what passes as knowledge, of its contextual specificity – returns to provide the ground of a relativist perspectivalism: "it is essential to be aware that our perspective at any given moment, whether it be in youth, in maturity, or in old age, is the perspective of the moment and not necessarily more valid than the perspective of other moments" (O: 317). Hence, Fernando can read as a Nietzschean, but Fernando's epistemic temper is less radical than Nietzsche's own:

Ideally, our understanding of reality at any moment should not deny but integrate our previous understanding of it. There is no point in going from black to white because there is always something essential in the understanding that the first moment provides and only very seldom is a radical change justified. The alternative is between being constant and consistent and being a weathercock and a turncoat. Our thinking should be flexible, but not inconstant or inconsistent. (O: 317–318)

The sensibility is fallibilist – liberal rather than epistemically revolutionary. Being truthful for its part has "intrinsic value" – if yet again with a ceteris paribus clause:

Lying is useful only on two sorts of occasions: the first, in order not to hurt others unnecessarily when they do not merit our consideration and, as with persons of very old age or very little maturity, it would no longer or not yet be worth the trouble; the second, in order to save our skin, but only in the cases of the sheer necessity of survival. (O: 323; the translation is slightly modified from the original English in accord with Fernando's advice)

Fernando calls upon the noble virtues in his defense of truthfulness – "ninety-nine percent of the time, truth is more loyal, more honorable to us and others" – but with truthfulness as with its contrary, questions of "what is useful and more constructive" are not out of order (O: 323).

On the matter of feelings, Fernando remains eclectic in grounding his ethical judgment. His epistemic relativism, however, stands in contrast to an emotive deontology that entertains the absolute, at least at its limits. The cheerful pragmatism that tinges his approach to truthfulness and lying is absent from his approach to the ethical regard of feelings – others' and one's own. In the background of his almost troubled seriousness of tone, one hears the echo of the emotional hero's grandest and most perilous hours:

Not to hurt other people's feelings is good, but it cannot be the single measure of your actions, and it is very difficult to know how much and when we should allow the feelings of others to affect our actions. We may take as an absolute limit on our actions only that we never intrude into another's private sphere. *If I feel like slapping someone, I shouldn't think that I have the right to do so, but rather that I most assuredly have every right to prevent others from slapping me.*

Within our own private spheres we have to keep a very careful eye on which of our concerns we can permit influence to be exerted by others. I think that we should allow the feelings of others to interfere only with what we do not consider essential to our self-fulfillment. (O: 321–322)

Fernando's psychologistic phrasing has nothing specifically Portuguese about it any more than it is idiosyncratic. He speaks of "self-fulfillment" as a Western modern. He assigns it the value he does as the same sort of modern, for whom the language of humanist psychology has become a standard discourse of the self since its origins in the early twentieth century and for whom the near-absolute ethical estimation of self-fulfillment has become themitical. He does not write as a Sartrean; his psychological essentialism points to a self to which more is given and of more substance than the self for which the only ontological given is that it exists for itself. He does not write as a Heideggerian; if he is sensitive to the role and weight of tradition in the formation of the self, his tradition is an open-ended and permeable one and always susceptible to transformation.

The genealogist notes that humanist psychology has its roots not merely in the secularized confessional of the psychoanalytic chamber but also in the Romantic fashioning of the essence of the self as "interiority." Fernando's appeal to "the private sphere" wants casting in at least a dim Romantic light, as does his assessment of the legitimacy of the self's resistance of external conventions, regardless of the intimacy of who might impose them:

If the harm that our actions inflict on others is caused only by the destruction of the image that they have created of us, then we have every right to do what we consider important for our self-fulfillment and what we believe is right, however much another might suffer from the shattering

of that image. If, however, our actions result only from secondary preferences and not from something essential, if it is a matter of mere appetite
and not of a life experience important to our fulfillment, then it's not
worth the trouble to distress those who love us or to shock those with
whom we live ... Altruism, more than anything else, is an intelligent form
of egoism. (O: 322)

Here again, the Enlightened melding of principle and consequence
informs the prism of Fernando's ethical vision. It comes with a note
of caution: "What we do can have the most unforeseen consequences"
(O: 320). Fernando does not aspire, however, to reside in the Land of the
Lotus-eaters, in that cosmos of pathic passivity in which Sartre the
armchair sojourner discovers his Flaubert. Fernando's ethics is an ethics
of decisions demanded and consequences, expected and unexpected,
faced as they arise: "There are always many choices, none of which is
perfect. Yet, sooner or later, we must decide; we have to make our choices
as best we can, but we have to make them" (O: 316). A reflexively modern
principle of the necessity of decision under conditions of incorrigible
uncertainty informs the pronouncement.

Schematically, Fernando's mode of ethical valuation and judgment at
first sight places him within the general tradition of philsophical prin-
ciplists, of those who grant priority to rights over goods. Rights are
themitically constitutive of Fernando's Enlightened, Romantic and
Euromodern ethical universe, though only the apparent right to self-
fulfillment is positively transhistorical. He owes a debt to Millsian
liberalism, as his preoccupation with harm attests. He is, however, not
a simple liberal, for whom duties are typically only negative – duties not
to violate the rights of others. Fernando's ethics includes positive
duties. Some of them we have met already – the duty to think independently and critically among them. Other duties like them await
attending.

Already, he looks a bit Kantian, though it would be a mistake to
relegate him to the Kantian league. His consequentialist valorization

of self-fulfillment allies him rather with the classical philosophers of virtue. His evidently more particularistic understanding of the good for any human woman or man and his historicist relativism are not classical but once again modern. At second sight, then, Fernando is difficult to place. His is a blurry, quantum ethical presence, defying the assignation of any single atomic weight, measurable only at the cost of distortion. Philosophical purism, the puristic drive toward rationalization that has dominated the philosophical enterprise in the West, is incompatible with such elusiveness – but the modern Western everyperson may well be Fernando's nearer fellow traveler.

Mode of subjectivation: scope, structure and priority

Already complex, then, Fernando's ethics takes on further complexity in its absorbing into the everyperson a subject who is anything but socially or culturally ordinary. Fernando is first a human being – a "mere mortal," as he regularly puts it – but someone else besides. He is a noble and understands the noble position ethically as a position of far greater responsibility and duty than the mere mortal must face: "We are human beings exactly equal to others and . . . have nothing more than a sonorous name and tradition: 'Noblesse Oblige.' Noble status does not confer on us any rights whatsoever, but only confers on us certain additional obligations" (O: 323). Nobility demands sensitivity to and the defense of one's honor, but never the pettiness of an excess of indignation at insult. It demands consciousness of one's "place in history," but also the awareness that "the balance sheet of life" is constituted only of what one has actually achieved and not of what we might dream of coming to pass in the future. It comes with the responsibility to "deal fairly with others," but a responsibility "in triplicate," because it brings privileges and advantages that mere mortals lack. Fernando thus derives an ethics of etiquette: "good manners are indispensable in our relations with everyone, and kindness as well, as much as possible, and ... we should be all the more considerate the more humble the condition of our interlocutor" (O: 324). Of bad manners, the consequentialist Marquis advises their deployment "with extreme parsimony and only when absolutely necessary, not least because if they are deployed too often they lose their efficacy" (O: 324–325).

To return, however, to principle: intrinsic to and the ultimate and only ethical rationale for nobility is "service":

Our name merely gives us the advantage of knowing who some of our forebears are. A name that some were able to win through their deeds, through service to country or king, and that others were able to preserve through their wisdom and through their continual service to the commonwealth.

This is to say that the respect and the consideration that our name often helps us garner or, if you will, the advantage that we have from the outset over the common run of mortals and that the latter, implicitly or explicitly, often accord to us, is paid for the whole length of our lives and from generation to generation. So it is and so it should be. (O: 325)

The hermeneuticist of suspicion is likely – and has every right – to read such a justification of standing as a rationalization or *méprise-ment*, a witting or unwitting apologia for privilege and advantage alike. The hermeneuticist of suspicion is, however, free and even compelled to read any ethical self-justification in precisely the same terms, thus offering an interpretation that may well be true (or not), but of no sociologically discriminatory power – as the astute herme-neuticist of self-suspicion Fernando in fact recognizes clearly. That reward for service – granted, broadly construed – has been the official rationale for the conferral of nobility is in any case a plain social fact. That the obligation to serve is the regnant obliga-tion of the noble is a presumption that Fernando himself has taken very seriously, though not without due consideration of the consequences of the courses of action that he has decided to take, including whether such courses might be advantageous to him and to his heirs.

To state the almost obvious: Marcus and Hill have reasonably generalized over Fernando's own case in positing that noble service comes with the proviso not simply of repeating the past, but instead of a controlled, individualizing effectuation of its continuation into the present and the future (Marcus and Hill 2005: 336). They generalize over Fernando's own case in positing further that the nobility's social reproduction centers on the maintenance of the house, this powerful actant whose ethical call dominates the noble project, sometimes to catastrophic end, and in many cases even after its crumbling. In short, the Portuguese noble qua noble must find a way to serve king or commonwealth in serving the house, and vice versa. At least, Fernando is and, from the immediate post-revolutionary period forward, has proved himself committed to finding the means and the resources that would enable him to do so. The post-revolutionary diminution of his income was itself acute enough to force Fernando to face a possibility that bordered on the unconscionable – selling the palace. Obviously, he did not do so, but is not ashamed of having considered doing so, precisely because "circumstances drove him to it" (O: 326). Yet, had he done so:

I would have broken a most important link in the chain of our family's tradition. I would have negatively affected the future and this present moment – this sermon – would not have taken place. And nevertheless, I would have done no more than what the members of another illustrious family did, the Almeida-Portugal family, whom we represent today, and of whom only the memory and some family relics remain; I ended up doing no more than the son of the builder of this palace, who was also once at the point of selling it.

Luckily, I did not sell the house, but I did sell – for I thought it necessary – many of the furnishings and objects of the house. The fifth Marquis of Fronteira also did as much when he needed money to restore and decorate it.

I am sorry to have done what I did, but in the same circumstances I would do it again in the bat of an eye. (O: 326)

Nor is this all that the Marquis has done in the name of the preservation of Fronteira – and of the service of the commonwealth at the same time.

In the summer of 1988, Fernando invited Frederico George, a Professor Emeritus of the Faculty of Architecture at the Technical University of Lisbon and his stepfather, to assess the condition of the palace and identify those of its architectural elements in direst need of care. Professor George's younger colleague Jorge Bastos assisted him in the assessment. History – especially recent history – had indeed taken its toll. Lisbon absorbed Bemfica in the latter half of the twentieth century. In the aftermath of the annexation, increasingly heavy traffic passed near the palace, which is on the way to and from the airport, less than a kilometer north of the municipal zoo and about the same distance south from the camping park on Mount Monsanto. George and Bastos blame the vibrations that the traffic generated for much of the damage the palace subsequently suffered. Of particular urgency at the time was the repair of the northern loggia, which was perilously close to collapse (George and Bastos 1993). Fernando's interest in the scholars' assessment was not merely academic. The properties of the Condado had been reconsolidated. Finances had improved. Fernando had also taken a further and most consequential step in order to see the palace put back on to its own feet. His solicitation of scholarly advice was part of a practical plan.

Formally in late February of 1982, by national decree, Fronteira was declared a National Monument and enfolded into the Portuguese patrimony, for the straightforward reason that "it is a living testament to Portuguese culture that must be preserved and enriched" (O: 331). In 1989, in order to carry out that preservation and enrichment, Fernando established with his closest circle of relatives and respected friends the

Fieldwork in ethics

Foundation of the Houses of Fronteira and Alorna. He did so with an important precedent in mind. Another of Fernando's cousins, Fernando de Sousa Botelho e Albuquerque, fourth Count of Mangualde, is heir to and the current director of the Mateus Foundation, the centerpiece of which is the Casa Mateus, which sits in the western interior of Portugal east and slightly north of Oporto. Casa Mateus is the most visited tourist site in the country, an elaborate palace, larger and built later than Fronteira, more characteristically Iberian in its architectural style, famous like Fronteira for its well-tended formal gardens. The Mateus Foundation is also among the country's major cultural benefactors, offering fellowships to artists, hosting dance festivals and musical performances at the Casa and offering tourists entry into its interior and gardens alike. The terms of the Foundation are the model for the Foundation of the Houses of Fronteira and Alorna. Ownership of the property remains in private hands; Fronteira remains Fernando's personal property, or more strictly it remains his in usufruct. [To have a personal property or a usufruct may appear pretty much the same from the outside, but believe me, it is quite different from the inside. The charter of the Foundation states who follows after me, the representative of the house, who is the bearer of the title of Conde de Torre: FM.] With the establishment of the Foundation, however, the same property is translated into what closely resembles a not-for-profit corporation. Among the benefits of doing so – for the owners of palaces in Portugal as well as those in many other European countries who inhabit the present without the benefit of the most materially pivotal of their ancestors' privileges and immunities – is a significant reduction of the rate of taxation.

Among the ends of the Foundation is also one of its means – Fronteira itself becomes one of the sources of income as well as the concrete entity on whose behalf such income is sought. At least as importantly, the Foundation facilitates the preservation of the family in its domestic embodiment, in the concrete edifice that is Fronteira itself. Hence, Fronteira's status as something quite other than a commodity: it is kept while nevertheless giving of itself, its interiors open like those of Casa Mateus to the ticketed public during select hours of most days, its larger rooms and gardens available during the period of Marcus' research for reservation and rental for such purposes as weddings. Its profits and its endowments also – and by obligation – serve the national interest. The Foundation is entitled to specify just what sort of service it will render. In the charter of the Foundation, Fernando's stipulations are at once precise and open to what the future might hold:

Its priorities rest with the humanities and with all that may contribute directly or indirectly to the understanding of the human being. At this particular moment, the Foundation is especially engaged with the following contemporary disciplines: history, art, and philosophy – understood in the broadest sense possible; all the intersections among these disciplines, including the history of art and the philosophy of history; and all other studies that might contribute to understanding them better. Of interest beyond these there is, of course, whatever else might contribute to the preservation of the Foundation's inalienable heritage. (O: 333–334)

The charter characterizes the Foundation as "erudite but not academic, flexible but self-consistent, independent in the face of social conventions but respectful of the prevailing standards of ethical conduct" (O: 334). The author of the charter could thus be writing of himself. Just so, the heir to Alcipe focuses the present and future ambitions of the Foundation on those lineaments that her particular life etched into the collective visage and more intimate familial consciousness of the Mascarenhas family. Art stands at the forefront and cultured refinement before battle and knightly bluster, however imposing the Room of the Battles may still be. Just so, the present owner of Fronteira fulfills his double obligation to sustain continuity with his ancestors and differentiate himself from them in the process. Just so, he achieves precisely what he offers as a summary of himself as noble. He remains sensitive to the past but always with an eye to the future.

That many of the central rooms of Fernando's home may be rented out to wedding and other parties is not altogether to his liking. He finds the events from which the Foundation derives some portion of its income an annoying distraction. They can be noisy. They can be messy. They demand anticipation even though he has a staff that largely takes care of the practical tasks they impose. José Maria's wife, Maria (de Assuncão de Castro Infante da Câmara), who lives in the bottom apartment of the palace with her husband and son, oversees catering. Fernando is disturbed when, entering one or another of the rooms, he finds furniture moved, his familiar pathways blocked or detoured, his habitual orientations in need of conscious readjustment. He dislikes fundraising. He tells Marcus that in fact he "hates" it. [About fundraising – I do hate it, but the Foundation does carry on its cultural mission without fundraising. There are very few instances in which we have used fundraising: first and foremost for the repairs of the roofs of the house, for which we succeeded in obtaining funding from the Portuguese state: FM.] So with service comes displeasure and in that displeasure some sacrifice of contentment.

Such a sacrifice is, however, petty – it amounts to next to nothing – in comparison with the sacrifice Fernando made in order to set the Foundation in motion. With its establishment, he signed over to it some 90 percent of the monies – most generated by the farm – that would have been his personal income. He did not offer Marcus or me a ledger to browse. He never told us what the typical sum of the 10 percent of his income – its sources in any event independent of the Foundation – that he retained might be. He did not sacrifice enough to bring about his own economic declassement. A palace that had a staff of twelve when his grandfather lived there nevertheless housed during my visits a staff of only three to five – and two of those were immigrants who worked for very little in order to have the Foundation sponsor their securing of permanent residency. Fernando told me that he regretted not having ever had a Ferrari (one of his father's possessions). He did have a driver (and man Friday, who among other things might greet a prowler in the gardens at night with a shotgun), but he rode in a Renault touring car. He told me that his mother thought him mad for forfeiting so much of his spending money to the Foundation's charge. He added that she simply didn't understand.

Between Fernando the mere mortal and the Marquis, then, between these two subject positions, one common to us all and the other that of a minority within the minority that is the contemporary Portuguese nobility and even more of a minority within the European nobility, a particular relationship seems to hold: within the mortal the Marquis has his nest. Mortal first, then Marquis: Fernando puts it this way in his Sermon. He advises António to "be first a man and then, only then, but immediately thereafter, a nobleman." He elaborates further:

Use your own head first. If you have doubts, think of what your ancestors would have done. But even when you sense that you must do that, never forget that the moment in which you are thinking is another moment, and a moment different from that in which your father or your grandfather or your great-grandfather or your great-great-great-great-grandmother were thinking. (O: 325–326)

Once again, Fernando is surely pronouncing on himself – but in an imperative mood the force of which is consequently less definite than that of self-description. The relationship between the subject position of the mere mortal and any other, less inclusive, is in any event not without variation. The self-sacrificial hero or heroine, the saint who dies defiant in the Roman arena, the Buddhist monk who self-immolates in protest, the captain who goes down with his or her ship – none of these subjects acts first and foremost as a mere mortal compelled to survive and none (ceteris paribus) is acting anethically, much less (ceteris paribus) unethically (cf. Evans 1999: 28).

Fieldwork in ethics

The question is whether Fernando himself conforms to the imperative
he delivers to his heir. When, far removed from the context of the
Sermon, I once asked him directly what the difference was between
Fernando and the Marquis, he was at first startled, then chuckled, then
responded, "well . . ." – which might or might not be taken as an answer.
Likely in any case is that the question is not for him entirely resolved, or
even resolvable. His cousin at Mateus is more certain. Marcus and Hill
write of their conversation with him, "He stated that he had never had
any choice but to run Mateus. It was drilled into him from the first
hour of his birth. Duty and obligation to the family and Mateus have
been with him always" (O: 371). The Count put it to Marcus and Hill
summarily: he did not own Mateus but Mateus him. As already noted,
Fernando said the same to Marcus and me of Fronteira – which
warrants the suspicion that the noble is in fact the nest of the man
rather than the reverse. The Count's eldest daughter, Teresa, heir to his
titles and to Mateus, asserted to me when we spoke that hers was the
first generation for whom being or not being a noble had become a
choice. Fernando belongs to her father's generation. Teresa's tie to
Fernando is warm; she knows him well. It would be surprising if she
did not have both her father and Fernando in mind when spelling out
for me the specific contemporaneity of her own condition.

Telos

Quantum-blurry, differently and multiply placed at one and the same
time, principlist and consequentialist, rights-driven and duty-bound,
attuned to independence but also to the inescapability of the weight
of the past, tempted by the universal but cognizant of the relativity
and fallibility of ethical normativity and ethical judgment, survivalist
in a double sense, eccentric, even contrarian, balking at labels, heroic
but with a twist, Fernando's mode of subjectivation is as good as

ineffable, but his ethical telos is in its general expression articulable enough. Being the subject that Fernando would be is being an innovative preservationalist of a familial heritage in both its symbolic materiality and its materialized symbolism. His project – and in this case, too, one is correct in deeming it a project – is that of seizing pragmatically and creatively the possibilities that come to him in order to sustain the symbolic and material contours of a familial past and to render them present through the cultivation of a service appropriate to its place and time as its ultimate ethical redemption, its paying of the debt it owes for the privilege that has come to and continues to be conferred upon it. The subject thus cultivated and constituted and set into autopoietic motion is a relational subject, its self-definition tied inextricably to the genea-logical network of the living and the dead who jointly determine its limits and its reach and who even if dead continue to have communi-cative life through it. Individuating, Fernando's is, again, not an indi-vidualist subject in the manner of the individualist subjects whom de Tocqueville encountered in the fledgling United States, always in danger of pressing their self-reliance to the disorienting extreme of finding themselves a law unto themselves and so rushing elastically back to the cognitive and affective comforts of themitical conformism (Tocqueville 2004). A fortiori, Fernando's is not an individualist subject in the manner of Emerson's more radical and – in principle – more clear-sighted aspirant to self-reliance, much less in the manner of the Trans-man of Nietzsche's *Thus Spake Zarathustra* (Emerson 2000; Nietzsche 2003). It bears a closer family resemblance to those modern (but not postmodern) middle-class English individualists of Strathern's *After Nature*, whose projects of self-definition and self-differentiation had their limits and reach within the coded stylistics of the themes and acceptable variations of the cottage and its gardens (Strathern 1992). They are Fernando's humbler and distant relations – but evidently influenced in their way by the noble taste-making that as Elias has shown has served the middle classes as a long-standing point of reference not merely in England but in a broad stretch of Western and Central Europe since their emergence in the sixteenth century (Elias 2000).

Concretely, the Foundation of the Houses of Fronteira and Alorna is the pièce de résistance of the telos of Fernando's subjectivation, all the more so because it binds together the farm and Fronteira into a unified and coherent autopoietic ecology. It requires upkeep in its own right. It is in need of practical managers, from caterers to tour guides to fundraisers. It is also in need of erudite and frequently even academic advisors and specialists to aid in fashioning the programs of which it is host or sponsor. The Foundation sometimes shares sponsorship of what the messages that it disseminates electronically (and through other media) refer to as *actividades culturais* – "cultural activities." The recruitment of restorers of the palace (some of whom are students of restoration and willing to work for the experience alone), poetry readings, film showings, musical performances and lectures spanning the humanities are its stock in trade. Its capacity for largesse rises and falls with income from the farm. In 2003, severe fires ravaged a great swath of both the north and the south of Portugal and inflicted major damage at the farm, especially on its cork oaks, which are its chief cash crop. Fernando told me that it would take a decade for production to recover. [True, but only in what relates to the trees that have survived. We had to cut down more than 65,000 cork trees and those that have replaced them will take some thirty-five years to begin production and, say, seventy years to reach full production: FM.] The Foundation is nevertheless an ongoing success. Fernando has fulfilled and continues to fulfill the service that he has set himself to perform. He has done so not least through the acquisition of bureaucratic skills and cultural capital in addition to that which his upbringing and his formal higher education have netted. Having overcome his initial distaste for the rusticities of Fronteira, having come genuinely to admire the virtuosity that its artisans exercised with the training and the materials they had at their disposal, the Marquis has become a gentleman scholar of the history of Portuguese azulejos. Though he does not give the impression of being an extrovert, he has also become a widely recognized presence in the national media – as actor (once), social commentator on television, and journalistic interviewee. In his earlier adulthood, he was approached to run for political office. In the end, he did not, though his political ambitions have not entirely disappeared. (As he has grown older, he has – to his mind, predictably enough – lost the red leftism of his youth. He has become "pink.") If sotto voce, he has ambitions to regalvanize the Portuguese nobility as a cadre of some common purpose. All of these ambitions are modest at most; contemporary realities tend to dampen them. The Foundation remains the primary object of his devotion – but of course, in the name of the house and the family heritage and of the service that is his lot.

Substance

Fernando's subjectivation could have been derailed as any process of subjectivation might be derailed – and not by bad fortune alone. Fernando does not use nor is he aware of Foucault's concept of ethical substance, but the latter is applicable without residue to the temperamental problem that already by his late adolescence he recognized to be in danger of paralyzing him. Call it the danger of emotional heroism become far too much of a potentially good thing. It is a danger that lies within the broader expanses of the realm of the senses. It includes some if not all of the carnal pleasures and does so for some of the same reasons that the carnal pleasures ethically troubled the Greeks. To repeat: Palácio Fronteira was never in Fernando's past and is not now a Calvinist commune – and as my colleague Diana Hill observed in another context, neither is the greatest part of Portugal, even – or, rather, especially – that part of Portugal that is piously Catholic (personal communication). The appetites are not always and immediately subject to suspicion there. Fernando gives little impression of the

Rabelasian. His appetites are not wide-ranging. He indulges relatively few innocent pleasures – and a few more that are not so innocent. Though he does not drink regularly, he enjoys the effect of alcohol. He follows soccer and Grand Prix racing. He is an avid player of a number of games, from the computerized Civilization to bridge. He has no ethical discomfort with sexual pleasure – in and of itself. He relays to Marcus that he smokes hashish. Marcus inquires further. Fernando responds: "there is a less difficult superego, there is a pleasant physical feeling, and there is a very nice mood" – but "nothing," he adds, "that I couldn't express with a slightly bigger effort" (O: 137).

Such apparent insouciance can, however, be misleading. Fernando is untroubled at his overstepping the bounds of bourgeois respectability, but some of his habits leave him with regrets. One of the latter emerges in the course of his admitting to Marcus that his memory is no longer at its full powers. He blames its decline on his having indulged in smoking hashish "heavily" for some four or five years, during a particularly stressful period of his second marriage. Then as with his more moderate consumption of it later on, the drug would drop "a softening veil" between the real and his experience of it that made stresses "easier to bear" (O: 137). The ethical – or at least, ethically relevant – problem at which this confession hints has its index in the cognitive damage that Fernando fears he has done himself, but it has its crux in his having failed adequately to consider the consequences of what he was doing and above all having failed to have exercised adequate self-control. The Greeks knew the problem well. They called it *akrasia*, "weakness of will." Fernando's idiom is no less ethically loaded, but is more psycho-medical. He tells Marcus of a "tendency towards addictions" (O: 42). That tendency has led him toward (and, with struggle, away from) cigarettes as well (cf. O: 152–153).

For all this, Fernando is not after all a Greek. He can agree that the carnal – or, more accurately, psycho-carnal – pleasures are not intrinsically evil, but he gives them his ethically concerted attention only in the negative, only for their potential to foster vices. He shows no inclination to think of them also as the substance of any of the virtues that he esteems. A surer clue to what that substance is comes by way of introduction and parenthesis in response to Marcus' solicitation in what otherwise could be taken as the merely aesthetic accounting of his musical tastes. Before setting them forth in detail, Fernando writes that listening to music was "an extremely important part of my life as an adolescent and young man, very heavily charged with emotion, in itself and as a medium of relationship to others" – a Foucauldian turn of phrase, though entirely by coincidence.

As I have already noted and whatever its bioethnographic shortcomings, saudade comes close to coding the emotional limit-experience that comes or ideally might come at the intersection of melody, lyrics and voice in the songs of the French chanteurs and chanteuses that Fernando admires as well as of the fado that he loves. It is more distant from the emotional alembic of the Brandenburg Concertos, but its agitated suffusion of pain and desire is very much the center of gravity under whose influence Fernando came during his adolescence and early adulthood in entering into that most perilous region of the realm of the senses – the erotic. The man who declares to Marcus that he "loves to love and be loved" deploys without worry and with full affirmation a broader concept that can embrace not merely his heterosexual sensibility and his homosexual corporeality, but also other affections and friendships devoid of eros or at least erotically neutral (O: 136). He writes with the same ease to Marcus of his (untranslated) "saudades" after a lapse in their correspondence (O: 126). He is barely less comfortable and positively enthusiastic in informing Marcus just short of a year after the beginning of their correspondence that, for his part, he has come to consider their relationship a "Platonic homosexual involvement" and his first "love affair" since his marriage to his second wife (O: 130). He can only add that "life is really something wonderful" – and that he has "just smoked some hashish" (O: 130). In such high spirits (if I may), in so blithe an outpouring of saudades, the emotional hero makes another appearance, all the more tellingly for wearing his potential downfall on his sleeve.

It is well worth recalling Fernando's emotional vertigo at the passing of his first (Platonic) homosexual affair: "Devastating jealousy, but I behaved with total decency so perhaps jealousy is not the right word; sense of loss ...?" (O: 129). "Devastation" is the key – not to emotional heroism per se, but to the consequences of its unrestraint. Responding to Marcus' request that he elaborate further on "how certain music" helps him to "construct himself as an emotional hero" (O: 117), he offers an emendation and a clarification that I have previously cited piecemeal:

You seem to pay little attention to past tenses. Anyway, music didn't help me to construct myself as a heroic figure but to live out the hero that there is, or I imagine there is, in me. I suppose the fantasy comes with the aristocratic inheritance (never asked anyone), but I believe it is also a very adolescent thing. There is a facet of this that I recall, which has more to do with the intensity of feeling (in a way, when you feel intensely you are being heroic [?]), the other a specific context that I was thinking about – when I was feeling cornered and attacked by nearly everyone I loved because of this homosexual affair with (...). (O: 119–120)

This heroism, the heroism of his second and only consummated homosexual affair, this testing and overstepping of conventional boundaries, is not evil in Fernando's mind – on the contrary. As the Greeks recognized centuries ago and as Fernando is aware, however, it is dangerous. It risks hubris – an outrage that such widely read adherents of the culture and personality school as Gilberto Freyre have alleged to be one of the tendencies of the Portuguese-cum-Lusotropical character and Lusotropical eroticism at large (Freyre 1956; cf. Vale de Almeida 2004: 46–55). No anthropologist now can or should affirm what Miguel Vale de Almeida appropriately labels such "culturalist essentialism" (2004: 49). As Vale de Almeida also notes, however, an anxiety about the hubris to which saudade among other putative lineaments of the Portuguese or Lusotropical psyche might lead is a preoccupation of culturalist discourse "since the writings of King Duarte in the Middle Ages" and of culturalist efforts to account for the specificity of Portuguese colonialism and its gradual decline from the glories of the Age of Discovery into the decadence of a spendthrift monarchy, isolation and marginality (2004: 51). The ethical problem at issue here thus cannot be reduced to something strictly personal, in however strictly personal a register Fernando's responses to Marcus' and to my own queries might be.

It is nevertheless in a personal register that Fernando articulates the problem in that refraction that he claims ethically as his own: "I am (was?) in my nature an extremely sensitive person and fell in love from sixteen onwards very easily and very deeply, suffering, most of the time excruciating pain until I realized I would become a boneless [i.e. spineless: JDF] personality if I didn't take steps against it" (O: 42). As an aesthetic disposition, the disposition toward the extreme intensification of saudade – and of the rest of the emotional family that it resembles – risks overflowing into an ecstasy incompatible not merely with stale social conventions but with the very foundations of civility. As an aesthetic but even more urgently as an erotic disposition, it risks carrying to excess, into decadence, into dissolute voluptuousness, the distinctively intense refraction of saudade that is the gravitational center of the substance of Fernando's emotional heroism itself. It risks precipitating the plunge into a voluptuous paralysis that is incompatible with the life of the man of action – a man that, very much in accord with the Hellenic and perhaps more pointedly the chivalric current of "Western civilization," if very much in his own way, Fernando would be. All the more as it becomes its own addiction, Fernando's extremity of sensitivity risks – or rather, risked – derailing what his fortune and his titles at once have afforded him and have called upon him to be.

Hence, it has demanded disciplining. It has demanded askêsis. It has demanded instruction and the operation of sometimes painful technologies of self-formation. Nothing less has been necessary for the transition from adolescence into ethical adulthood as Fernando has realized it. He has had to come to grips with himself. He has had to impose upon his flights of feeling a rigorous exercise of stylization. In doing so, he has gathered together, contained and given grace to a potentially scattered and volatile temperamental affliction within the bearable lightness of virtuous composure.

Askêsis

Pedagogy

Machiavelli might come closest in the European tradition to composing a guidebook for the man who would be king or even manager of his grand estate, but he is not among the authors that Fernando professes to hold close. The contextualist and idealist Collingwood, who understood the historical imagination to consist of the recollection and (as Fernando urged me to stress) critical and transformative re-collection of the thoughts and deeds of the past, is the author to whom he appealed most frequently in his conversations with Marcus and me – and even then, not often. As one would, again, expect of someone whose symbolic capital is largely inherited, Fernando does not point to specific books or authors as eminent *magistrae vitae*, one or another teacher of life. Occasionally, he has derived lessons directly from his ancestors: "My 7th grandparents, the Marchioness of Tavora and her husband ... were executed at the orders of the Marquis de Pombal (Prime Minister) and King Dom José I. That was a decisive factor in my thoughts about how the 'powerful' should be dealt with" (O61). Fernando accordingly advises his heir António to be courteous to the powerful, as apparently his ancestors were not. Among his teachers, past and present, are also living relations and friends, most but not all of whom have sat or sit with him on the board of the Foundation. Their circle is small: José Maria – especially on matters concerning the farm – and his wife, Maria; his friends Regina and António Baião; his former student Felipe, who now busies himself with the everyday affairs of the Foundation. During his marriages, his wives were also his counselors. He has taken lessons away from psychoanalysis. When they were alive, his stepfather and – of much longer duration – his mother were important pedagogical resources, each in their own way.

Fernando's reminiscences of his mother's pedagogical interventions arise here and there in *Ocasião*, and not only at such critical moments as that of the possibility of his being consigned to a military school. If appalled at his homosexuality, Fernando's mother was a more benign influence in many other respects. She did not inhibit but instead supported his particular demons. She played a part in selecting for him the ancestors who suited him best. She was among those who "pointed out Alcipe to me as being the origin of my 'intellectual' tendencies" and of whom, "as far as I can remember but particularly since I had Portuguese literature at school (at 16), I was very proud" (O: 60). Or as he puts it with his now customary self-irony: "out of necessity, Alcipe was the 'excuse' I could resort to, to explain the blatant difference between my father's relatives and me" (O: 61). Fernando's mother oversaw his making the proper social connections in his youth. He was not mindlessly obedient. He recalls one conversation: "'Mother, if I have to go [to parties] anyway, then why do you ask me?' To which she would answer, 'Because I always hope that you will give the right answer'" (O: 34). He is less certain whether he remains obedient to her in his adulthood. He writes (the fallibilist and, here again, the herme-neuticist of self-suspicion) to Marcus before her death: "My mother would say that she is not at all a sort of 'consiglieri' for me, for she claims that I never follow the 'tons' of advice she gives me. My wife claims the opposite. Who am I to judge?" (O: 109). In any event, she deserves leading credit for his primary socialization. Fernando also credits his finishing his degree in philosophy to her "persistence and insistence" (O: 94).

Fernando's stepfather Frederico's presence seems to have been consistently beneficial, even nurturing, when his mother could be stern. Frederico also directed his stepson toward Fronteira. He was more influential than any of Fernando's other pedagogues in his coming to love the palace, to appreciate its charms and idiosyncrasies and to explore its architectural and aesthetic history. Frederico was by Fernando's own pronouncement "a great teacher" and was a trained architect, "with a special knack for the restoration of historical buildings." He was "the closest thing to a father" that Fernando ever had (O: 93). He nurtured Fernando's understanding of Fronteira as a "jewel which is simultaneously erudite (there is some debate as to how erudite – I haven't yet studied the subject well enough to decide) and naive" (O: 92). Fernando "had to learn to love" the palace – and as we already know, he did with time do just that.

Reflexive

Here, however, Fernando's askêseis had already begun to shift from being in the hands of pedagogical others to being in his own. His embrace of Fronteira also came through his undertaking his own studies – of the azulejos that decorate it among other things. His studies are of ethical relevance precisely because he understands them to be part of his being a responsible "master" of the house – or responsibly mastered by it, as the case may also be. Fernando now knows – at least he is very familiar with – Fronteira and with that very knowledge comes the distinctively ethical wisdom of his ties to a familial past to which he is indebted and his carrying into the future a debt that he must find the means of redeeming. Such a familial tissue of successions, of which Fronteira provides both a concrete mnemonics and a concrete foreshadowing, thus constitutes the temporal schematic of Fernando's subjectivation as mere mortal and as Marquis alike. It is a schematic for which, as Reinhart Koselleck has argued, history itself can still serve as a magistra vitae (Koselleck 1985). Koselleck diagnoses such service as pre-modern – which reflects his Kantianism more than a convincing dichotomy between the pre-modern and the modern. The schematic is in any event at complete odds with any millenarianist sensibility, which I would argue (and have argued) depends on the detachment of temporal sensibility from every continualist framework and its focus instead on the linearity of the individual course of life and its embeddedness within an indexically particularized generation – its own (Faubion 2001b: 99–109). Fernando expects no Second Coming. He does not expect history in its contingent march to cease. Nor is he bleak about what is to come; he is anything but a tragedian. He is in contrast – this reader of science fiction – the only person who has ever told me that he would like to be immortal, to live forever. He is intrigued by what might – for better or for worse – come to pass. He would like to be its witness. He is curious, and is so with an ethical inflection: "the questions that 'buzz around my ears' are, perhaps, those I like best, because I don't know the answer to them, and therefore those that make me think" (O: 102).

Such a stance demands composure in its own right, but the askêsis that Fernando has plied in acquiring his composure is not a proleptic meditation on future evils – or goods, for that matter. It has rather been an exercise – in important part under pedagogical supervision, but now largely as a technology of autopoiesis in his own command – of a self-ironization of an originally more brutal than comic sort. His description of it is disturbing – and perhaps merciful in its lack of specific details:

I was helped by Bli (she is some 3 years my elder) ... She taught me how to deal with emotionally charged objects through extensive and often cruel use of irony. As a sort of final exam, which lasted only a few days, she also led me through a descent into hell, or as she put it, "to drink the chalice of bitterness to the last dregs" – it was a mutually conscious process, and I am infinitely grateful to her for what I have learned (I know because I have recently tried it with a friend in need). Simultaneously, I started a process of trimming my sensibility to the point of becoming frightened with my inability to feel... Bli also helped me recover my ability to feel, but after all these processes there was an enormous difference: I was able to control my feelings and adjust them to my needs and wishes. In time, I further refined this trait so that my sensitivity became almost automatically adapted to circumstance – more or less like these automatic cameras which adjust the shutter to the amount of light. (O: 43)

Fernando demurs from Marcus' construal of his irony as outward-looking, toward the world at large. He objects to being attributed so "academic," so general and abstract an ironic attitude. His gaze is instead inward. Lacking details – both Marcus and I were hesitant to ask for them – it is difficult to trace its sources. It recalls the Christian exercise of the examination of conscience, though it looks to be more exhaustive, is entirely secular and has neither piety nor purity of soul nor the Augustinian surrender to divine will as its ethical imago. It suggests an exercise of (self) humiliation, though whatever humility it instills once again seems not to be Christian in its derivation. The man who writes to Marcus that he wrote his Sermon to António in order to leave him "the legacy of my thoughts about the subject of a nobleman's role in the world, which I am presumptuous to believe ... could hardly be better expressed by anyone I know" has no excess of humility – and Fernando is happy elsewhere to admit it. One might be tempted to call his work with Bli and with himself sado-masochistic were there any suggestion of pleasure in it. It is neither a Manichean nor an existentialist downward cascade – utterly without irony – into corruption, though it shares with both the quest for a certain truth about the self. The anthropologist would like to render it of a collective order – but here, Fernando proves to be an anthropological frustration.

As an enthusiast of psychoanalysis, Fernando is anthropologically more accessible – the good Western modern, resorting to his therapeutic pedagogues but also taking up their devices as a proper technology of self in its own right. He writes to Marcus that he found the idea of "unveiling unconscious assumptions" a "particularly exciting" one, adding as supplement the confession: "as you may have guessed, I am fascinated by my quest for my inner self and grasp at any chance to know it better" (O: 30). He reports not unhappily less than a week later: "I am beginning to feel that this exchange of letters with you is becoming my 3rd experience in a sort of psychoanalysis and wonder if this is any use for you; after all you are an anthropologist and not a psychologist" (O: 43). He is not rejecting here the plausibility of a Lacanian idealization of the unconscious as an intersubjective symbolic order – but he is not endorsing the idea, either.

So Fernando writes as well. His exchange with Marcus sometimes has the character of a psychoanalytic dialogue, but his writing is not always a technology of psychoanalytic production:

Yes, I do write, as you have been able to observe these last few months … For what purpose? The first answer that comes to mind is for posterity. I still feel that I have not established my place in history as an individual, and would very much like to be someone regardless of who I was born. Of course creating the Foundation, to a certain extent, guarantees my place in history, but in a way that is much too dependent on [who] I was born. I would like one day to be able to say to myself I have gained my place in history "above and beyond" the fact of being born in my family. In a way it would have been easier if I didn't have this background that tends to lull me into laziness. (O: 95)

Trazimundo echoes in this declaration, as once again does the imperative – merely mortal but also noble – of individuation. Fernando writes. He does produce his Sermon to António and he does author an occasional scholarly paper on azulejos – but he does not manage to write five volumes of memoirs. He is "lazy." He is not, however, quite so lazy that he abandons a six-month-long epistolary exchange with Marcus that results in what has all the trappings of a memoir. *Ocasião* indeed.

Pragmatist but no Calvinist, Fernando is also a regular player of a number of different games, some solitary and some in the company of others. In part, they are simple diversions, an escape from "loneliness" and a stage on which to act out his "sense of competition in a harmless way" (O: 122). They are a sedative: "they focus my attention with very little emotional involvement and therefore are very restful. For instance, at bridge, I never get angry at a partner's mistake, though I may point it out, and worry about my own (but more intellectually than emotionally)" (O: 122). They are in danger like other pleasurable distractions – such as hashish – of becoming addictions, but if addictions "they are relatively easy to deal with." Relatively: "Mind you, I've had my critical moments with Civilization; I played for many months almost without interruption except for meals (not necessarily) and for office hours, which I even skipped for a few days" (O: 122).

Even or perhaps precisely in the dangers they hold, however, games are for Fernando also technologies of the self, stimulants of reflexivity and tools of the cultivation of just that lightness that facilitates composure even in the face of crisis. No tragedian, Fernando tends – now at least – instead toward the comic, but this *Homo ludens* can play deeply. Of his favorite computerized entertainment, Civilization, he remarks: "I gradually grow attached to the civilization I'm building" (O: 122). Addiction threatens – but in the very threat, Fernando has the opportunity to regain his grip, and most often succeeds in doing so. He may need what parents are now framing as "time out": "when at the height of war I feel I'm getting too emotional, I interrupt and return later. Once in a very difficult battle I had to interrupt for 3 days – when you get too emotional you start making mistakes" (O: 122). He keeps coming back, however, for the self-reflection it provokes: "There is always something to make me think, sometimes just about itself, sometimes bearing on 'outside' life, like a battle (they last centuries in this game) I won when I was very nearly out of my tethers (no idea if I'm saying what I mean)" (O: 122).

Fernando finds similar self-technological assets in games generally. They polish psychological discernment and self-discernment. They allow Fernando to observe his behavior, "either with other people (therefore including their reactions) or with a neutral subject (the computer or the program or the authors of the program or what-ever...)" (O: 122). They, too, are magistrae vitae in their way. They are an escape from life, but also a model of and model for it; Fernando answered my querying whether he thought life itself was a game in the affirmative.

Yet the man of composure cannot bring quite the attitude to games that he must bring to everyday ludic life. We can leave Fernando with the most regulative of the lessons that he has learned and cultivated and the technology of self that has gradually instilled his composure within him as a second nature: "it is true that my naturally excessive sensitivity has made it necessary for me, with Bli's help, to always introduce a touch of 'lightness' in anything serious (and inversely, perhaps as compensation [?], to take [relatively] seriously any game)" (O: 63). Winning isn't everything.

Afterword

I have not seen Fernando since 2002 though as the chapter now complete attests, have often been in touch with him. I have learned that Fernando has lost a substantial amount of weight. I remain on the email list of the Foundation and have noticed that its activities and sponsorships have proceeded in an ever greater flurry. Its resources must be increasing – though in the current downturn are likely com-promised. At some of the functions at the palace, Fernando is himself the star. Diana Hill recently wrote me to report that she had visited the palace to find Fernando dressed in a poet's shirt, displaying to visitors and potential buyers a collection of jewelry featuring semi-precious stones from all parts of the globe and of his own design, "holding court," as she put it, in the Room of the Battles. What would the knights valiant think if they could see the twelfth Marquis of Fronteira at his table of jewels? Nothing too untoward, one has to conclude.

FIVE

An ethics of reckoning

What first brought me to the bit of property in the near middle of the Texas prairie known as Mount Carmel was a curiosity bordering on the lurid that had as fuel a long-standing interest in millenarianism, a widely publicized and lethal confrontation, a lecture, an unexpected academic appointment, and the possibility of a day trip in a new home state. In 1980, I graduated with a BA in anthropology and philosophy from Reed College. While at Reed, I joined a long line of anthropology majors before me in coming under the spell of the formidable Gail Kelly, who was herself under the spell of the anthropology of millenarianism. Enough said, except that Professor Kelly was under its spell for what she unabashedly regarded as its primitivism, its exoticism and its irrationalism – the binary opposite, thus, of all that she regarded herself to be (exoticism excepted). I was not thus bewitched. In 1990, I returned to Reed to teach in the anthropology department and in the program in the humanities. On March 2 or 3, 1993, I was slated to offer a lecture in the humanities program on early Christian millenarianism. Some three days prior to that lecture, agents of the US Bureau of Alcohol, Tobacco and Firearms raided the Branch Davidian compound and engaged those inside in a gun battle that left four of the agents and six inside the compound dead. A standoff ensued. I thought I had the rare opportunity to render a topic set some two millennia in the past of contemporary relevance. Following good Reed tradition and as had been my own habit when enrolled there, the students in the lecture hall had not been watching the televised news or reading the newspapers and so knew nothing of the Texas event. I remained for my part fascinated – and increasingly appalled – with the standoff as it unfolded. Some twenty days before its climax and much to my surprise, I was invited to Rice University as a finalist for a position in the anthropology department, which I was ultimately offered and quickly accepted. In July, I arrived in Houston to settle into an apartment and prepare for my classes. In October, I traveled with my partner and a friend who had also recently taken up residence in Houston to Waco, where the staff of the Visitors' Center kept discreetly out of sight but offered to anyone who asked a map of directions to Mount Carmel. We arrived at the site to find a chain-link fence surrounding a bevy of bulldozers whose drivers were methodically pushing concrete, wood and metal into the deformed footprint that would remain long after they had departed and the fence had been removed. A few moments later, we found Amo Paul Bishop Roden.

The ungiven

So take one part anthropologist: James D. Faubion, "James" to some, "Jim" to most, male, white by most accounts, nearing middle age, permanently employed, persistently depressive, anxious, gay, (too?) sensitive to disapproval, easily overstimulated, none too courageous, poor traveler, intellectual snob, serious cook, (too?) obedient to expectation, something of a homebody, admirer of Aeschylus, Johann Sebastian Bach, Ruth Benedict, Ingmar Bergman, Harold Bloom, Aretha Franklin, Giancarlo Gianini, António Carlos Jobim, Margharita Karapanou, Claude Lévi-Strauss, Vladimir Nabokov, Wallace Stevens, Alice Waters, Max Weber, Lena Wertmuller, Walt Whitman, Ludwig Wittgenstein, Virginia Woolf, and so on, fond of seashores, forests, the Doric order and Ionic style, Mediterranean landscapes, occasional snow, tomato sandwiches, New Orleans, Athens, a gardener and botanist manqué. Mix with one part anthropologized: Amo Paul Bishop Roden, "Amo" to many, female, middle-aged, college graduate, erstwhile systems analyst, divorced mother proud of her intelligent son – whose custody she had lost – widow of George Roden and mother enchanted by the vivacious and blessed daughter she had with him – whose custody she had also lost – without the usual sort of employment but far from idle, assiduous writer, agrarianist, admirer of Jimmy Carter, Daniel, Victor Houteff, Isaiah, Jeremiah, Jesus, Saint John the Divine, Lyndon Larouche, Ben Roden, Lois Roden, Ellen Harmon White and so on (I never thought to ask her about her tastes in film or music; somehow it didn't seem relevant), sympathetic to sinners like herself, advocate of militias, polygyny, polyandry and scrupulous honesty, champion on behalf of the Rodens of the ownership of the Mount Carmel property, fierce critic of the Bureau of Alcohol, Tobacco and Firearms, Bill Clinton, concupiscence, the love of money, the US court system, the US govern-ment, the followers of Vernon Howell – who would come to name himself David Koresh – oppression, persecution and Janet Reno, too horny to be a saint in her own explicit judgment, vegetarian, Branch Davidian, militant in a church militant, millenarian, Biblicist, herme-neut, figuralist and allegorist, appealing to descent in her routinization of spiritual charisma, called and chosen to purvey the Present and Final Truth, ultimate antitype – to her light – and hypostasis of the sixth angel of the Book of Revelation, preoccupied with ancient origins and immi-nent ends, often worried that They would poison her and convinced that They had already done so, twice briefly confined to psychiatric hospitals, holding vigil at Mount Carmel, talking with the curious tourists, posting a history of the events that had led to and that followed the conflagration at Mount Carmel on April 19, 1993, in which – should one count the unborn among them – eighty people died, posting lessons and warnings, posting other histories, other lessons, other warnings, resting when she could.

As it turns out, the whole is rather less than its parts. Nor is such an outcome atypical of such relationships, which some anthropologists nevertheless seem to believe should aspire to the mutual intimacy and openness of the best of friends and longest of lovers. The whole for its part is ragged, porous, piecemeal, open to wind and rain, and so not a proper whole at all. I have argued that the ethics of the anthropological fieldworker – of such a subject position considered as an ethical position in and of itself – is an ethics of connection between fieldworker and other whose particular form and substance always bear the inflections of the fieldworker's own triangulation of themitical-affective, epistemological and ontological investments (Faubion 2009). The anthropologist–anthropologized dyad is another animal. It is constituted of connection, but its connectedness bears the inflections of the anthropological triangle and its anthropologized counterpart alike, if more now than in the past. It is inevitably heterogeneous – the fieldworker's motives and modes of connection and those of the other cannot fully coincide. Hence, in the going terminology, it is an assemblage, or at least is so if it is productive, at the very least of itself.

The same dyad is also communicative – so long as the fieldworker or the other manages to render it public in one or more of the fora available to him or her or – in the logically simplest case – the two of them. Because it is in principle communicative, it belongs in principle within the domain of the ethical, emergent from the reflexive practice of the mutually oriented freedom of its internal motors. It unquestionably has its charismatic moment – though whether the anthropologist or the anthropologized is the charismatic leader admits of considerable variation. Margaret Mead, for example, seems to have been leader far more than follower. This anthropologist was definitely a follower. It must also have an internal themitical resolution – again, as long as it lasts and should it in fact achieve and sustain autopoiesis. In some part, that resolution hinges generally on "informed consent." In any event, it does so officially or at least as an official requirement. Almost needless to say, in actual practice consent admits of many degrees, informed consent a matter of the unsaid as much as the said, and the forms and signatures meant to secure and attest to it often the very causes of its refusal. Method impresses itself on the themitical normativity of autopoiesis as well. It is the channel – and so both the conduit and the restriction – of the communicative dynamic internal to the anthropologist–anthropologized dyad and so ultimately to the communication in which the dyad as subject engages and can engage with its external interlocutors. Almost needless to say, in actual practice method is every bit as much a matter of degree – and art – as consent. However well planned and prepared it may appear to be in one or another grant proposal, it is almost always ad hoc, situationally specific and vulnerable to circumstance. It, too, is not one but many things.

The conclusion that the dyad at issue – as a subject in its own right – has little or nothing of the given about it thus seems to have ample warrant. Its internal subjects and so the ethics within its ethics are creatures of the given, if never of the given alone. The dyad they form is, however, a creature of contingency, a topological particularity that the fieldworker and very likely the other as well would like to see its way to enough commensurability with and comparability to its fellow creatures to achieve the status of a singularity, an accident that was never really waiting to happen but turns out to have happened after all and not to have been nothing more than an accident after all. No one is born an anthropologist and no anthropologist is born to undertake the fieldwork that he or she comes to undertake. Much less is the other born to be the fieldworker's informant or interlocutor or consultant. That fieldworker and other meet and meet again is rarely a sheer coincidence. Most fieldworkers are drawn to their field – if not by intellectual curiosity then by that mixture of sensuous fascination and repulsion whose object is what we are no longer supposed to admit to experiencing as the exotic. I suspect that such a mixture continues to play an important role in the fieldworker's increasing choice of a field that is in many respects familiar – as in the case of the American fieldworker conducting research in the United States or the medical student among his own cohort (Konner 1988). Whatever the motives of its emergence and however less than coincidental, the dyad-subject in any case remains a thing of chance intersections. It has no proper parentage. It has no proper kinship. It has a genealogy, but its genealogy is Nietzschean and Foucauldian.

My relationship with Fernando Mascarenhas was and potentially remains a cooperative, even a collaborative relationship (cf. Kelty *et al.* 2008). It endured for a number of years and, I hope, will endure for many more. I enjoy Fernando's good humor, his honesty, his polished manners, his blend of egoism and lack of pretension. Before engaging him, I had a cursory knowledge of Portuguese ethnography, barely any knowledge of Portuguese history, no knowledge whatever of the Portuguese nobility. I could neither speak nor read Portuguese (and still only read it). I am, however, fond of adding to my store of scholarship and scholarly skills. I had once briefly been to Brazil, but had never been to Portugal. If a poor traveler, I usually adjust well after arrival. Usually. Initially, someone else was paying my way. Nor was I busy with another research project. With Marcus' encouragement and Fernando's welcome, I found myself with an ocasião that I could barely refuse.

For all that subsequently unfolded, however, I cannot deem my relationship with Fernando to have generated a dyad-subject in its own right, an emergent and enduring third party of which he and I were the catalytic ingredients. I like Fernando; I suspect that, if asked, he would count me among his friends. I was always aware, even so, that I would never be counted among the inner and tight circle of those friends with whom Fernando has genuine communion. I did not approach the relationship with expectations of communion. Nor was the barrier I encountered as daunting as those I more than once encountered in my original research in Greece. It was perfectly civil – but formal enough to preclude the merging that, speaking strictly for myself, would have been necessary were a genuine catalysis to have transpired between us. The relationship was in this respect typical of many of an anthropologist–anthropologized sort. Potentially generative of an autopoietic third, it was not generative in fact.

A further inhibition to such a merger lay in what proved to be – in my case, again – a difference of sensibility. Fernando's attitude to history is, as I have pointed out, prevailingly comic. Mine, in contrast, is prevailingly tragic. Fernando finds nourishment in the past and, with that nourishment, energy for the future. I tend to look at the past as a Satan that I would most like to get behind me and at the future as the promise merely of becoming the past. Fernando pursues repair, restoration, revival. I am attracted to ruins, decline, poetic meditations on death and finitude. I went to Lisbon hoping to find a Pessoa; I found someone more like Alexander Pope. Perhaps I also went to Lisbon expecting to find a fellow homosexual traveler; deviance always loves company after all. Fernando's sexual experience, his erotic mode of being in the world, the objective possibilities available and those unavailable to him sexually and erotically were, however, not at all my own. In this respect as well I found him quite interesting, but also a touch pitiable (that tragic sensibility again, here with an arrogant undertone). That pity – which he would not for a moment have countenanced – further stood between us. Last but by no means least were Fernando's privileges, his life of privilege, which I could taste but could not share. This is not to say that I regard myself as without privilege, much less underprivileged – but the privileges of a titled and wealthy Portuguese and those of an American academic allow of remote comparison at best. I know how deeply, how far before and how far beyond the instrumental, identity runs – but I have to admit that I sometimes avertedly rolled my eyes when talk of survival was on the table. Between Fernando and me, there was rapport, and at least as much rapport as the usual anthropologist could hope to cultivate with even his or her key informants. I could nevertheless not recognize enough of Fernando in myself to transform that rapport into genuine synergy.

The psychoanalyst might smile, but the issue was not simply personal. It was one instead of objective and ultimately collectively grounded incommensurabilities, of habitus at a distance not easily bridged. Once again, I suspect that ethnographers have, more often than not, encountered similar incommensurabilities, especially in the disciplinary past, rendering the potential emergence of any dyadic third party an all the more unlikely outcome. Habitus can change. Perhaps, if my engagement with Fernando had not been so much second-hand and had our actual face-to-face interactions been more sustained, both of us would have adjusted more, each to the other, and the synergy necessary to sustain that third party would have taken effect. Perhaps not. These days, anthropologists of an activist inclination who focus their investigations on populations of similarly activist inclinations might more often find just that synergy. At the very least, a common commitment, a common telos (if immediately only of a political and not necessarily of a distinctly ethical sort) lies within their interactive grasp. More than a common telos is required for the synergy at issue to take effect, but it is required nevertheless. Fernando and I neither had nor found that point in common. Fernando wanted biographers among other things; in Marcus and, under other metrics, in me, he got them. He wanted them not merely to establish the record of his own works and days. He wanted them further to establish a record that could occupy a place in a genealogical past and future whose tissue and whose horizons were not remotely my own. For my part, I was seeking willing subjects of ethical bioethnography and I got what I wanted as well – but academic relationality is not noble relationality and the temporality of academic production and the durability of that production not at all the temporality of inherited and inheritable titles. So it went. So it goes.

With Ms. Roden, affairs took a very different turn.

Mode of subjectification: selection and recruitment

The trouble with any genealogy of the Nietzschean or Foucauldian sort is that it offers no resolute starting point. The genealogy of Western asceticism and its potential transvaluation may begin with the archaic Greeks. The genealogy of the scientific codification of sexualities may depart from classical Athens. Just as likely, however, such beginnings are simply matters of methodological and evidential convenience. The textual archive that begins to accumulate from the archaic period forward is full of ambiguities, but it is far less ambiguous and far more detailed than the material and plastic archives that precede it. The Greeks bear sometimes striking resemblances to their neighbors around the Mediterranean and the Near East, though we are not now accustomed to consider the latter "Western." Reconstructing such resemblances nevertheless requires the investment of a measure of methodological good faith that the more suspicious genealogist might regard as too trusting. No genealogist, moreover, can be competent in every dead language in the region, but instead only in some of them. The trouble is not one of infinite regress, but of a regress into increasing obscurity and complexity and thus uncertainty. One has to draw the line somewhere.

Hence, I will not begin the genealogy of my own integration into the subject that yielded *Shadows and Lights of Waco* (hereafter 2001b) at the literal moment of my birth. Of greater relevance are the circumstances of my religious upbringing – or rather, of the almost complete lack of it. The sociological profile of the religiosity of the very small southwestern Oregon town in which I was raised was typical of other towns of similar class and size in the region. It was a pot of dislocation and enclavement still far below the melting point but interfused enough to approach the oxymoronic: enclaved dislocatedness; dislocated enclavement. It was organizationally too stable to nourish explicitly millenarian activism, though not so stable that it starved the eschatologically inclined. It was socioeconomically marginal. Within its municipal borders, its population of schoolteachers was the cadre of highest status and highest income. Beyond its borders lived a sizeable population of farmers and ranchers, several of solid economic resources and income but only a very few even semi-industrialized. The majority of the area's population found their work in the lumber industry or in trades and businesses dependent on that turbulent and contracting industry. Their income was seasonably variable: good when the nearby forests were accessible; poor or non-existent during the months when for one reason or another – weather, court injunction on behalf of the preservation of an endangered species – they were not. A good month might see the purchase of a pick-up truck or a speed boat. A bad one might see an even further descent into the indebtedness that belonged to a body of customs that the uncharitable outside observer might well and sometimes did label "white trash." The town was a poor and self-defensive cousin of cities and middle-class suburbs that could seem much farther away than they actually were. The religious correlate of such multi-dimensional poverty was so precise that one might suspect that some sociologist had engineered it in order to prove the point. At the time of my upbringing, the town and its rural surrounds lacked even a single church from among the standard denominations. Its six or seven small churches were instead either non-denominational or New Denominational, two of the latter Pentecostal and another a Church of Latter-day Saints.

My parents for their part would probably have characterized themselves as Christians if asked, but we never attended church at any point in my childhood. We had no expressions of piety among our collectibles. We did not engage in any ritual manifestation of religious commitment or belief. We did not, for example, say prayers of thanks before dinner and frankly thought that people who did so were a touch fanatical, all the more so should they enjoin us to do so with them as guests at their dinner table. Pentecostals – I learned to call them "Holy

Rollers" – were beyond the pale. Our Christmas decorations included a Nativity scene. If I recall correctly, it was I who insisted on acquiring and displaying it – though less in the name of revering the event it commemorated than in the name of the sort of authenticity that also led me, callow anti-consumerist, to insist for several years that our Christmas tree could bear only ornaments that we made by hand. (No electric lights, either.) My mother harbored the bitter memory of the experience of her own mother's excommunication from the Episcopal church upon divorcing my rakish grandfather. Perhaps as a consequence, she would have nothing to do with religious congregationalism – not Episcopal congregationalism, though we could have traveled just a dozen miles to find it, and certainly not Pentecostal or Mormon congregationalism. My father joined her in expecting that religion – theirs, such as it was, and that of others – be kept a very private affair. If nothing else, it was good business; both were the solidly petty bourgeois owners of what was then the sole grocery in town and interested in courting as many customers as they could. My mother could, however, carry her own privatism to occasionally unsociable excess. Responding to the solicitations of one or another of the New Denominational proselytes who appeared frequently at our porch, she would sometimes pronounce that "she had her own religion!" and slam the door.

Anything might have happened – or almost anything. What actually did happen was in broad strokes the more expected outcome. I did not become a believer. My mother sent me once to a non-denominational Sunday school so that, at the unripe age of seven or eight, I could "make up my own mind" about whether I wanted to "go to church." The playing field was already far from even. I hated the experience. I found the teacher's story-telling beneath my intelligence and sophistication (as intellectual snobs go, I was fairly precocious). I found the other children in the room almost as alien as they must have found me; we did not speak to one another even once. I found the class in its entirety a horrible and vulgar breach of the privatistic etiquette that I had evidently already internalized. I found it quite enough. Even so, I did not rush to take up the atheistic cause. I credit my brother for my restraint. Ten years my senior, my brother was himself an atheist and an atheist at the highest and loudest pitch of adolescent arrogance. Ours was a rivalrous relationship. I could hardly do anything but oppose him.

I should, however, add that my drift beyond or above or below belief was not emotionally untrammeled. I am a rigorous agnostic, but I neither have been nor am a blithe one. My father died after a protracted and gruesome affliction with cancer when I was fifteen. In the aftermath of his death, I irregularly attended a Catholic church, at first with all the awkwardness and discomfort of someone new in ice skates and then with increasing pleasure as one of my cousins, a member of the church, saw to it that I was welcomed into a youth group that met in the early evening once or twice a week for a catechism very much in the spirit of Vatican II, if catechism it was at all. My relationship with the church was brief. It ended abruptly after the presiding priest sternly reprimanded me after I confessed that I did not and could not believe in God. My longing to be able to believe, if not in some god then at least in the abiding reality of an ethically oriented cosmos, did not cease, even so, and it has not yet ceased. I could still readily embrace both the burdens and the redemption that such a cosmos would bring. I would still be ready and willing to pay the costs of the resolution of the great paradoxes of meaning – the suffering of innocents, the co-implication of right and wrong, the inevitability of mortality – that Weber found at the heart of the problematics of the world religions and Geertz subsequently appropriated in giving an anthropological account of religions of both global and local scope (Weber 1946c; Geertz 1973: 100). Asad has argued that in granting such diagnostic priority to the paradoxes, Geertz – and so, by implication, Weber – is guilty of affirming too exclusively Christian an understanding of religion itself (Asad 1993: 45). Asad does not convince me, but

I am willing to grant him his point here for the sake of argument. If I thus consign myself to the category of someone who is "too Christian" in conceiving the object of his longing, then so be it. Like Weber and Geertz, I am thus too Christian – but a Christian without portfolio.

I would in any event be in anything but good faith were I to leave my subsequent interest in religion and the religious just here, an apparent matter of temperament, nearly of nature. I do not hold the religious of any stripe – qua religious – in contempt. I tend instead to hold them generally in a double regard: as beings for whom I have a certain sad, passive envy; and as beings whom I think that I can know in (dare I say?) some objective sense of the term but still cannot really fathom. I hesitate to declare such a regard as definitive of my particular anthropological gaze, of what attracts it as well as of its mode of resolution. I can at least say that it is characteristic of the subjects that have most enduringly sustained my anthropological attention. I hesitate further to identify a single current of my socialization as the source of such a sentimentalized attention. I can at least say that it has an important homologue – whether reinforcement or determinant – in the regard in which I used to hold the more thematically outstanding of the boys and men of my youth. Even the lay sociological reader has been able to infer that the town of my upbringing was not a cosmopolis. Instead, it was overwhelmingly white, if with the occasional Native American ("Indian") in at least passing residence, in its majority racist, traditionalist and anti-progressivist, unbendingly heteronormative and authoritarian and not infrequently violent in its enforcement of the separation and elaborately coded mutual inversion of gender roles.

I did not conform to thematical expectations. The story of my deviations is boringly similar to a thousand other stories already told. There is no need to carry it any further, except in order to effect a more precise mise-en-scène of the many acts and scenes of the book of revelation that – for me at least – *Shadows and Lights* would become.

Fieldwork in ethics

Human beings respond diversely to their stigmatization – rebelliously, in flamboyant complicity, by retreat to the closet, with despair. Cavafy (see my website) spans the whole spectrum of such responses, but my own response to stigmatization was nearer the last in the list and coupled very closely with the longing to be what I was not but also what I was convinced I could never be. Gender conformity and religious commitment were homologous in my schemas of perception and experience just there. To call on terms that I am now well aware are at once sociologically, technologically and physiologically off the mark, they both seemed to me to "just happen." Off the mark, such terms also might formerly have served me as a mask, not with which to disguise myself to others but with which to disguise myself to myself. I have since let the mask of the naturalization of sex and gender slip, if not fall entirely. I have done so in more or less direct correlation with the fading of my concern over my lack of conventional manhood – which has in any event proved to be of far more variable and mutually inconsistent conventions than as a child and early adolescent I was experientially aware. I seem still to cling to the mask of the naturalization of religious commitment with a tenaciousness that survives my having come to be well aware that it has a greater depth and staying power the earlier it is induced and that it, too, is of variable conventions and so of variable criteria of expression, among them the criterion that many of my religious friends deploy – the sincere declamation that one "just knows" as a matter of experience that the divine (in any of its greatly variable conceptions) exists.

Some of my best friends are indeed religious – and the great majority of them do not frighten me for being so. My religious longing has nevertheless come to be the companion of a countercurrent of dread. Mine is a dread of a counter-Dostoevskian sort – not that without but that instead with God anything at all might be possible. I have in mind not only what human beings have proved capable of doing to one another and to themselves in the name of their religious commitments (see Faubion 2003). I also have in mind what I could become were I to find religious commitment someday just happening to me.

I am open to two interpretations of the dread in question. One would hold that what I fear is the transformation of the self that lies at the center of my own ethical investment – and so of my identity – into its opposite, of finding myself passing from the secure rationalist moorings of my ever so academic agnosticism into the open, uncharted and unchartable waters of a belief beyond reason, of belief as Unreason, belief beyond belief, in which any and every inconsistency might reign and so anything and everything might follow. The other is that I am a believer not, as I claim, without portfolio but rather so far and so darkly in the closet that I cannot recognize myself within it and so have to face the possibility that I might come out of it. Of course, I prefer the first interpretation. Every hermeneut of suspicion will prefer the second. System-theorerically, the two are moot, since they amount in communicative practice to strict equivalents.

In any event, whichever is more correct, my dread found what might be thought of as its specter incarnate in Amo Paul Bishop Roden, there on the Texas prairie, holding vigil and court at Mount Carmel, one day in the bright late autumn of 1993. Mount Carmel was dreadful enough in its own right, the compound within its perimeters that once housed the followers of David Koresh a gruesome ruin of cement and rebarb and charred splinters of wood with which the blank-eyed, growling, over-built bulldozers were having their way. Nor was Ms. Roden the only self-designated Branch Davidian asserting rightful title to the property. Those of David Koresh's followers who had left or escaped from the compound before it burned were also making their claims. A third faction opposed both Ms. Roden and Koresh's followers with claims of its own. Relations were not amicable. Gunshots and fires belong to Mount Carmel's history beyond the conflagration in April 1993. Ms. Roden, however, struck me with a quite particular terror – she reminded me in a great many ways of myself, and of far too much of myself. Hence, I could not cease returning to her, even if I aborted a good half of the trips I made to her before I actually arrived at Mount Carmel itself. (I take the opportunity to apologize to my partner, who was my driver and photo-documentarist throughout the project, who put up with my frequent failure of nerve, and who relieved me of what would have been the intolerable burden of being alone at Mount Carmel with all of my demons and Ms. Roden's as well.)

On my first visit to Mount Carmel, near the entrance to the property, my companions and I initially met not with actors but definitely with actants – an array of hand-painted signs, some of them ominous quotations of Ms. Roden's favorite Old Testament prophets, others interpretations of such Biblical encryptions as the *mene mene tekel Upharsin* of the Book of Daniel, still others documentations with photographic or mimeographic illustrations attached of the destruction of the compound and insinuations of cover-ups and conspiracies. To the left of the entrance stood a rectangular stage, which one of Koresh's followers had built in order to continue the musical performances that Koresh, "the rocker messiah," had himself regularly offered while he lived. At its back stood a stage building and at the entrance to the building stood Ms. Roden, actively in conversation with another of the curious or outraged or aggrieved or amused who came and went in a steady trickle through all of my subsequent visits. I did not seek to engage Ms. Roden in conversation that day; her interlocutor had detained her at great length. Or perhaps she had detained him. Or perhaps the detention was mutual. In any event, I merely approached Ms. Roden when she was once again free. I did not introduce myself as an anthropologist – every anthropologist knows to what misimpressions our professional title can give rise, unless he or she happens to truck in stones and bones. I introduced myself instead as a professor at Rice who was interested in her church and in the comparative study of religious traditions and asked her if I could pay her a future visit and discuss her church with her then. She said that I could of course do so, that she was always happy to talk – a most true and sincere remark, as it turned out. I left with my companions. We were certain – quite certain – that the car that followed us for the next several miles was tailing us.

What had brought Ms. Roden to Mount Carmel was a series of coincidences and quasi-compulsions that I cannot recount as thoroughly as I can – or could, if I thought it worthwhile – recount my own. Ms. Roden nevertheless offered me her own recounting and though I have already reviewed it in *Shadows and Lights*, I will review it again here, if in different terms, my own terms instead of those of the dyadic subject whose voices are those in *Shadows and Lights* itself. She responded to my initial posing of the question of what had brought her to the Texas prairie with casual reference to a taste for warm summers. What had taken her to many other places previously was above all anxiety. Its persistent object was nuclear holocaust. Ms. Roden was born on January 20, 1943. Mushroom clouds would soon be in the air. She would also have been nineteen, just beginning college, at the time of the Cuban missile crisis. She would further have grown up in the suspicious atmosphere of ideological antagonism and atomic saber-rattling that suffused the Cold War. She was far from alone in her worries. Paul Boyer has meticulously documented the nuclear turn of the proleptic and millennialist Christian imagination in the United States with the bombing of Hiroshima, an irresistible figura of the violent tremors and all-consuming fires that the Book of Revelation presages as the inauguration of the eternity in which time and the suffering that is its measure "shall be no more" (Boyer 1992). Whatever else, such an event would be an emphatic resolution of one at least of the most enduring paradoxes of meaning.

Ms. Roden's imagination was, however, not the tutored Biblicist's imagination in her early adulthood. She had a casual religious upbringing. She described her mother as a "lukewarm Christian" and her father as religiously indifferent. Her cast of mind in that period bore closer comparison to those thousands of good middle-class citizens who trusted their civic leaders to demarcate fallout shelters of allegedly secure refuge or, if not that, invested in backyard shelters of their own, allegedly more secure. We tend not to think of such citizens or their leaders – from the most humbly local to the presidential – as mad. We now think of them merely as mistaken – if not in their concerns about the likelihood of nuclear war, then at least in their optimism that their shelters (with the exception, perhaps, of Iron Mountain) could ever save them. In any event, their concerns were common and dynamic. The Cold War put a great many people into motion, erecting their shelters and stocking them with supplies but also ferreting out internal enemies, fashioning bigger and better bombs and the bombers and submarines and silos facilitating their delivery to one or another enemy target.

Ms. Roden, for her part, took a bus from Boston to Washington in order to join a protest against the Vietnam War. She expressed to me her conviction that the file that "an FBI agent" informed her to be in the bureau's archives and to identify her as a "subversive" dates from that excursion. She would travel further and farther:

At the end of the sixties I was so distressed ... that I left the country and went to Canada. When I was in the country before I went to Canada, I was a very normal kind of person. I just had regular jobs, and I went to work, and I watched t.v. All the things that normal people do, you know. (2001b: 4)

She spent a decade in Canada "being a normal person." She met in Canada the man who would become her first husband, married, bore her son, and divorced. She noted that she remained very much out of touch with the United States there, "because it got so much worse between the late sixties and when I returned in '80." She moved to Texas to a farm about twelve miles from Waco proper in December of 1980 – odd timing at the very least, since it coincided with the end of

Jimmy Carter's and the beginning of Ronald Reagan's more bellicose presidency. Perhaps the nuclear industry had something to do with it: the breakdown at Three Mile Island occurred in late March 1979. Canada had long been an enthusiast of nuclear power. By 1979, eight reactors were in operation in Ontario alone and more were in one or another stage of planning. In 1979, no reactors were in operation in Texas. I can only speculate. Perhaps she really was in search of warm summers – though southeastern Canada has enough of its own. She spoke of her arrival in uncharacteristically serene terms: "it just came over me as I was here in all this beautiful, peaceful country, that I owed God a lot, and I said, 'OK, God, take the rest of my life'" (2001b: 3). She "felt a call" to find a church. She came upon a Pentecostal congregation and, within it, a woman who "taught the Bible some, and she took my hand that first day and talked me into going right down and being saved, taking communion there." If without nuclear reactors, the Texas prairie was amply supplied with churches.

Whether or not anxiety pressed Ms. Roden to Texas and whether or not it pressed her further through the doors of a church, it came again with a vengeance in due course. In 1983, she began to have dreams. She began to have what she sometimes characterized as "visions" (2001b: 4). She saw the holocaust of her fears unfold in an imminent future. She was inspired to undertake an analysis of the "likelihood of a surprise nuclear attack … using a Russian point of view" (2001b: 4). She offered no firm predictions, but spelled out her reasoning and its "alarming bottom line" (2001b: 5) in a letter that – "feeling the need to warn people in Waco to prepare" – she sent to local government officials and circulated among her acquaintances. Most government officials – among them, it would seem, those to whom she wrote – no longer take dreams and visions as evidence of anything other than wishes or, indeed, anxieties, or perhaps psychosis. Ms. Roden received no replies. She was nevertheless certain that she had not gone unnoticed:

I suspect that I was reported to the government by my landlord, but that's just a hunch. The day after I gave him a copy, I was under surveillance. My food was poisoned, my house was sprayed with chemicals, people who hid their faces from me started fishing in my landlord's pond. Alarmed, I told my family... Between the visions, and the concern that someone was trying to kill me and my reputation for honesty, I was easy prey. (2001b: 9–10)

A deputy sheriff would shortly arrive in the company of one of Ms. Roden's sisters. The two conveyed her to a psychiatric facility, where she proved to be an uncooperative patient, determined to be released without agreeing to acknowledge formally the diagnosis she faced: "the government of this country thinks that it is necessary for anyone remotely expected of being subversive to have a mental health record" (2001b: 10). Shortly afterward, she lost custody of her son.

The tale continues in much the same vein, but two of its episodes merit special mention. The first is her devotion to the study of the Bible and her conversion to Biblicism. She told the woman who had urged her to take communion of her vision. The woman told her:

if it was true, it would be in accordance with Scripture. And so that's how I got into Bible study... I hadn't ever read it, and I started heavily studying it. Hard-core Bible study for four years ... I found the visions in the Bible. It was like being given a key. (2001b: 20)

The second was her meeting with and eventual marriage to George Roden, "son of Ben and Lois Roden and elected president of the Branch Davidian Seventh-day Adventists" (2001b: 20). It's a long story. George was at least the lineal heir apparent of the Rodens' ministry, itself a revival of the precedent of Victor Houteff, the schismatic founder of what was at first known as the Davidian Seventh-day Adventist church (much to the displeasure of the Seventh-day Adventists, who had expelled him) and whose original and substantial community resided for several decades in a city unto itself – known as Mount Carmel Center – within the precincts of Waco. A few of its edifices remain standing in the city. The rest have given way to a municipal reservoir. Houteff's community fell in the wake of his widow Florence's errant prophecy, or endorsement of an errant prophecy, of the date of Christ's return. Well before the mistake, Florence oversaw the move to a nine hundred acre expanse of prairie property, a "New" Mount Carmel, and lived there with a diminished band of the remaining faithful. In 1962, she and her counselors voted to dissolve the church and reduce the Mount Carmel property to seventy-seven acres. Florence retained enough of the proceeds from the sale of the property to finance a move to California. She subsequently – so it is put – "became religiously inactive."

In 1965, Ben and Lois Roden undertook to purchase the acres that remained and undertook a revival on them soon thereafter. Ben had been having his own visions throughout the prior decade, among them the vision (and ensuing Biblicist demonstration) that he was the "Branch" whom God had appointed to rebuild His temple. His follow-ers were few; only some fifty people would live under the mantle of the Rodens at Mount Carmel. Ben died in 1978, but not before anointing George responsible for the rebuilding of the temple and acting as the New King of the Branch. In the year preceding Ben's death, Lois had herself had a vision of the Holy Spirit as a female aspect of the Godhead. She accordingly understood the mantle as hers alone and was unwilling to pass it to her son, with whom her relationship soon soured. It would sour further in late 1981, when then Vernon Howell became a permanent boarder at the compound. He soon became Lois' favorite. Though her junior by more than forty years, he soon became more than merely her spiritual favorite – or so the rumors had it. The affair – if there was an affair – came to an end in 1984, when Howell married the fourteen-year-old daughter of a longtime resident of Mount Carmel. (In 1984, a girl of fourteen could be legally married in Texas with parental consent.) He traveled with his wife to Israel in 1985 and, while there, appears to have had a revelation of his distinctive spiritual mission (Tabor and Gallagher 1995: 42). Even before he left, a majority of the residents of Mount Carmel had already become convinced of his spiritual gifts. When he returned, George nevertheless succeeded in evicting him and his loyalists from a New Mount Carmel become "Rodenville." The exiles subsequently set up camp in nearby and aptly named Palestine. George had made Amo "a Branch Davidian in an hour"; the two married by way of "spiritual," not recognized civil contract and began living together at Rodenville in the autumn of 1987.

The Branch Davidian ethics of daily conduct is an expression of what I have called "spiritual biopolitics" (Faubion 2005). Most contemporary theorists of what is often called "life politics," and of biopolitics within it, would have difficulty with the classification. For most such theorists – Giorgio Agamben (1998), Michael Hardt and Antonio Negri (2000), and Nikolas Rose (2006) among them – biopolitics is a resolutely secular affair. I will not repeat here the argument of *Shadows and Lights*: that such secularism is not merely at odds with the empirical evidence but also dependent on the Principle of the Separateness of Estates, the theoretical axiom and axiomatically modern principle of the autonomy of religion from politics and politics from religion (2001b: 70–71). Foucault for his part was better aware than his followers in the analysis of biopolitics that such a principle is of tangential relevance. Instead, he traces the clinical and psychoanalytic pastoralism of the biopolitical "anatomo-politics of the human body" (1978: 139) in large part to a Christian confessional that he characterizes as being in the seventeenth, eighteenth and nineteenth centuries and as still being "the general standard governing the production of true discourse about sex" (63). Yet, in the course of becoming a properly biopolitical technology, reworked in the pedagogy of the eighteenth and the medicine of the nineteenth century, "it gradually lost its ritualistic and exclusive localization; it spread" (63). The confession became secular *as well as* religious and sex a secular *as well as* a religious concern along with it (116). The Reverend Wesley's teachings approach the threshold of the transformation. Beyond that threshold lies a coordinated array of discourses and practices that for the most part "escaped the ecclesiastical institution" if never entirely "the thematics of sin" (116). Their collective tenor is vitalistic, and so bears the mark of an ascendant bourgeoisie that gradually converted "the blue blood of the nobles" into the "sound organism and healthy sexuality" of those best suited to rule (Foucault 1978: 126). The conversion in question has its most purely extra-ecclesiastic realization as a thoroughgoing medicalization of political and social legitimacy. The concepts, disciplines and domains of intervention that Foucault includes within the broader Western European universe of biopower suggest that it has no more purely extra-ecclesiastic realization than in nineteenth-century France. Biopolitically normalizing physicians abound there, as (often in translation) do sexologists and psychoanalysts from Kraft-Ebbing to Freud to Reich. The church and its clerics are remarkable for their absence.

Across the Atlantic, however, the universe of biopower takes a different path. Its expansion in Europe and in America has the same impetus – the cholera epidemic of 1832. A good many physicians are among its American executors, but its great popularizers are with few exceptions ardent Christians, though sometimes Christians very much of their own cloth. Religious biopolitics thus belongs to the history of the refractions of the modern apparatus of governmentality as they mingle with the voluntarism, sectarianism and pragmatic utopianism of an America that has long interposed between the individual body and the general population its ever fissile array of Protestant congregations. The combination that results is, moreover, far more sustained and symbiotic in the New World than it is in the Old. Nor should this be unexpected. The United States has never been a land noted for the number and prominence of its Enlighteners and atheists. On the contrary, it is a land in which, as de Tocqueville first noted, religious precepts and religious devotion can so deeply infuse the rest of thought and practice precisely because no single church can claim title to being the church either of the state or of its correlative regime of truth.

In the United States, the dominant strands of religious biopolitics might heuristically be condensed into two poles. One of these can be called Thoreauvean. To the other I could apply a number of particular names. I could, for example, refer to it as Whitean, after Ellen Harmon White, the founding prophetess of the Seventh-day Adventist church and still a central prophetic and ethical authority within the Branch Davidian church in all of its factions, including Ms. Roden's. Ms. White is, however, only one of many prophetic and visionary spiritual adepts of the early and mid-nineteenth century to whose corporeal and spiritual exercises substantial congregations were drawn and to whose exercises they continue to be drawn in ever increasing numbers still today. Not alone but in the variety of their programs they articulate what can summarily be called a transcendental hygienics.

Thoreau, for his part, hardly thinks or acts alone. Emerson and Whitman and their aptly so-called Transcendentalist brethren are his spiritual companions and enough has been written about them all that an elaborate doctrinal reprise is unnecessary. I merely repeat the obvious in recalling the debt these supernaturalist naturalists owe to German and English Romanticism (cf. Abrams 1971). What they add to the already incipiently biopolitical premises of eighteenth- and nineteenth-century moral physiology and the Romantic critique of the debilitating aspects of civilized existence, however, is a recognizably American valorization of the self-sufficient individual, for whom a vital Nature serves in her own sublime self-reproduction as the magistra vitae, at once a gymnasiarch and a spiritual advisor. If they are not yet ecologists, this is because neither the preservation of a pristine landscape nor the reduction or elimination of the pollutants of a clean environment are at the forefront of their this-worldly concerns. Liberty has pride of place. This is recognizably American as well, but has not itself yet reached the extreme of a libertarianism so self-centered as to permit indifference to the plight of others. The Thoreauveans were Unionists. They were abolitionists. Their heirs are now devoted to the Sierra Club.

Born in 1827, ten years Thoreau's junior, Ellen Harmon White was also an abolitionist, though she and her husband, James, largely avoided any direct involvement in what they thought of as "politics." Her early life unfolded in just those decades and under the influence of some of the very thinkers that Foucault has identified as being of crucial significance for the institutionalization of the disciplines of the anatomo-politics of the human body in France. In the United States, the 1830s and 1840s were rife with medical innovation but also with the revivalist campaigns of what is known as the Second Great Awakening. The most influential of the revivalists of the period was William Miller, whose arguments for the imminence of the Christ's return touched a broad stream of populist anxiety and converted it for a time into a stream of hope. Miller was ultimately pressed to specify the precise date of the Second Coming and his sizeable Adventist following dissolved rapidly in the famously "disappointing" aftermath of his mistaken pronouncement. Well before that, however, Ms. White had attended at least one of his exegetical sessions. A frail young woman who seems to have had more than one ecstatic and visionary episode in her early twenties, she came to adopt Miller's methods and amend his errors. In 1863, she formally established the Seventh-day Adventist church on her own charismatic credentials.

Ms. White published voluminously during her long lifetime, mingling her own writings with those of hundreds of others into a collective and revelatory whole. Among the topics to which she gave especially copious attention and the extant scholarship that she mined with special eagerness were health and the healthy maintenance of the body. She, too, has a debt to the moral physiologists of the eighteenth and of her own century. She was an enthusiast of hydrotherapy and – like many of the other women and men of the same period who would establish their own representatives of what have subsequently been gathered together under the label of the New Denominations – of a carefully selective vegetarian diet abundant in whole grains. Here, she has no greater debt than to Sylvester Graham, originally a New Jersey minister who found a more successful calling as the popularist of what his magnum opus summarily entitled *The New Science of Human Life*. Published in 1839, its teachings came uncredited but largely intact from the physiological writings of none other than François Broussais, disciple of the "empirical" vitalist Xavier Bichat and with Bichat a founding member of that primordial hotbed of biopolitical discourse, the *Société de Sante de Paris*, the Paris Health Society (Nissenbaum 1980; Sokolow 1983). White incorporated Graham's dietetics into her own writings without revision and with the explicit approval of such eminent physicians as Dr. John Harvey Kellogg, who was among the first devotionalists of the Seventh-day Adventist church. Graham has given us the Graham cracker. Kellogg is the father of the inventor of that celebrated whole-grain morsel and icon of the budding health food industry, the cornflake. Seventh-day Adventists continue to this day to proscribe imbibing alcohol or taking in tobacco or narcotics. They continue to prescribe vegetarianism. Ms. Roden follows faithfully in their train, seeking with special vigilance to "eat foods that provide all twenty-two amino acids to get ... accelerated healing" (2001b: 148).

Such phraseology reveals commitments directed less at keeping as distant as possible the evils of the flesh than at sustaining the most pious possible care of a body god-given in its health and vitality. Accounting for her own practices, Ms. Roden herself recalls the habits of the Jewish patriarchs, but not in order to repeat the obligations attendant on the Covenant:

> Everything the Bible says you can eat is clean, and can be eaten. But if you look at the years before the Ark, before the flood, when they lived eight or nine hundred years, you will see that God gave them the herb of the ground, and right after the flood gave them all the animals and the herb of the ground, and the difference in diet is particularly shown by Abraham, who lived to be a hundred and seventy-five. And Joseph, eating from the flesh-pots of Egypt, lived to be a hundred and ten. If you get away from animal foods, except perhaps for eating very young animals on ceremonial occasions, and that's your meat consumption, then you will live a lot longer. (2001b: 148)

Even this schismatic offshoot thus preserves an ethico-religious consequentialism often ready to accommodate itself to the latest advice of nutritional science. Seventh-day Adventism remains unusual among the New Denominations – which include the Church of Christ, Scientist, the Church of Latter Day Saints and Jehovah's Witnesses – in establishing training hospitals and contributing actively to medical research. Several but not all of those denominations have instituted strict codes of dietary practice. Between the physicians and the Christian Scientists, between the physicians and the Jehovah's Witnesses, relations have been and remain strained. Yet even such strains, which revolve around the optimal means of the maintenance of health and the response to disease, reveal that biopolitical concerns and biopolitical values are at the forefront of the collective ethical consciousness of physicians and New Denominationalists alike. In just that meeting of minds lies, I suspect, an account of why the biopoliticization of the conduct of daily life has proceeded so much farther in vitamin-obsessed, almost tobacco-free America than it has in still Gauloises-perfumed France.

A final observation is in order. It is that the division between Thoreauvean vitalism and transcendental hygienics, however liable to mediation and even to occasional collapse, seems to point to a division of class, or rather of class fractions. It is well known that the majority of the participants in the New Social Movements have backgrounds that are comfortably middle class. They are in their majority also relatively well educated. They are social actors who are likely to see themselves as entitled and who are objectively capable of exercising an entitlement to a modicum of social power. They are likely to experience their social status as fairly secure even if age and such other variables as the short-term fluctuations of the career market may compel them to adopt programs of austerity (or as we're now speaking of it, "flexibility"). They have opinions. They vote, but their individuality is probably sufficiently cultivated to render them proud and jealous of their independence, at least of their independence of mind. If transcendental vitalists and practitioners of a politics of transcendence, they are likely to be Thoreauvean in their outlook. They are far more likely to be metaphysical or cosmicist New Agers than theological and ecclesiological New Denominationalists. If the New Denominations are in fact of diverse class composition, their doctrinal and pastoral credos still resonate most loudly with the frustrations and the expectations of the members of a middle class less sure than the typical Thoreauvean of the security of either their status or their means and less confident of their individuality as well. If they are largely a petty bourgeoisie, they are in any case still a bourgeoisie; the New Denominations do not tend to attract the majority of their numbers from the working class, much less from the underemployed or unemployed poor, groups who, like the elite, are both more loyal to the older denominations. The elite may regard any too immediate or this-worldly promise of salvation as insufficiently sublime, insufficiently distant from necessity; the working classes and the poor appear to regard it as implausible. Between the two, Ms. Roden found in her schismatic offshoot her spiritual, ethical and political home.

Fieldwork in ethics

Ms. Roden is not a direct descendant of Thomas Münzer, that sincere, millenarian Lutheran who won Luther's scorn and, largely as a consequence, lost the Peasants' Wars that he had incited and led. The doctrines that Ms. Roden embraces give expression even so to a sense of disenfranchisement of a double order. One part of that order is in the control of those managers and brokers of material goods and resources that we tend – whether or not we actively seek them – to take for granted as goods and resources worthy of pursuit. Call it "the One World Government" or call it something else: for Ms. Roden it brooks no alternative. It is global and globally in command. The other part of that order consists in that "regime of truth" – this phrase of Foucault's seems particularly apt here – that dictates the categories, the terms and the narratives at once of personal and of collective legitimacy.
Ms. Roden is just short of convinced that the alternative regime that she supports – one grounded in "Bible truth" – is the only regime of the truly true and the really legitimate. With an almost sociological precision, she is equally aware that hers is a utopian commitment; in the perverse present in which she understands herself to be living and writing, her appeal to Bible truth is an appeal that is destined to fall largely on deaf and hostile ears. As inevitable or as merely possible, she envisions a future of battle. A primitive rebel she is not, but she is a spokesperson of the discontented *paysans* of the current cultural and political economy who envision as did so many of her historical predecessors that the world of their redemption would be a world in which the enervating forces of an oppressor with which they are all too familiar should give way to the fecund forces of a sacred liberator. It is not just any war that they anticipate, then, but a war of the holy against the unholy. If peace will come, it will be a peace whose politics has an indelibly transcendental cast.

George and Ms. Roden's honeymoon did not last long. I cite again a long passage that appears in *Shadows and Lights*. Determined to prove his charismatic superiority, a reliable source reports:

George ... dug up the body of Anna Hughes, a Davidian who had died at eighty-four and had been buried for twenty years on the Mount Carmel property. He put the casket in the [community's] chapel and challenged

Koresh [the name deployed here *avant l'heure* – Howell did not legally
change his name to Koresh until 1990] to a contest to see who could raise
her from the dead. Koresh asked the McClennan County sheriff to arrest
Roden for corpse violation but was told that he would need to bring
proof. Koresh and seven of his loyal followers tried to sneak on the
property to take a photo of the corpse. They were dressed in camouflage
and heavily armed. A forty-five minute gun battle ensued, each side
blaming the other for firing first. Roden was wounded slightly in the
hand. Koresh and his men were charged with attempted murder, and
surely one of the stranger trials in Waco history was held in 1988. The
jurors found the others not guilty but were split over Koresh's guilt.
The judge declared a mistrial. Six months later George was charged with
the murder of a fifty-six-year-old man in an unrelated incident. He was
found not guilty by reason of insanity and was sentenced to an indeterminate stay in the state hospital in Vernon, Texas. In the meantime Koresh
came up with the money to pay the back taxes on the Mount Carmel
property, and his group returned triumphantly and began to rebuild.
(Tabor and Gallagher 1995: 43)

Ms. Roden could only return to her farm, where the symptoms of the
persecutions that she had suspected in the past became more acute.
She remained loyal to George and to his claim to the title of the
Mount Carmel property, even though she did not accept his spiritual
anointment. She came instead to recognize her own anointment, if not
at first and never primarily as a prophetess but as an "angel," a
"messenger" of the Final Days. She found ample Biblical resources with
which to interpret the conflagration at Mount Carmel as yet another
step in the march toward the end of time – and as punishment for sin as
well. Soon after the conflagration, she moved again to the Mount
Carmel property and began her vigil there, antagonist of those surviving Koreshites who were asserting their own rights of occupancy, filer of
several lawsuits on George's behalf, greeter and guide for as many of
the visitors to Mount Carmel as she could manage, Biblicist typologist
(cf. 2001b: 46–47) of no secular or aestheticist turn at all, daily
filling typewritten pages with her identifications of the figurae of the

culmination of Biblical eschatology, the figurae of herself prominently included. There and thus, to close the circle, I found her. So transpired our mutual selection and recruitment to, our initial enfoldment within, the dyad-subject of which Ms. Roden was usually the far better half. The rest wasn't merely anthropology, but it was anthropology among other things.

Mode of judgment: ethical valuation and justification

I am compelled for the sake of brevity and the avoidance of ambiguity to give the Faubion–Roden subject position a proper name. Call it Araucaria, after the pseudonym of one of the setters of cryptic crosswords for the *Guardian* newspaper and the designation of the genus of the monkey puzzle tree. Quite unlike the current Marquis of Fronteira and Alorna, Araucaria has never in its jointliness produced a sermon, has never established a foundation in the service of the national patrimony, has never undergone psychoanalysis, has no title, no holdings, no celebrity. Unlike Cavafy, it has never written a poem. For all this, it is not without roots. It has such ancestors as James Mooney and Wovoka (Mooney 1965 [1896]) and, much more recently, Roland Littlewood and Mother Earth, Christopher Morgan and Hayara, and Susan Harding and one of her evangelical intimates (Harding 2000; Littlewood 1992; Morgan 1997). It does not have many more; the great majority of the contributions to the anthropology and sociology of millenarianism have been grounded in historical research rather than fieldwork and have focused on collectivities rather than individuals (Behrend 1999; Cohn 1970; Hobsbawm 1963; Lindstrom 1993; Robbins 2004; Wilson 1973; Worsley 1968; for a partial exception, see Pessar 2004). It seems not to have many successors, either, perhaps because millenarianism has fallen out of academic fashion with the turn – uneventful cosmically, in spite of many premonitions to the contrary – of the twentieth into the twenty-first century. (Robbins [2004] is an exception to this rule.)

I suspect, however, that it will have them in the future; millenarianism may fade but, if the past is any teacher of life at all, seems also always to have its new day. If with less certainty, one or another anthropologist is likely to be there to encounter it when it does.

Araucaria acquired its particular constitution for a number of contingent but compelling reasons, all of which influence its conception and extension of the ethical chrism, its mode of the justification of ethical decision and conduct and the particular mode of its relation to the themitical that came to orient it. Prominent among those reasons was that my visible attachment to the representative of one of the schismatic factions of claimants of the Branch Davidian altar rendered my contact with any of the other factions and factionalists effectively out of the question. I may not have been trailed the first time I departed from Mount Carmel, but I had been watched and would be scrutinized again and again with every further visit I paid to Ms. Roden. I have reported in *Shadows and Lights* that one of Ms. Roden's rivals hostilely dismissed me as a "reporter" when I arrived at Mount Carmel in the late summer of 1994 to observe a Solemn Assembly of Branch Davidians of one commitment or another not merely from Texas but from many other states as well. Ms. Roden and her rival – who was presiding over a ceremony with all the restorationist accoutrements of a rabbi – had come to an impasse earlier the same day. Ms. Roden had sought to preach at the ceremony. Her rival succeeded in preventing her from doing so. After that, any investigation of the Branch Davidian community such as it fracturally was remained perhaps objectively possible but well beyond my personal powers of negotiation and capacity to endure suspicion, tension and conflict. Ms. Roden would accordingly be my primary interlocutor, though I also had the benefit of an enormous archival store of the writings of Houteff and the Rodens, photocopies of which Ms. Roden peddled to whoever, for whatever reason, might buy them, for a nominal fee. With the other Branch Davidians – at least with those of the locale – Araucaria thus proved to be in something approaching a state of war.

The analysis to which I have committed myself in the first part of this book would compel me to conclude that Araucaria did not confer the ethical chrism on what it could only constitute as its enemies. Fortunately, the matter was far less ideal-typical than any that would warrant such a conclusion and in its empirical ambiguities liable to much qualification. First, Ms. Roden might continually find condemnatory types among the Bible's personages and events through which to render many of her contemporaries. At one point, she found cause to identify not merely one of her fellow claimants to Branch Davidian leadership but also her husband George as manifestations of Satan (2001b: 65). (In many other contexts, she cast George, who was well known for his foul mouth and to whom she herself attributed Tourette's Syndrome, as the "rough wind" of Isaiah 27:8.) She did pronounce her rivals and their followers in error, sinners and – on what she took to be further Biblical evidence – unfavorably judged. She declared that drunkards are damned, that the medical establishment and doctors should be shunned, that the wicked should be avoided, that those in love should marry "lest they fornicate," and that the "death decree" of taxation should be paid "in bullets" (2001b: 142–143). The themitical Ms. Roden is not shy of severity.

Her severity must nevertheless be balanced against – or at any event juxtaposed to – her insistence that she, too, is a sinner, a backslider, often overwhelmed by circumstance in her quest to be worthy of her god's call: "Trying to be righteous while living in a ditch [as, for a time, she did] is like standing on a banana peel in an ice rink" (2001b: 151). It must be juxtaposed to her insistence – and it would be decidedly anti-Biblicist to insist anything else – that God alone is our final judge and his judgment transcendent and inscrutable. It must finally be balanced against and juxtaposed to a Ms. Roden who was perfectly willing to treat me with respect and wit and grace even though I knew that she knew that I was in several respects far astray from her principles. I never gave her any reason to think that I was myself a believer of any sort – though more on that matter in due course. I knew that she had soon surmised my sexuality, not least because she exercised considerable care not to mention it. Thematically, she was unquestionably heteronormative, but with the more nebulous extension of the chrism, she proved ready to accommodate the apostate and infidel anthropologist and perhaps even her religious rivals – enemies of sorts, but not quite enemies to the death, since she understood her eschatological role to come to an end with the full articulation of her message. She did not see herself as among the remnant who would heed that message and join the returned Christ in his great and final battle with the forces of the Antichrist. In any event, she sometimes wrote as if she expected herself to die before that event. Sometimes not.

As I indicated in *Shadows and Lights* (2001b: 158), her extension of the chrism to me may well have had instrumental motives. I am fairly certain – and came to such certainty not long into my fieldwork – that in both a secular and a religious sense, she came to see me as a source of the legitimation of her personhood, her voice, her sensibility, if not quite her theological and cosmological commitments. Only once I had concluded fieldwork did I also come to suspect that she might have thought me unwittingly (altogether unwittingly, I should add) godsent to promulgate her message to a broader world. In composing *Shadows and Lights*, I did indeed attempt to lend her a certain legitimacy – and not merely by insistently referring to her with the honorific "Ms. Roden" rather than by her first name. I avoided at every step a diagnostics of pathologization that would effectively silence her. I further adopted a style and a theoretical apparatus of such high and elaborate seriousness that the non-specialist reader could (I now realize) only find inaccessible. The latter choice was unfortunate, perhaps – or in any event, not in full accord with Ms. Roden's interests, at least if it is to blame for the very limited readership that the sales of *Shadows and Lights* suggest she and I have garnered. In any event, I did further include extensive passages from her own writings, entirely in her own voice. I included all of those passages in which – not without considerable revision along the way – she gradually articulated the message that, as the antitypical sixth messenger of the Book of Revelation, would and could only reach its culmination with the identification of the returned Christ himself and the fateful battle with the Beast already done.

Or rather, I included almost all of them. When she was not writing as if she expected an early death, Ms. Roden read the deaths and destruction at Mount Carmel as the final and so literal figura of Armageddon, even if she found every reason not to read the government agents and forces that stood in opposition to the Koreshites within the compound as a Christly army. That she could not identify a Christ returned among any of the personages on either side of the standoff thus led her to continue her search and, in the course of it, to suspect that what she had initially thought to be the Present and Final Truth of the world's end was partial at best. Only after I had ceased visiting Ms. Roden did I receive what would constitute her last angelic testament. At length:

[Whether] V. T. Houteff [was] the second coming of Christ is not a question that many have asked. Christians should. Houteff was the founder and prophet of the Shepherd Rod church, the Davidian Seventh-day Adventists, a small man with no beauty that made him desirable, a Bible interpreter who created a solid foundation for Bible students, an immigrant to America from Bulgaria [a light rising from the east].

Did he come as a thief as Christ said he [himself] would? (Rev. 3:3) Yes, indeed, Houteff came in the footsteps of Christ. Christ stole the righteous of the flock from the duly-appointed but corrupt priesthood (Num. 18:1–7) and justified himself because he was the true shepherd (John 10:1–11). So Houteff stole the righteous flock from the duly-appointed but corrupt priesthood of the Seventh-day Adventist church . . .

Not only was Houteff the Lamb that opened the seals, he was also the Lamb in the third angel's message of Rev. 14 [a forewarning of the punishment of the unrighteous, the "smoke" of whose torment will ascend "up for ever and ever"]. Houteff announced the beginning of Ezekiel 9 [a forewarning of the

slaughter of the unrighteous among the residents of Jerusalem] in 1930: ...
The prophecy of Ezekiel gives the information in detail from the beginning of
Luther's reformation to Ezekiel 9.

That the Holocaust fulfilled this prophecy went unnoticed in Houteff's time.
God closed Houteff's eyes to it just as he hid the seven thunders from him
so that Houteff might fulfill the suffering servant of Judah, Christ come as
a thief, rather than Christ come in glory ...

The application of Ezekiel 9 foretold by Houteff actually took place [in
accord with the prophetic chronology of Ezekiel] four hundred and thirty
years after Luther's personal reformation. Luther was ordained a priest in
1507 and posted the Ninety-five Theses on the church door in 1517. That
corresponds to the ten-year period from 1937 to 1947, the years of Holocaust that preceded the formation of Israel in 1948 ...

... Houteff's sealed flock, which included Ben and Lois Roden of the
Branch, stood as the holy angels that they will rise up to be, and Houteff
stood as the Lamb he was during the Holocaust, and the smoke of the
crematoriums arose in a sorrow and a horror that will never be forgotten.
And because Houteff himself was the Lamb that took the Bible from God's
hands, and also the Lamb on the earth during the Holocaust, he can be
none other than Christ come as a thief, the second coming of
Christ. (2001b: 97–98)

Perhaps it is all but obvious: among the ellipses that I inserted is one
that deletes Ms. Roden's explicit pronouncement that the Jews who
were put to death in the gas chambers were being punished for their
sins. I could not bring myself to include it. Or rather, Araucaria – that
quasi-whole less than the sum of its parts, whose own last testament is
Shadows and Lights – could not bring itself to say it. Sometimes banally,
as with the suppression of the actual names of many of the persons
that Ms. Roden included in her writings, sometimes not so banally,
Araucaria was a censor of itself.

So Araucaria – like many of the rest of us – was occasionally of two
minds. My own sense of the extension of the ethical chrism is a
straightforward example: I attribute it much greater breadth than
Ms. Roden did and I am much less certain than she was of its limits.

In fact Araucaria was not only of two minds but often of three or sometimes even of four. One of them was Ms. Roden, angel and occasional prophet. Another was a Ms. Roden who could and did shift into an entirely secular idiom. So, in response to my asking her how she spent a typical day, she spoke of tending the memorial that had been erected to honor the Mount Carmel dead: "It's a lovely place. I'd like to see it made into a park. I'd like to see it all mowed and … not landscaped but cut down the thorn trees and emphasize the beautiful trees. Just make it beautiful." She concluded with an acknowledgment of taking occasional advantage of the therapy that was available to her at a Waco clinic, and of the other means to which she resorted in order to "keep [her] head on straight" (2001b: 157). The millenarian should hardly care – should she? – about transforming Mount Carmel into a park. For that matter, with the end so imminent, she should hardly care about passing some four and a half years in the occasional company of an anthropologist, or plying lawsuits against her rivals in the McClennan County court, or advocating on behalf of George Roden's rightful title to the leadership of the Branch Davidian church even after his death in 1998 – in the course of escaping from Big Spring hospital, a higher-security facility to which he had been transferred after escaping from the facility to which he was originally assigned – and with no further heir apparent clearly in sight. I had to conclude in *Shadows and Lights* and still maintain that the millenarian would have no such cares. I still maintain that Ms. Roden was not only or exhaustively millenarian but – once again like many of the rest of us – had accommodated herself "to a world so shot through with epistemological and [ethical] alternatives that none but the perceptually or logically most self-evident of beliefs – much less systems of belief, much less systems of [ethics] – can be given full credit, accorded categorical certainty" (2001b: 158). Such a world is one in which commitment thus always entails taking a risk. Ms. Roden's is a limit-case in point. Hers are matters of eternal life and eternal death.

Another of Araucaria's operative minds was of course my own, which had its own internal fissure (translated more or less faithfully into the fissured text of *Shadows and Lights* itself). On the one side was me, the very one, not only a subject-in-position but a particular subjectivity, with my own particular course of life, my own memories, my own traumas and (in between one and another depressive episode) joys, to my own mind an academic refugee, far more comfortable in a library and the liminoid ambience of the ivory tower than in what the anti-intellectual like to call the "real world," mocked in my adolescence for my effeminacy and still not altogether comfortable with my body, much less what one would politely call my "orientation" or (worse) "lifestyle," thus always a touch distrustful of strangers, thus always keeping my distance, thus overdetermined for the anthropological life, however poor a traveler I might be, phobic of dirigibles, phobic of heights and during my fieldwork with Ms. Roden not driving a car, not made for life on the Texas prairie and often scared witless there, but coming back again and again because in Ms. Roden, in her wit and humor – in spite of everything – and her humiliations, in a Biblicist obsession with finding import in everything and a refusal of coincidence that carried my own interpretive penchants into the realm of extreme sport, in her arrogance and her fallenness, in her suspicion of government and in her paranoia, I saw, as in a glass darkly, an image of myself, there but for the grace (as it were) of God.

On the other side was the anthropologist, rigorous infidel, professional believer in nothing except contingency, critic of biologism and psychologism, second-order observer, diagnostician of the collective in the individual, always at risk of offending his diagnostic subjects for seeming to exercise, perhaps even to exercise – poaching here from T. S. Eliot – those eyes that fix their victims in a formulated phrase, leave them sprawling on a pin, pinned and wriggling on a wall. Anthropology so practiced – and I do admit to so practicing it once in a while – is an obvious technology of domination (which is not to say that it is inevitably in error), all the more so when it is fortified with a conceptual apparatus of sufficient density to be almost bullet-proof. However dense my conceptual apparatus, I am not practicing that sort of anthropology here; my diagnostics is not and cannot effect sociological reduction because it is itself a post-philosophically contingent technology of the address of phenomena that are – in their openness – themselves irreducibly contingent.

Yet I am – or was, in my enfoldment within Araucaria – unable to employ even such a less symbolically violent apparatus all the way down, to myself or to Ms. Roden, the very one, in her own particularity, with her own irreducibly unique course of life. I could not do so intellectually, because my diagnostics remained and remains in the rather more violent tradition of Bourdieu: it cannot generate mechanical but only statistical models (see Bourdieu 1977). I could not do so existentially because I continued to reach an impasse at which matters simply became too personal and the communicative locks threatened to close. I am not an Augustinian hero; try as I might, I cannot put light in every last dark corner either of my consciousness or of my unconscious (if such a thing exists). Nor am I so nosy that, for example, I could bring myself to pursue explicitly with Ms. Roden a most delicate matter that her rivals circulated as a rumor in accounting for her particular repulsion with David Koresh and at which certain of her own writings (pointedly not quoted in *Shadows and Lights*) hinted – that her father had abused her sexually. Everyone has his limits and some things are better left unsaid.

That Araucaria emerged from such a mess as a sustainable subject was thus as far distant from the given as could be imagined. Yet for all the fuzziness – which, if more resolved, might well have taken the form of inconsistency – of its constituents' ethical sensibilities, it gradually yielded what was in effect an extension of the ethical chrism of its own, identical neither to Ms. Roden's conception of its extension nor to my own. Araucaria is not the sort of subject that has its own personality (at least not literally), its own consciousness, capacity for self-reflection, or conceptions or perceptions. Its mind, properly speaking, was not its own; it was rather the somewhat schizophrenic mind of that of its dyadic constituents, the Vladimir and Estragon waiting often at cross purposes and with Sartre's Flaubert for their Godots, its chartless pilots, the anthropologist and Ms. Roden and Amo and me. As a subject in its own right, it was a thing of practice. In practice, however, it realized a conception of the extent of the ethical chrism every bit as definitely as we all realize even – or perhaps especially – our non-conscious epistemic and ethical commitments in our unreflective practices. Araucaria's ethical universe was and remains a universe of readers.

That it would be such a universe is no more given than any of its other conceptions-in-practice, but was among its objective possibilities from the outset of its active existence and, at least in hindsight, one of few possibilities that had any great likelihood of coming actually to pass. Like the Rodens before her, Ms. Roden wrote. She wrote daily and by the pound. She wrote well – in fact, very well, with the ease of someone who had indeed completed her college education with a BA in mathematics and a minor in psychology and often with the distinctive cadences of the King James Bible, which was her constant reference and most constant inspiration. She talked as well, but she had actually answered a great many of my questions long before I began talking with her and had already put all of them on paper. My interviews yielded novelties now and again, but most would soon have Ms. Roden leading me to yet another of her papers or pamphlets or bound volumes, which I would purchase and take home. Such materials became my richest and my primary resource and that was just as Ms. Roden would have it. She very much wanted me to use them. She wanted me to reproduce them and wanted me to give them the attention that would do them justice. She wanted that justice done in writing.

So, I hope, I did at least some of her bidding. The result – which lingers beyond Araucaria in its active phase as its artifactual afterlife – is a book that I can hardly claim to be exclusively my own any more than I can claim it to be Ms. Roden's. Its voice is at once religious and secular. I would be disingenuous and dissembling were I to insist that it is religious and secular in equal measure. I wrote *Shadows and Lights*. Its prevailing tones are my own. Its voice nevertheless remains neither mine nor Ms. Roden's, much less both of ours in a unison at which we did not and could never have arrived. Its ethical call is to the reader and its ethical embrace an embrace of anyone who would read it seriously.

Mess aside, Araucaria also realized two overarching principles of ethical judgment, a standard of ethical critique. The principles themselves – or more accurately, the critical turns of mind of which they are an abstraction – may have been what allowed my relationship with Ms. Roden to unfold as a relationship, at least as one that could move beyond the confines of my own self-absorbed fascination. They might also mark a genuine meeting of minds, even though the minds in question extended in directions quite different from the point of their intersection and even though they mark that point only in their abstraction. Once again, the whole that was not one was less than its parts. The millenarian Christian and the anthropological infidel nevertheless found themselves agreeing with one another regularly on three normative positions: that no one should be so confident of his presumptive knowledge that he acts upon it without hesitation; that oppression is never warranted; and that ceteris paribus people should leave one another unharmed. We found ourselves to be ethical fallibilists and ethically bound to a commitment to tolerance of a broadly humanistic if not quite humanist stripe. Our own divisions of mind could find us being nothing else, Ms. Roden's ardent Biblicism and my equally ardent secularism notwithstanding. Of course, our substantive differences remained; fallibilists we were, but our fallibilism had different grounds and different foci. Though the term never explicitly arose during our conversations, we also found ourselves themitically to be libertarians. Once again, our substantive differences were patent. She thought that we should be free of the harms perpetrated and the strictures imposed by our uniformly imperfect governments and that we should do no harm to one another – but God might appropriately step in to punish sinners of one errant path or another. I expect our uniformly imperfect governments to exercise control over the institutional production and increase of arbitrary inequality – a more strongly interventionist and politically more leftist stance than Ms. Roden's. I think that we should do no harm to one another except in retaliation or retribution for or restitution of harm already done. I am unwilling to wait for a god to intervene, much less save us. Rhetorically, as libertarian, Araucaria sounds more like me than like Ms. Roden. Here, too, however, its voice is more complex and less resolved than my own. Ms. Roden adds her own timbre to it. Araucaria thus resembles a religiously inflected Millsian in its mode of ethical judgment, though its voice is less utilitarian than principlist. It is not silent on consequences – if you listen to its Rodenesque timbre, you will hear for example that "honesty is the best policy" – but it drifts, if still far from the Kantians, then somewhere within and between consequentialism and principlism and more toward the themitically universalist than the particularist. It is a scatter, so many quanta; like the Marquis of Fronteira and Alorna, Araucaria is an ethical modern.

Mode of subjectivation: scope, structure and priority

The scope of the human is very wide. The scope of the open and – for a while – autopoietic system that grew out of my relationship with Ms. Roden is much more narrow. The position that it occupied is not one that it occupied uniquely, but relative to the human, it has only a few iterations. Its nearest iterations include the ancestral precedents in the anthropology of religion that I have already cited. At a greater level of abstraction and so of lesser complexity, it has a few more. Araucaria emerged concretely out of a method that was pre-ponderantly life-historical. It might thus be placed in co-occupancy with such dyadic counterparts as Sidney Mintz's relationship with Taso, Vincent Crapanzano's with Tuhami, Majorie Shostak's with Nisa, Ruth Behar's with Esperanza, Michael Herzfeld's with Andreas Nenedakis (Behar 2003; Crapanzano 1980; Herzfeld 1997; Mintz 1960; Shostak 1981). Even more abstractly, it belongs to the anthropology of religion, and still more abstractly to social-cultural anthropology. Even yet more abstractly, it has at least one foot in social and cultural theory. In all but the first two of such positions, however, it can hardly be conceived of as an autopoietic system. Its latter locations depend on that bit of objectified mind that is precisely its literary afterlife. It was not in any event a nested subject-within-a-subject in the manner of Fernando's noble humanness or human nobility. In this sense, at least, it was simple. Its active home was on the Texas prairie and the place of its afterlife the multi-sited if always somewhat cloistered preserves of scholarly libraries and ivory towers and my files and desk at home. Many collections of Cavafy's poems have found their way to Borders and Barnes & Noble. I am fairly certain that *Shadows and Lights* did not.

Structurally and themitically, Araucaria owed much to the consti-tution or contract that I put forward to Ms. Roden early in our relation-ship and to which, after a couple of months' delay, she gave her blessing. The constitution or contract in question took the form of a letter that I wrote not merely as a means of seeking my interlocutor's informed consent but also as a means of proffering a rough and ready definition of our situation in relation to and with one another with which I at least could live. The letter – which came on official departmental paper, and so explicitly identified me as the anthropologist that I had initially demurred from introducing myself as being – read:

I would ... be very grateful to hear from you at some point in the near future – if not about the "need" for such a book as the one I have in mind (for I fear that you and your fellow congregants are all too modest to admit of any such "need") then at least about your willingness to participate with me in the writing of it. Let me emphasize that I can certainly understand your exhaustion. I can certainly understand your thinking that you have better things to do with what time you have. I also recognize that you may have no particular reason to trust my intentions; after all, I am seeking not to join your church but instead to record its past and present situation in the world. I am an "outsider." I cannot be your Matthew. At best, I can be your "translator," someone who tries to render your situation in terms that might do it proper justice and that even outsiders might understand. I would ask (though I grant that even this might be too much after all that you have endured) to be given the benefit of the doubt. I'm merely a scholar. Whatever else I may or may not be, I'm quite sure that I'm not evil. (2001b: 157–158)

I am reasonably certain of the latter still – though not a naif, either. I am still grateful finally to have received Ms. Roden's affirmation that she "would be happy to participate" in my "study." I am now inclined to think that she never fully affirmed the terms in which I put that study forward to her, terms that I would not enclose in quite so many quotation marks were I to write the letter again. I also should have said that I was interested in the past, the present and the future situation of her church. The anthropologist had not yet fully appreciated the native's point of view.

The letter was a pitch, but not a fraudulent one. I made a point, obviously enough, not merely of acknowledging the hardships that Ms. Roden endured but of suggesting implicitly that I was ready to acknowledge even those hardships – those poisonings of her food, those strange, burning substances that airplanes dropped from the sky, those noxious gases that They sent on the wind to Mount Carmel in order to debilitate her lungs, her good health – that many others might and even more others surely would merely have dismissed as paranoid fantasy. I made an effort to communicate my acceptance of her church as a church, even though it had not officially been recognized as being one from the point at which Florence Houteff and her council dissolved its Davidian predecessor. I did not promise to do so in the letter, but I regularly made donations to that church when I visited; I paid Ms. Roden for her publications and always gave her something in addition, which on one occasion she plainly accepted as a divine deliverance, glancing upward with a smile when I put it into her hand. That was simply one occasion when I entertained the suspicion that she did not see me as the mere scholar that by my own account I was.

Above all, I did not for a moment pretend or want to pretend that I was or could ever be a fellow believer. I could not have proceeded with the relationship under such a pretense. After my first work in the field, an investigation of social and cultural reformism in Athens in the aftermath of the 1967–1974 military junta (Faubion 1993), I was in need of another project. When I encountered Ms. Roden, I did not have one. In the encounter, I thought I might be at the verge of one – but I would never have pursued it further had I not passed muster as and in spite of my being an infidel. Every relationship between anthropologist and significant other is partial, but few can be sustained in complete anthropological disguise. I wore many masks – I always do – but with Ms. Roden, I could not wear the mask of the potential convert. I thought of many of my personal traits and orientations as beyond being Ms. Roden's necessary business. I thought that any disguise or silencing of my secularism would constitute an intolerable lie. I would like to think that I did so because I understood such dissemblance to constitute a complete betrayal of the reciprocity on which the relationship between the anthropologist and any contemporary significant other must depend. The gift I sought from Ms. Roden was her testament. In return, I would have to offer my own – empty though it was.

Constitutions and contracts are typically ambiguous. Our need for judges and lawyers would be drastically diminished were this not so. A contract as brief as a letter and without the prior negotiation of its terms was bound to be both ambiguous and incomplete. My contract with Ms. Roden was notably incomplete in its leaving the structure of our practical relationship without any specification whatever. Professions of faith or the lack of it do not in themselves constitute any practical directive. Ms. Roden and I accordingly had to provide the structure of our time together as time passed and with considerable cybernetic attention along the way. From the outset, we both intuited that our interlocution could not take the form of argumentation, of dispute. At the outset, we had already agreed to disagree and to do so in one specific respect – over the matter of faith – absolutely (or so I thought). My capacity to act as a participant-observer was constrained in the same breath. Nor, however, could I adopt the traditional role of the recorder of exotic customs and habits, effectively freed from their impact. Above all because of its requisite refusal of reciprocity, the Bourdiesian mode of "reflexive" fieldwork was not available to me, either – if it is any longer available to anyone at all. The themitical alternative that arose early in our conversations may not have been the only alternative, but it had the virtue of relegating disagreement to the practical background and resolving what could otherwise have been an intolerable dissonance of disparate epistemic doxologies. It was a reversal of what obtained in the real world. Ms. Roden would assume the role of my teacher. I would assume the role of her student. Shades of Marcel Griaule and Ogotemmêli (Griaule 1965).

Araucaria was thus pedagogical in its internal, its constitutive dynamics. In its actualization and in its actuality, it took its direction from what might also be characterized as a pedagogical project, of which *Shadows and Lights* was the primary expression. The organization of its changeable structural features is, however, better characterized as that of theater. Such a characterization has every likelihood of being doubly misleading if it is understood as implying that beneath such a composite and emergent subject lay a real actor, rationally and calculatively putting on a show for a presumptive audience, managing impressions and pursuing the alliances that the ethnomethodologist or actor network theorist might claim to discern. First, Araucaria is not the sort of subject that permits of the distinction between appearance and reality. Ms. Roden and I may both have had – we surely did have – our reasons for inaugurating and sustaining our relationship. The flexible arrangement, the interactive simplification at which we arrived, however, never resolved itself into a consistency sufficient to amount to a collusion of which Araucaria could serve at once as instrument and mask. At the very least, if the being of Araucaria was in any respect dramaturgical in Erving Goffman's sense, then it was flatly a dramaturgical failure (Goffman 1959). Ms. Roden and I may occasionally have made an impression, especially on the rival claimants to religious authority who were also coming to and going from Mount Carmel. We did and could do next to nothing to manage whatever impression we made. We were an ambiguous couple and coupling, but ambiguous in a manner so ingenuous that we had to pass for whatever joint subject our audience took us to be.

Second, Araucaria was not an actor. It was rather theater itself. It included roles – teacher and student among them, though not exhaustively. Teacher and student we resolved ourselves into being for one another, but wearing my anthropological cap I was simultaneously casting Ms. Roden in many other roles – millenarian, disenfranchised quasi-citizen, marginal, socially branded as deviant among them. As I have already mentioned, I am sure that she did the same with me – I was "Dr. James" explicitly, but not that alone. It had a normative scenario – Ms. Roden would deliver her message and I would record it. It had its scenes, each of them another over the course of those four and a half years of meetings and conversations on the prairie. It came in due course to have its climax. It came subsequently to have its denouement – in *Shadows and Lights*, even if that constituted more a whimper than a bang.

Marcus has repeatedly referred to the textual representation of the definition of the situation of fieldwork, customarily in the introductory or first substantive chapter of the standard monograph, as its mise-en-scène. Much the same attribution is appropriate to the definition of the situation of fieldwork in the field itself, now almost always a negotiated definition, however rarely it amounts to a genuine consensus. Just as the monograph does, so also fieldwork itself has its poetics, its parameters of stylization, and with them another homology with subject positions of a more conventionally ethical order. What is notable about the mise-en-scène of my fieldwork with Ms. Roden – which was also Ms. Roden's with me – was that it was far from being the first of the poetic registers that our relationship resolved. First came our initial encounter, an event of most uncertain consequences. Next came the *mise-en-scénario* – the setting of our mutual expectations, each of the other, of the normativity of the relationship, of the productive parameters and limitations of whatever plot it might acquire. Next came the roles that we assigned one another, or at least those we assigned one another by mutual acknowledgment.

Next and only next came the mise-en-scène of fieldwork – if it ever quite came at all. Our meetings and conversations on the prairie might be said to have their staging, but the staging was different from one of my visits to the next. I initially found Ms. Roden presiding on a literal stage, with a cyclone fence and bulldozers in the near distance. The next time I arrived at Mount Carmel, I again found Ms. Roden, but she had constructed an office – a very small hut, equipped with a bed and a desk and her typewriter and a minimal supply of electricity – and was busy working on the construction of a museum, a larger building into which many of the flyers and writings and many of the twisted tricycles and other artifacts of the conflagration would be placed. The cyclone fence had been decorated with crosses commemorating each of those who had died in the conflagration, with wreaths of artificial flowers and with signs of dire warning. It had several apertures through which a human being could easily pass. When I next visited and for a few visits thereafter, Ms. Roden was in the company of a man, another church-contracted husband, whom she said George had sent to offer her protection and who was shy in my presence but evidently very handy with a hammer and skilled in carpentry. The museum was up and running and looked sturdy enough. The cyclone fence had disappeared and the now open perimeters of the compound had been transformed into a series of posted footpaths, each marker along their way identifying one or another site of interest, from the compound's arsenal to the chamber to which women and children had fled but in which they had become entrapped as the April fire had spread. Ms. Roden and her husband were sleeping in a broken-down Volvo, the doors of which they somehow managed to chain shut during the night. A local militia was financing the construction of a memorial of gravestones and crepe myrtles at the near edge of the remains of the compound. Ms. Roden had constructed an altar nearby. Subsequently, she and her husband became the owners of a camper, where she cooked and wrote, though the Volvo remained their sleeping quarters.

Then the husband disappeared, apparently at Ms. Roden's bidding, after he proved to be incapable of overcoming his addiction to alcohol. When I next visited, I found that most of the signs that had been posted along the footpath had been removed, Ms. Roden's altar damaged, and another altar constructed to challenge it. Not long after, I came upon a scene dramatically transformed: no stage, no museum, no office, no Volvo, no camper. Ms. Roden had set up a billboard of her postings near the entrance to Mount Carmel. Copies of Ben and Lois Roden's and of her own writings lay on the ground beneath it. Ms. Roden herself was sitting under the shade of a tree at road's edge. She was living in a pup tent and both bathing in and taking her drinking water from the pond that the property held. She told me of a fire – yet another fire, which had destroyed her office and museum among other things. In the background, a building was nearly complete – a Visitor's Center of whose financing the income from a local conservative radio host's charity campaign was the chief source. It would belong to and have as its staff the Koreshites. To its left and just beyond the Mount Carmel property another edifice was under construction, a church that the leader of the third surviving faction – the man who had presided as priest at the Solemn Assembly that I had briefly attended – had determined to build on property that he had purchased. Though my partner, interested in filming a documentary, would do so, I did not return to Mount Carmel and never met Ms. Roden face to face again. A few months later, I learned that Ms. Roden's mother had died. She left her daughter an inheritance and a trust fund. With the monies, Ms. Roden purchased a recreational vehicle and departed from Mount Carmel. I next heard that she was in Maine. I also know that she returned to Waco two or three years ago to file a multi-million dollar lawsuit against the Koreshites in the interest of reclaiming Mount Carmel. The suit has subsequently languished.

Scenes thus had to be reset, redefined, assessed and reassessed for the possibilities they afforded, the roles they permitted and those they required. As Ms. Roden's situation became more tenuous and her rivals more assertive, I found myself increasingly in the role of a charitable contributor and my partner and I both in the role of chauffeurs and assistants, taking Ms. Roden to the copiers where she would be able to reproduce her writings, fetching and delivering her paper and postage stamps and other supplies. She had come to trust us perhaps as much as and perhaps even more than she could trust anyone else in her local surroundings. Among other things, I had taken care always to alert her in advance of my plans to visit, always using my department stationery to do so. Very early into our relationship I recognized that surprise would be corrosive. She did not, however, trust us without qualification. At the very least, she did not always trust us to know exactly what we were doing. After finding her beside the road and witnessing her "tank up," as she put it, with water from the Mount Carmel pond, my partner and I were compelled to rush to Waco to buy her provisions. We were not so unknowing that we thought that she would accept food from us; she had previously made it clear to me that she ate only food that she herself had selected. Instead, we bought several gallons of water – distilled, capped and sealed – at a Waco supermarket. When we set it before her, she refused it. I thought at the time that she did so because she thought it poisoned. I was troubled that she might also have thought that I was the agent of its poisoning. I now think that she refused it because she thought it insufficiently pure. She once told me that she had moved to Mount Carmel to live with George instead of remaining on her farm because she was in need of the "particularly pure" drinking water that Mount Carmel produced and that, so many years later, only the murky waters of the pond could apparently still provide.

Araucaria was theater, then, but its mode of subjectivation continuously improvisational. It was a performance, a subject-as-performance. Its Butlerian performativity was, however, vague at best; its citational resources were few and far between (cf. Butler 1993). Every fieldwork-generated subject may be of the same mode, more or less. If so, then Araucaria is illustrative if not exemplary. In my experiencing of it, in my partially being the substance of it, I nevertheless found it improvisational in the extreme. My first fieldwork, among the cultural elite (and other instantiations of the culturally controversial) of Greece, had a diverse array of scenes and the array was by no means of a piece. Even so, each scene had its regular contours. I did not discern all of them, but that was simply a matter of my own failings. The dramatis personae among whom I circulated were also diverse and often very different from me, but we often had similar levels of education, or similar sexual orientations, or both in common. I never mastered the local stylization of interaction and I am still in most Greek eyes the stuffy and overly formal and insufficiently self-assertive Anglo-Saxon that I have always been. I never mastered a lot of other local competencies, but it was not because the competencies were inconstant that I did not do so. It was more a matter of my sometimes more, sometimes less consciously not wanting to do so. In any event I must leave the matter of whether Araucaria was more rather than less typical of its ilk to future collegial discussion. Suffice it to say that it was a subject often on the wing.

What can be said even of a whole that is not one in relationship to its parts can be said of an assemblage in relation to its bits and pieces: the totality has priority; the bits and pieces are subordinate to it. Once again, such subordination may be the typical situation of the field-worker in relationship to the relational fabric of fieldwork itself. Indeed, logically it must be so, at least if fieldwork lasts long enough and its threads and seams have sufficient cohesion actually to constitute a relational fabric, however ragged and of loose ends it might be and whether or not it is actually autopoietic as such. Looking back on it, I have to conclude that the assembled fabric of Araucaria also had a certain staying power. After all, it survived actively for almost five years. I nevertheless retain the sense that I constantly had while still pursuing fieldwork – that the fabric was likely to tear or fray irreparably at every new shift in the relational wind. Its improvisational mode of subjecti-vation was the provocation of my many ongoing anxieties, though not because I was an especially poor improvisationalist. On the contrary, both Ms. Roden and I became ever more adept at improvising as the time between us passed. The problem lay rather with the ambiguity of the definition of both role and situation that made improvisation necessary in the first place.

In fact, such ambiguity proved deadly. During my penultimate visit with Ms. Roden – when I still found her in her camper and not yet in a pup tent – I was discussing with her a doctrine that may have come as one of Lois Roden's revelations or have come instead with the arrival of one of her last acolytes (the man who was building his church just beyond Mount Carmel's boundary, the priest at the Solemn Assembly). Ms. Roden endorsed the former of the two alternatives. The doctrine in question was that of a fourth and once again feminine aspect of the Godhead, that of the Holy Spirit Daughter. The lovely mysteries of the resulting gender and numerical symmetry aside, I wanted to know whether such a quaternary Godhead was imagined to be singular or plural in its essence. Ms. Roden was uncharacteristically without a ready answer. She paused and then replied that "you would have had to ask Lois about that" – though of course that was out of the question. (I am not a competent spiritist.) Soon after this in our conversation, she announced to me: "You could be a Branch Davidian."

To my mind, the terms of what, from my first letter to her on, I had understood and wanted our engagement to be were violated. The contract was breached. Until this revisiting, I have always thought that the breach was Ms. Roden's. I now realize that the breach was my own. I had taken the perilous step of pursuing beyond the limits of Ms. Roden's own writings a topic on which she found herself to have no light. This angel called to reveal the Present and the nearly Final Truth, this passionate seeker of the light, had encountered a limit and its darkness. As she had seen previously, she would have to cede to another the quest for the Final Truth itself. I now think that she may have been ceding at least the possibility of undertaking that quest to me. Just so I, too, could be a Branch Davidian angel – or at the very least, give it a try.

Telos

Araucaria thus had the flesh of a full script only posthumously, with the completion and publication of *Shadows and Lights*. Its telos had its most enduring footprint in the same event – which is not quite to say that its telos was *Shadows and Light*, the very book itself. Ms. Roden and I may both have had projects toward whose achievement our relationship was at once means and end. Our subject-in-relation did not; Araucaria was not a purposive but an autotelic subject. Its raison d'être was itself, or more carefully, itself under a certain description.

Ms. Roden had a message. She wanted to have it broadcast much farther than she herself had the resources to do. She wanted my attention and the benefit of the social and cultural capital that I had at my disposal. She wanted someone to take her seriously. I had my own agenda: self-examination in the mode of Alice in Wonderland; windmill-tilting against the demons of disenfranchisement and delegitimation; critique of the congregationalism of prevailing anthropological conceptions of religion and the misplaced essentialism of the social-theoretical division between the religious and the political; contract with a distinguished academic press and the securing of promotion to full professor; and so on. Needless to say, as with every other feature of our relationship, synergy was not something that we could take for granted. Its probabilities were low, if they could be registered at all.

Nevertheless, synergy was what brought Araucaria into being as a subject whose immanent telos could appropriately be described, perhaps only be described, as "publicity." Even this description has misleading connotations. It should not be confused with what we are now calling "ink." Nor should it be confused with the "visibility" that is part and parcel of political and other sorts of media celebrity. I admit it: I had a daydream or two of Ms. Roden and I and our remarkable collaboration being the feature of an unmitigatedly favorable review in the *New York Times* Sunday Book Review. I doubt that Ms. Roden had quite the same fantasy; I suspect she occasionally dreamed of her message being recited and declaimed before some suitably world-historical assembly. Such fantasies gave Araucaria some of its life force, but they were too disparate to endow it with its raison d'être. The millenarian and the infidel anthropologist had incompatible worlds of their dreams. Their synergy could not emerge from the oneiric. It could only emerge instead from the joint labor of proffering and recording with what both hoped to be the most accurate possible detail the events of the recent past and the near future. Ours was thus an enterprise of a distinctively contemporary inflection (cf. Rabinow 2008; Rabinow *et al.* 2008), even if we did not agree at all on the matter of their true import and significance. It could emerge only as the joint labor of producing and keeping and then bringing to light just those events, as each of us interpreted them. Araucaria thus has as its immanent telos a making public and a publicness. It had as its immanent dream that it would also gain and so – as Michael Warner persuasively has it – make a public in the very process (Warner 2002). But that would take work. That would require askêsis.

Substance

Araucaria had as its ethical substance a substance to which I have already alluded and what I will now explicitly call "voice," though I might be accused of a certain phonocentrism in doing so. To characterize its substance as that of recording alone is in any event insufficient. The record that Ms. Roden and I compiled was a necessary condition of publicity, but it was not sufficient. Nor was it yet communicative, not yet the communiqué that it would ultimately need to be in order to have a public not merely as its formal object but also as its concrete receptive corpus, in the present or in the future. It was in fragments. It was of disjoint chronologies of disjoint scales. It was replete with terms desperate for definition – not least, to the anthropologist himself. It was, in other words, thin and badly in need of thickening. On the one hand, it was far more extensive than *Shadows and Lights* would itself prove to be. The archive that I have on file includes what I would estimate to be some three thousand pages and measures some four hundred sixty cubic inches. My monograph is of much more modest dimensions. On the other hand, the record is much more minimal than *Shadows and Lights*. It is often redundant. Only in part – in its textualized parts, in Ms. Roden's and her predecessors' writings – does it have analytical direction. It certainly has no anthropological direction. Above all, it is a cacophony waiting to acquire the sonant virtues that would or at least could be exercised for rhetorical effect. The record that Ms. Roden and I compiled was meant to constitute the notes of an oratory, even if our expectations of the sort of assembly before which that oratory would have its delivery were, once again, notable for their divergence.

Giving voice has been in anthropological fashion for a couple of decades now and is usually understood as a giving of voice to those who are unable to gain a hearing – to the poor, the resourceless, the excluded; to the subaltern, the downtrodden, the displaced, the destitute. Endowing the voiceless with their voice is usually understood as a matter of the anthropologist acting as an agent – which is to say, a representative and an intermediary – on behalf of his or her subject. The anthropologist is a broker who has mastery of those competencies requisite to bringing his or her subjects' interest before their proper court. Or he or she is an intellectual, whether more traditional or more organic, articulating for subjects who cannot effectively do so what their objective interests are. Or he or she is a vehicle of recognition, of his or her subjects' right to be recognized, to be accorded dignity or respect or at the very least civil standing, to be extended the ethical chrism, to be brought in from the ethical cold. Acting in any of these capacities deserves recognition in its own right; it is itself in full accord with the themitical values of professional practice. Those who so act – I among them – also deserve reminding not merely of the risk of condescension that they run but also of the hubris that consists in being overconfident of having an impact of any consequence. These days, anthropologists tend to attract the attention largely of other anthropologists – if even that.

Whether for better or for worse, then, voice has all the trappings of the candidate for an ethical substance. It exists as a potential and a potential that permits of a large variety of modes of actualization. There is nothing about it that invites its being diagnosed as inherently evil or inherently good across all ethical domains.

System-theoretically, voice – giving it, being permitted to have it, actually having it – has a peculiar and perhaps unique intimacy with the most general conditions of communicative autopoiesis and so with the ethical domain as such. With the ideal-typical slave, who is precluded from any exercise of the conscious practice of freedom, the voiceless subject, or more precisely the subject precluded for one of any variety of reasons from exercising its voice, is by that fact alone incapable of acting as a constituent of communicative autopoiesis. The point stands even if voice is construed merely as its most literal manifestation – the direct or mediatized human voice. It can be made with greater force and more exhaustively if voice is construed as any technology of communication, from all of those we already know – written exchange, signed exchange, iconographic or even abstract aesthetic expression so long as it conveys meaning, or at least that it means something or other, in its design – and those that are yet to come. Yet just so, the universal distribution of the license of voicing is far from being a requirement of communicative autopoiesis. Systems theory renders understandable the temptation – and it is not merely an anthropological temptation – within the ethical cosmos in which we live, a cosmos dominated by generalized media of communication, to reify the universal distribution of voice as a cardinal themitical obligation. It allows us to understand how and why the capacity to have a voice, whether or not that capacity is in fact capable of actualization, can operate as a distinctively modern modality of the ethical chrism, satisfying at least the demand for a secularization of the chrism and of its indiscriminate humanization even if it proves of inadequate scope to those more vitalistic or utilitarian ethicists who care to extend the chrism well beyond the talkative precincts of the human itself.

Once again, however, systems theory falls short of providing a ticket with which to cash in an ought from an is. Not everyone needs a voice for autopoiesis to proceed apace. Indeed, the suppression or deprivation of voice can sometimes promote communicative autopoiesis. As has already been mentioned, a chorus of liars does not ceteris paribus promote the interests of autopoiesis. Many modern legislators of the themitical have correlatively found cause to suppress voices of "hatred" or "incitement" or "destructive falsity" – consider German and Canadian laws banning the denial of the holocaust – even if they run directly counter to the "freedom of speech" into which the themitical normativity of voice often finds modern translation. (It might be added that the revisionists from David Irving to Mahmoud Ahmadinejad who insist that the holocaust never really happened raise with particular acuity the problem of the application of the ethics of parrhêsia. The revisionists no doubt believe that they are speaking truth to power, or simply speaking the truth in spite of everything. Parrhêsia nevertheless requires of them – doesn't it? – to be speaking the truth in fact. Such objectivism imposes a strong condition on the practical realization of an ethics of parrhêsia. Foucault's devotion of so much of his final lectures at the Collège de France to the practical requirements and guarantees of an objective parrhêsia indicate that he was well aware of just how strong a condition was at issue. It is all the stronger if the parrhêsiast no longer has his daimon or patron deity to provide the imprimatur of his pronouncements.) The sheer – functionalist, nihilist – requirements of communicative autopoiesis are in fact probably compatible with the suppression of the majority of voices in a communicative collective, all the more so when voice has the autopoietic benefit of technologies of its production and reproduction that have minimal need of talkative operators. Such suppression also increases complexity, or does so to the extent that it meets resistance among the vocally suppressed – and it has often done so, even before the dominance of generalized media of communication and the abstractions they invite. We cannot legitimately infer even so that "we" – whoever or whatever that might be – are meant to voice. Carmelites remain among us and their vows of silence are not ceteris paribus either inhibitive of communicative autopoiesis or evil per se.

Voice is malleable. Proper voicing – whether aesthetically or oratorically or ethically proper – demands training and practice. It demands coaching and so pedagogy. It also invites if it does not always require the further directives and refinements of reflexive technologies. In all of these respects it is a precise ethical homologue of carnal appetites for the classical Greeks, the will for Augustine as for many others, or extreme sensitivity for Flaubert – though Sartre did not approach Flaubert's emotional affliction as an ethical substance – but more straightforwardly in any event for the Marquis of Fronteira and Alorna and even Constantine Cavafy.

Askêsis: pedagogical

Araucaria would have to be trained to speak as a millenarian – if by no means speaking in that voice alone. Nothing else was compatible with the autopoiesis of the communicative relationship in which it subsisted. Its psychological steering mechanisms – especially this one, writing now – thus had to face an initial problem of potentially unconquerable proportions. Good members of society hate listening to millenarians, much less giving them center stage. That they hate listening is not really very mysterious – though perhaps because of my early shock at the rabidity of the demonization of David Koresh (Faubion 1999a, 1999b) and my later enchantment with Ms. Roden, I have only recently come with full clarity to see the obvious for what it is. To wit: millenarians at their most consistent call for the abandonment of and imply the triviality of the most basic of those commitments that the good member of society – qua good member of society – embraces and must embrace. Millenarians have little time – literally and figuratively – for routinized institutions. They have equally little time for the themitically established, for legalism, for economy, for equality, for compromise. They dwell within the primal scene of crisis and the charismatic. They are unabashedly sovereigntist and there is almost always a sovereign among them, who far more rarely performatively sustains his or her charisma through the production of miracles than through the transgression of the themitical order, including the themitical order that at any particular moment he or she or it might have declared to be the law. Good citizens do not like the transgression of their themitical orders, and so sovereigntist a transgression of that order as the most self-consistent of millenarian transgressions are – thus the bulk of the empirical evidence warrants concluding – is very likely to provoke the good member of society's rage and disgust.

In our particular age of reason, the front line of assault on millenarian recalcitrance is not typically martial. The opinion that millenarians will eventually do away with themselves is for one thing widespread, even though their doing so is rare when not under martial assault. That opinion is itself a thing of the front line, at which the millenarian is precisely an enemy of reason, depraved or mad. It is not merely popular. In that earlier age of reason of a sort that was late imperial Rome, Tacitus famously attributes to the early Christian abominations and evil and things horrible and shameful (Tacitus 2009: 4.2–4.4). Norman Cohn offers an analogous if more psychologistic and thus more modern assessment of the millenarians of medieval Europe (Cohn 1970). A legion of professional psychologists continue to offer the same assessments of the millenarians in our contemporary midst. The diagnosis of madness is a declaration of the illegitimacy of voice. As Foucault has famously argued, it is a diagnosis that reduces the mad voice to the sole intelligibility of the symptom and so communicatively silences it (Foucault 2006). Araucaria's voice could not be informed by such a reduction. Had it been so, it simply would not have been the voice of the subject-in-relation that it was. Or to put the matter differently: had I written *Shadows and Lights* under the influence of the psychologists, Ms. Roden would have had no voice and Araucaria would not have existed. Instead, I wrote it under the influence of Foucault's *History of Madness* – a long-standing influence, needless to say.

As I trust I have already made clear, Ms. Roden was not the most consistent of millenarians, but was vulnerable to psychologistic reduction even so. What was the anthropologist to do? He let her speak, in written inscription, and did so at length. Or at least he reproduced her written inscription in an effort to let her speak. The effort seems not to have been a uniform success. At least some of the readers of *Shadows and Lights* (or so I've had word) do and can only hear Ms. Roden's speech as symptomatic. In his afterword to a volume in which, after *Shadows and Lights*, I had called again on Ms. Roden's example,

Robbins admits to as much in print (Faubion 2006; Robbins 2006). In any event, to further the same effort, counter-insurgently, the anthropologist developed a three-pronged critical analysis. It rested first in a genealogy of the hermeneutics of figurae, of type and antitype, from St. Paul forward, which informed Ms. Roden's Biblicist interpretation of the world-historical significance of events and persons past, present and future, including the person and antitype(s) that she was. That genealogy did not come off the top of the anthropologist's head. Professional and personal infidel, he had read passages of the Bible – either for the anthropological interest that such of his predecessors as Mary Douglas and Edmund Leach had found in them (Douglas 1966, 1999; Leach 1969) or as historical documents or, as we say, "as literature" – but had never studied it. He could recite certain of its pithier phrases but none of its lengthier passages. He had to learn its galaxy of details, just as he had to learn the history of the themes and variations of figural hermeneutics. It required lengthy and diverse askêseis.

Second, the anthropologist's counterattack rested in an argument extrapolated from though not explicitly made in *The History of Madness* and in *The Order of Things*, fairly obvious once you see it, that the rise of reason as we know it has gone hand in hand with the retraction of the sphere of legitimate gnosis – of experientially grounded knowledge – to an ever smaller and ever more this-worldly perceptual kernel. Third, it rested in the argument that the relatively recent delegitimation of millenarian gnosis – to which the mechanist-Biblicist and by all accounts paragon of sanity Isaac Newton had made what in his time was recognized to be a serious contribution – had its quite abrupt onset with the movement known as the New or Higher Criticism or, indeed, "hermeneutics." The New Critics insisted on reading the Bible as a historical document, the product of its multiple authors and their lives and times, a text of human production even though it might allow of a certain idealist access to properly religious truth. At the head of the movement were Protestant theologians ensconced in leading German universities in the latter half of the nineteenth century. The most likely of their inspirations – so the anthropologist had and would still have it – was the increasingly positive and increasingly widespread Jewish preoccupation with emancipation and, with it, the doctrines of the seventeenth-century messianic millenarian Sabbatai Sevi or Zevi or Levi (cf. Scholem 1971). The anthropologist had no idea whatsoever that he would be arguing for such an anti-Semitic inspiration of anti-millenarianism until his inquiry into the history of the epistemic delegitimation of millenarian reason in Europe brought him to the conjuncture of the emergence of the New Criticism with Sabbatian messianism. The revelation demanded further askêseis, largely of a scholarly sort. (It should be added that, as already suggested, the anthropologist is himself a practitioner of the New Criticism, and not only in his reading of the Bible; but [good scientist?] he refuses to regard it as God's truth.)

Training Araucaria into final form and full voice further required finding some means of giving voice to the more secular Ms. Roden as well as to the timid city boy who couldn't quite keep himself away from Mount Carmel. The askêsis demanded was less scholarly than stylistic – less a course in letters than in music and gymnastics. It had many false starts. It involved much shuffling of pages, codings and recodings, linearizations and relinearizations. It underwent much inscription and reinscription. It was not always informed by confidence in its progress or its rationale. In the end, it produced the only subject that its beings-in-relation could yield. It emerged as a thing of fragments. I would not go so far as to propose that it is schizophrenic, either in a pathological sense or in the more positive sense with which Deleuze and Guattari have endowed the schizophrenic of their post-subjectivational utopia (Deleuze and Guattari 1983). If only an assemblage, Araucaria sustains – at least to my mind – sufficient unity of voice and of form and function to merit the title of an integrated subject (thus this account). I would not go so far, either, to propose that Araucaria's voice is polyphonic, at least in the form and with the functions that Bakhtin advocated (Bakhtin 1984). At least, its voice is not the democratic multitude of Bakhtin's Dostoevskian epics. It might have been – but only at the cost of leaving Ms. Roden's writings without any defense but themselves. Democracy does not always incorporate and enfranchise its participants, much less its participants-in-relation, as vigorously as more socialist forms of governmentality, however much the latter risk condescension.

Araucaria's voice has its articulation somewhere between Deleuze and Guattari's and Bakhtin's utopias. If it is not quite of this world, this is because it has the timbres at once of the millenarian, marginal and liminal, and of the high seriousness of a forever small and minor science and of the academy at its most academic, privileged but still marginal, liminoid if not properly liminal. It is also an artifice – not merely the *fictio* that we now presume every monograph to be, but an apparition, the ghost of those conversations on the prairie in which the being-in-relation of which it is the voice was at its most animate. It shares the fate of every transubstantiation of field into text. It is doubly denatured, a voice at once displaced and disembodied. Not quite of this world, then – but it has no other world, either, in which to have an alternative hearing. Such is its reckoning.

Pedagogy: reflexive

In the field, in conversation, one reflects consciously only in pausing, if even then. More subliminally, if successfully and synergistically carried out, conversation is nevertheless itself a continually reflective enterprise, a mutual consideration that demands listening and, with listening, a mutual reconsideration, which may result in coming to know something that one did not previously know or in the realization that one does not really know what one previously presumed to know. In either case, conversation is thus a pedagogical exercise. Plato was the first to formalize its pedagogical dynamics. Like all such dynamics, all such askêseis, conversational dynamics take at least two to proceed. They constitute a technology of self, but also a technology of the formation of a subject-in-relation that, again, is irreducible to its relata. The conversational dynamics that Ms. Roden and I generated and sustained were of a modal piece with our being-in-relation. Ours was an improvisational pedagogy that resolved itself into a more routinized pedagogical partnership. It floundered at the moment that the structure of that partnership threatened a reversal of roles into which at least one of its constituents – or rather two, the anthropologist and I – could not even begin to find a way to settle.

Thus Araucaria began its afterlife and only in that afterlife came to its telos as public voice. That an ethical telos might be achieved only posthumously is a common conception. It is, for example, central to any Christian or Islamic ethics for which askêsis in this world or in the liminality of a purgatory has its ultimate ethical redemption in entry into paradise. Martial and other sacrificial ethics often meld the ethical telos with death itself – or at least with dying in the right way. Zen and certain Brahmanistic ethics conceive of an ethico-spiritual telos as being fulfilled in that death-in-life that is liberation from the wheel of desire, from passion and want and thus from suffering. None of these ethical systems is autopoietically bankrupt. The quest for an other-worldly paradise sustains a this-worldly conversation of impressively expansive proportions over such matters as how to gain access to it, how to know that one is able or likely to gain access to it or, if unable, how to live with the anxieties and limitations of ignorance. Martial ethics and their pacifist counterparts are in their successful autopoiesis ethics of the exemplary and very often of exemplars whom all might admire and praise and memorialize but relatively few – perhaps only extremely few – can ever fully exemplify. Creatures pass; communication in its cold comforts can nevertheless survive.

Such creatures as Araucaria might remain ethically active even in their posthumous purgatory, though they have available only a single technology of self-formation and self-reformation available to them. Moreover, such a creature rarely inspires the psychological steering mechanism or mechanisms that survive it to risk descending into the deeper levels of purgatory to deploy that technology on its behalf. The technology in question is that of revision. Its deployment is a strain at best, though the aspiring scholar fails to master it at his or her own peril. So, too, the aspiring scholar had better find the courage to make use of it at least in the limbo of what some of us euphemistically call the "pre-publication process" even if he or she remains too leery or too exhausted or too bored to proceed in the face of published reviews and commentaries to take the downward purgatorial stairs to the restudy or additional study, the revised edition or the subsequent article or monograph. As Marcus has observed, anthropologists used to undertake such extended labors far more frequently than they do at present (Marcus 1998: 233–245). I doubt that this is because anthropologists were formerly more courageous (well, perhaps) or less liable to fatigue or boredom than they are now. Sites have grown vague – all the more in the case at hand, when one of their most fascinating denizens has taken to the road in a recreational vehicle for parts mostly unknown. Anthropological programmatics have grown long in the tooth – though by way of partial conclusion, I deliver a polemic for their renewal. Questions have become more idiosyncratic or pro tempore. So, in the aftermath of the collapse of the World Trade Center towers, I spoke and wrote a generalist essay on the religious justification of violence (Faubion 2003). I have spoken on the idea of holy war and what I call "cosmologicopolitics." I have published another generalist essay on the semiotics of sacral action (Faubion 2006). Attending to the dietetic practices to which, through Seventh-day Adventism, Ms. Roden applies herself, I have formulated a plan of inquiry into the ethics (which should be understood in the plural here) of the godly body across the New Denominations of the past, the present and the near future. In all of these endeavors, my being-in-relation with Ms. Roden continues, but its key is increasingly minor. As for Araucaria, I would prefer that it not rest. I would prefer that it continue to have its haunts. But if it must rest, may it rest in peace.

Concluding remarks: for programmatic inquiries

In his dismissal of the historical anthropology that Jean-Paul Sartre develops in his *Critique of Dialectical Reason,* Claude Lévi-Strauss pronounces of historical inquiry itself:

It consists wholly in its method, which experience proves to be indispensable for cataloguing the elements of any structure whatever, human or non-human, in its entirety. It is therefore far from being the case that the search for intelligibility comes to an end in history as though this were its terminus. Rather, it is history that serves as the point of departure in any quest for intelligibility. As we say of certain careers, history may lead to anything, provided you get out of it. (Lévi-Strauss 1966: 262)

I do not advocate a return to the high rationalism that in part motivates Lévi-Strauss' relegation of historical inquiry to the domain of the mail clerk and short order cook. I do, however, want to suggest (and have good reason to believe that I am following Lévi-Strauss in doing so) that much of what Lévi-Strauss pronounces of such inquiry should also be pronounced of ethnographic inquiry, into which what used to be thought of as sociocultural anthropology has increasingly dissolved from the mid-1970s forward. The catalysts of that dissolution are diverse. Its outcomes are countervailing but their poles increasingly constant: on the one hand, a dogmatic cleaving to a conceptual repertoire of the anthropological past that is poorly suited to the anthropological present; on the other, the importation of conceptual repertoires from without, which often glitter but are rarely of the ethnographic indissolubility of anthropological gold – far from it. We are in need of giving the reconstitution of the anthropological at least a try, even if the effort does not and will never yield pure gold. I hope that in the preceding pages I have been able in at least one domain of inquiry to suggest how, why and with what risks and gains we might do so.

A perusal of my mental card file has yielded not a single instance of an ethnographic monograph that has succeeded through the deployment of its own substantive resources alone in establishing a generative programmatic – not just an analytical category or two, but a technology of disciplined question-formation. Those that have succeeded in doing so in the glorious Dreamtime of the anthropological past – from Malinowski's *Argonauts* (1922) to Leach's *Political Systems of Highland Burma* (1956) – have in every case had the support of one or another of the vastly abstract dichotomies, the master tropes or myths, in which we can no longer believe: traditional vs. rational; preconceptual vs. conceptual; the economy of status vs. the economy of material capital; above all, the primitive vs. the modern. Our disenchanted present began with a young generation of European intellectuals discovering in the immediate aftermath of the Second World War that the two prevailing programmatics of the first half of the twentieth century – Marxism and Freudianism – had both become licenses for the perpetration of abjection and slaughter. We are even more disenchanted – more bereft of the mythic scaffolding of vastly abstract dichotomies – now that we live in an epistemic and affective ecology whose hallmarks I have already suggested elsewhere include the collapse of the Soviet geopolitical system; the expansion of a geopolitical Europe and globalization and disorganized but culturally ever so thin capitalism; the double impulsion of both toward the deterritorialization of what remnants there might be of coherent cultural systems and the ever more normative individualization of the ever more normatively flexible citizens and subjects of a planet very much on the move; the ballooning of the suspicion that one has neither culture nor society to which to belong and so the increasing frequency with which anthropologists have been finding themselves summoned to act as secularized spiritual advisors to the human subjects of their research, which is often otherwise to be known as the blind leading the blind (Faubion 2009). Our contemporary ethnographicocentric ethnographies may well be full (chock full, speaking not only for myself) of analytical categories – they might indeed be called "theoretical" in just this sense – but their ecological fate seems consistently to be, and as Marcus has himself noted several times, that of the flash in the pan. Those that have the virtue of affirming the going moralistic fashion may hang on for awhile. The rest rapidly descend into the great mythological void in which nothing survives but history itself, which is to say the mere recording of one damn thing – and often more or less the same damn thing – after another. If our contemporary ethnographies are theoretical, then they are so without solid footing, and instead most often rely on a moralistic footing, which is one of the prevailing footings of which history itself can boast.

I had the recent opportunity – such as it was – to take a reading of the depth of our current descent when delivering a relentlessly programmatic lecture, mysteriously entitled "The Themitical in the Ethical: Groundwork for an Anthropology of Ethics," at one of the United States' leading universities. The response to the lecture – and I assure you that I took pains to define the "themitical" – was one that I estimate to be of the purity of Ivory soap – 99.44 percent. It was 99.44 percent bemused and even a bit hostile. What I have taken away from that experience – beyond yet another reminder of my esotericism – is that we have lost the conventions of the reception of the programmatic (though we're quite good at theory shopping) and, a fortiori, the art of fashioning it. The anthropology of ethics as it has emerged in the past eight or nine years is a limit-case of such loss, precisely because it is so perilously close and always in danger of subordinating itself to one of the most programmatic discourses we have and have ever had – that of the ontology and the metaphysics of practical reason, or what, again, passes in summary as moral philosophy or ethics. I hope that in the preceding pages I have established the programmatics not of the only but of one generative alternative.

Though I reserve a more complete development of the theme for a later publication, I end here with the beginnings of an explicit clarification of four distinctive modes of the construction of theory – of conceptual apparatuses of broader scope than that of the empirical illustrations or evidence on which they call – that, rendered explicit, might facilitate at once the readier and more clear-headed reception of theoretically driven analysis and the programmatic construction of such analysis. The four modes are not mutually exclusive, but do allow of being distinguished. I am not the first to make note of or to take the steps formally to characterize one or another of them. I offer all four here, however, as distinctive genres of programmatization, each suitable to particular purposes, none without its shortcomings, but each of passing legitimacy in its own right. I do not pretend to be exhaustive, but claim only that at least these four genres remain current. One I call referential – structured above all to sustain strict commensurability between concepts and the empirical tokens they encompass. Another I have been calling and continue to call here model-theoretic – structured above all to articulate the systematicity of phenomena that may but more often do not exhibit systematicity stricto sensu. The third I call tendential – structured above all to highlight processual tendencies within broader empirical fields, whether or not such tendencies are fully realized in the field under review. The last I have been calling and continue to call here diagnostic, but it could also be called interpretive – structured above all to bring to static as to processual phenomena categories that illuminate them contextually but are not determined by them.

In anthropology as in social and cultural theory self-appointed as such, purely referential conceptual apparatuses are now rare. They are the least current of any of the genres I have in mind and are so in part because they too easily attract the disparagement of being "positivist." In the USA, their primary social scientific nests lie within such disciplines as sociology, political science and experimental psychology. They are marked by and intimately compatible with statistical methods of representation and statistical inference. They give pride of place to the epistemic virtue of reliability – of empirical determinacy and empirically confirmable replicability. Just for that reason, they are often wanting of robustness – of conceptual reach and connectivity and of programmatic generativity. They are often micro-scalar: much of the work that passes as actor network theory is referentialist in character. I am not a devoted referentialist (a pronouncement that can come to the reader who has made it this far as no surprise). In addressing many of the questions that my empirical investigations dare not beg, however, I cannot do without referentialist results. Such results allow for the sketching of broader structural contexts that the periscope of fieldwork itself can only glimpse in small part. As a Europeanist, I have to have frequent resort to Eurostat.

Model theoretic apparatuses are very much with us, though they often attract referentialist criticism for being too abstract, too far removed from the plain facts, logical when well wrought at the expense of being adequately empirically sensitive. Bourdieu's theory of practice – as Bourdieu was aware, even if many of his readers have not been – is a model-theoretic apparatus of commanding order. Durkheim's inquiry into the elementary forms of the religious life is its ultimate ancestral precedent, though not an exact homologue. Bourdieu's presiding purpose is that of articulating the logic of the causality of the reproduction of both symbolic and material domination. It is a statistical model in Bourdieu's own considered reckoning in operating with variables that are a selection from but not exhaustive of the variables (of individual human actors and particular human actions) that are immanent to the empirical domain of which it is the intended model. It can incorporate statistical methods of illustration – Bourdieu makes a good show, but only what statisticians proper can regard as a show, of doing so in *Distinction* – but as supplementary devices, as monitors of the proximity of the model to what it is intended to model. Habermas' chief later works are model-theoretic. Luhmann's systems theory is also model-theoretic – to the hilt. The scope, range and sheer bulk of Bourdieu's, Habermas' and Luhmann's conceptual work is testament to the typical robustness of the model-theoretic genre. Unsympathetic readers may take it also to be a testament to its typical unreliability.

Tendential theorists are legion in contemporary social and cultural thought. Anthony Giddens is a model theoretician in *The Constitution of Society* (1986), but is a tendentialist in *Modernity and Self-Identity* (1991) and *The Transformation of Intimacy* (1993). Peter Sloterdijk is a tendentialist in his *Critique of Cynical Reason* (1987). David Harvey is a tendentialist in his *Condition of Postmodernity* and Michael Hardt and Antonio Negri are tendentialists in *Empire*. Foucault's genealogical investigations of the birth of the clinic (1994) and the prison are largely tendentialist. Like their model-theoretic cousins, tendential apparatuses favor robustness over reliability. Like those cousins, they attend to systematicity, but their models are always models of open systems and so of necessity referentially indeterminate. Again like those same cousins, they may or may not devote themselves to the interpretive enterprise of understanding the subjects or objects of their analysis, but are always directed toward accounting for how those subjects or objects have come into being; they are intended whatever else to be explanatory. What they cannot yield is the whole picture of their investigative field, even of its logic. They are thus often charged with being partial – which they are.

I borrow the term diagnostics from Geertz, who borrowed it in turn from medicine and chose it as one if not the only characterization of his own interpretive enterprise. He distinguished it from "cryptography" and put it forward instead as:

> a science that can determine the meaning of things for the life that surrounds them. It will have, of course, to be trained on signification, not pathology, and treat with ideas, not with symptoms. But by connecting incised statues, pigmented sago palms, frescoed walls, and chanted verse to jungle clearing, totem rites, commercials, or street argument, it can perhaps begin at last to locate in the tenor of their settings the sources of their spell. (1983: 120)

Geertz's is a stylish way of casting the dynamic of interpretive context-ualization and, with diagnostics, the more general model of its cardinal directive. It is, it seems to me, as good a way as any to cast the lineaments of a genre that allows of much internal plurality and even some measure of internal inconsistency. More recently, Paul Rabinow and Gaymon Bennett have formulated a "diagnostics" that derives neither from Geertz nor from medicine but instead from John Dewey and many others – Foucault included. (Find their work at en.scientificcommons.org/paul_rabinow.) Across the board, diagnos-tics range over a phenomenal domain that is always underdetermined by its empirical manifestations; they are thus never strictly referential. As Geertz plied it at least in his earlier interpretive career, it is not concerned to model. More carefully, it is not concerned to explicate the formal logic or the grammar of semiotic fields (in Geertz's endur-ing opinion, no logic of a formal character informs such fields), nor to explicate their semantics. It is instead an enterprise in semiotic pragmatics, concerned first and foremost with semiotics in practice. Diagnostics thus construed tends to fill rigorous referentialists with scientistic horror. Bourdieu consigned them (not very fairly, at least in Geertz's case) to the dungeon of subjectivism. Diagnostics nevertheless shares with its model-theoretic and its tendential counterparts a favoring of the robust over the reliable. Moreover, should model theoreticians or tendentialists seek an understanding of the semiotics of the practices (discursive and non-discursive) over which their models are intended to operate, they will have to find themselves tapping at least some of the array of specifically diagnostic resources. Only diagnostics can lead to the understanding that is for Geertz the epistemic telos of an interpretive anthropology. What it cannot yield in its own terms is an accounting, an explanation of any of the phenomena that it scrutinizes. Explanation must come generically from elsewhere.

The program that has been operative from the second through the fifth chapters of what has preceded is a combination of model-theoretic and diagnostic genres, with a bit of the tendential thrown in to boot. It tilts strongly – though not, I think, to the verge of polar mania – toward the robust; it favors the formation of questions over the definitive resolution of their answers. It is strongly invested in understanding, which I would follow Geertz and many others in characterizing as unfolding and possibly unfolding only on the plane of the intersubjective. In the interest of avoiding the epistemological limitations and the ontological excesses of many of the diagnostics – Geertz's included – currently available, it is just as strongly invested in venturing the beginnings of an accounting for, of a model-theoretical explanation of the range of the possible variations within the ethical domain in both its semiological and its practical realizations. It might look to be the apparatus of someone who wants to have his cake and eat it, too – but then, why shouldn't someone want that, at least so long as he or she might get it?

But rather than close on such a dangerously rhetorical note, I will close instead as I began. The apparatus that I have fashioned in the course of inquiring into how ethical subjects come into being as ethical subjects and what becomes (of) them once they do is simply one apparatus among many possible others. It is simply one combination of many other possible combinations of the referential, the model-theoretic, the tendential and the diagnostic modes of thinking about and thinking through the phenomena that lie within – and for that matter, that must lie outside of – the ethical domain. I sincerely hope that other combinations, other recipes of inquiry come to fruition – not at all least, because much work still remains to be done.

References

Abrams, H. M. 1971. *Natural Supernaturalism: Tradition and Revolution in Romantic Literature.* New York: Norton.

Abu-Lughod, Lila. 1986. *Veiled Sentiments: Honor and Poetry in a Bedouin Society.* Berkeley: University of California Press.

Adkins, A. W. H. 1960. *Merit and Responsibility: A Study in Greek Values.* Oxford: Clarendon Press.

    1972. *Moral Values and Political Behaviour in Ancient Greece: From Homer to the End of the Fifth Century.* New York: W. W. Norton.

Agamben, Giorgio. 1998. *Homo Sacer: Sovereign Power and Bare Life.* Trans. Daniel Heller-Roazen. Stanford University Press.

Aischines. 1919. *The Speeches of Aischines.* Trans. Charles Darwin Adams. Loeb Classical Library 106. Cambridge, Mass.: Harvard University Press.

Althusser, Louis. 1971. *Lenin and Philosophy and Other Essays.* Trans. Ben Brewster. New York: Monthly Review Press.

Anacreon. 1988. *Greek Lyric II: Anacreon, Anacreonta, Early Choral Lyric.* Loeb Classical Library 143. Ed. and trans. David A. Campbell. Cambridge, Mass.: Harvard University Press.

Anonymous. 1911. Hartmann, Karl Robert Eduard von. In *Encyclopedia Britannica.* Volume XIII. 11th edition, p. 36. Cambridge University Press.

Arendt, Hannah. 1998. *The Human Condition.* 2nd edition. University of Chicago Press.

Aristotle. 1934. *The Nicomachean Ethics.* Trans. H. Rackham. Loeb Classical Library 73. Cambridge, Mass.: Harvard University Press.

    1944. *Politics.* Revised edition. Trans. H. Rackham. Loeb Classical Library 264. Cambridge, Mass.: Harvard University Press.

Asad, Talal. 1986. The concept of translation in British social anthropology. In *Writing Culture: The Poetics and Politics of Ethnography,* ed. James Clifford and George E. Marcus, pp. 141–164. Berkeley: University of California Press.

References

1993. *Genealogies of Religion: Discipline and Reasons of Power in Christianity and Islam*. Baltimore: Johns Hopkins University Press.

Ayer, Alfred Jules. 1946. *Language, Truth and Logic*. New York: Dover.

Badiou, Alain. 2001. *Ethics: An Essay on the Understanding of Evil*. Trans. Peter Hallward. London: Verso.

Bakhtin, Mikhail. 1984. *Problems of Dostoevsky's Poetics: Polyphony and Unfinalizability*. Ed. and trans. Caryl Emerson. Minneapolis: University of Minnesota Press.

Barnes, Jonathon. 1979. *The Presocratic Philosophers*. Volume 1: *Thales to Zeno*. London: Routledge and Kegan Paul.

Battaglia, Debbora. 1995. *Rhetorics of Self-making*. Berkeley: University of California Press.

Baumann, Zygmunt. 1993. *Postmodern Ethics*. Oxford: Blackwell.

Beck, Ulrich, Anthony Giddens and Scott Lash. 1994. *Reflexive Modernization: Politics, Aesthetics and Tradition in the Modern Social Order*. Stanford University Press.

Behar, Ruth. 2003. *Translated Woman: Crossing the Border with Esperanza's Story*. Boston: Beacon Press.

Behrend, Heike. 1999. *Alice Lakwena and the Holy Spirits: War in Northern Uganda, 1985–1997*. Trans. Mitch Cohen. Oxford: James Currey.

Bellah, Robert. 1957. *Tokugawa Religion: The Cultural Roots of Modern Japan*. New York: The Free Press.

1972 (1964). Religious evolution. In *Readings on Premodern Societies*, ed. Victor Lidz and Talcott Parsons, pp. 31–50. Englewood Cliffs, N.J.: Prentice-Hall.

Biehl, João. 2005. *Vita: Life in a Zone of Social Abandonment*. Berkeley: University of California Press.

Boddy, Janice. 1989. *Wombs and Alien Spirits: Women, Men and the Zâr Cult in Northern Sudan*. Madison: University of Wisconsin Press.

Boellstorff, Tom. 2005. *The Gay Archipelago: Sexuality and Nation in Indonesia*. Princeton University Press.

Boltanski, Luc, and Eve Chiapello. 2005. *The New Spirit of Capitalism*. Trans. Gregory Elliott. London: Verso.

Bourdieu, Pierre. 1977. *Outline of a Theory of Practice*. Trans. Richard Nice. Cambridge University Press.

1984. *Distinction: A Social Critique of the Judgement of Taste*. Trans. Richard Nice. Cambridge, Mass.: Harvard University Press.

1990. *The Logic of Practice*. Trans. Richard Nice. Cambridge: Polity Press.

1991. Genesis and structure of the religious field. In *Comparative Social Research*, Volume XIII, ed. Craig Calhoun, pp. 1–44. Greenwich, Conn.: JAI Press.

Boyer, Paul. 1992. *When Time Shall Be No More: Prophecy Belief in American Culture.* Cambridge, Mass.: Belknap Press.

Bradshaw, Leah. 1991. Political rule, prudence and the "woman question" in Aristotle. *Canadian Journal of Political Science* 24:3(September): 557–573.

Brandes, Stanley. 1980. *Metaphors of Masculinity: Sex and Status in Andalusian Folklore.* Philadelphia: University of Pennsylvania Press.

Brown, Peter. 1980. *The Cult of the Saints: Its Rise and Function in Latin Christianity.* University of Chicago Press.

——— 1982. *Society and the Holy in Late Antiquity.* Berkeley: University of California Press.

——— 1988. *The Body and Society: Men, Women, and Sexual Renunciation in Early Christianity.* New York: Columbia University Press.

——— 1995. *Authority and the Sacred: Aspects of the Christianisation of the Roman World.* Cambridge University Press.

——— 2003. *The Rise of Western Christendom: Triumph and Diversity,* AD 200–1000. Maiden, Mass.: Blackwell.

Butler, Judith. 1993. *Bodies that Matter: On the Discursive Limits of "Sex."* New York: Routledge.

Canguilhem, Georges. 1989. *The Normal and the Pathological.* Trans. Carolyn R. Fawcett, in collaboration with Robert S. Cohen. New York: Zone Books.

Certeau, Michel de. 1984. *The Practice of Everyday Life.* Trans. Steven Rendall. Berkeley: University of California Press.

Cohen, David. 1991. *Law, Sexuality, and Society: The Enforcement of Morals in Classical Athens.* Cambridge University Press.

Cohn, Norman. 1970. *The Pursuit of the Millennium: Revolutionary Anarchists and Mystical Anarchists of the Middle Ages.* Revised edition. New York: Oxford University Press.

Connelly, Joan Breton. 2007. *Portrait of a Priestess: Women and Ritual in Ancient Greece.* Princeton University Press.

Crapanzano, Vincent. 1980. *Tuhami: Portrait of a Moroccan.* University of Chicago Press.

Daniel, E. Valentine. 1984. *Fluid Signs: Being a Person the Tamil Way.* Berkeley: University of California Press.

Davidson, James. 2007. *The Greeks and Greek Love: A Radical Reappraisal of Homosexuality in Ancient Greece.* London: Weidenfeld and Nicolson.

Davis, Elizabeth. Forthcoming. *Bad Souls: An Ethnography of Madness and Responsibility in Greek Thrace.* Durham, N.C.: Duke University Press.

Deleuze, Gilles, and Félix Guattari. 1983. *Anti-Oedipus: Capitalism and Schizophrenia.* Volume 1. Trans. Robert Hurley, Mark Seem and Helen R. Lane. Minneapolis: University of Minnesota Press.

References

Derrida, Jacques. 1974. *Of Grammatology*. Trans. Gayatri Chakravorty Spivak. Baltimore: Johns Hopkins University Press.

Diogenes Laertius. 1931. *Lives of the Eminent Philosophers*. Volume II. Loeb Classical Library 185. Ed. Jeffrey Herderson. Trans. R. D. Hicks. Cambridge, Mass.: Harvard University Press.

———. 1972. *Lives of Eminent Philosophers*. Volume I. Loeb Classical Library 184. Ed. G. P. Good. Trans. R. D. Hicks. Cambridge, Mass.: Harvard University Press.

Dodds, E. R. 1951. *The Greeks and the Irrational*. Berkeley: University of California Press.

Douglas, Mary. 1966. The abominations of Leviticus. In Douglas, *Purity and Danger: An Analysis of the Concepts of Pollution and Taboo*, pp. 41–57. London: Routledge and Kegan Paul.

———. 1970. *Natural Symbols: Explorations in Cosmology*. New York: Vintage Books.

———. 1999. *Leviticus as Literature*. Oxford University Press.

Douglas, Mary, and Aaron Wildavsky. 1982. *Risk and Culture: An Essay on the Selection of Technical and Environmental Dangers*. Berkeley: University of California Press.

Dover, Kenneth J. 1974. *Greek Popular Morality in the Time of Plato and Aristotle*. Berkeley: University of California Press.

———. 1978. *Greek Homosexuality*. New York: Vintage Books.

Dreyfus, Hubert. 1992. *What Computers Still Can't Do: A Critique of Artificial Reason*. Cambridge, Mass.: MIT Press.

Dumont, Louis. 1980. *Homo Hierarchicus: The Caste System and its Implications*. Revised edition. Trans. Mark Saintsbury, Louis Dumont and Basia Gulati. Chicago University Press.

———. 1986. *Essays on Individualism: Modern Identity in Anthropological Perspective*. Translation of *Essais sur l'individualisme*. University of Chicago Press.

Durkheim, Emile. 1995. *The Elementary Forms of the Religious Life*. Trans. Karen E. Fields. New York: The Free Press.

Elias, Norbert. 2000. *The Civilizing Process: Sociogenetic and Psychogenetic Investigations*. Trans. Edmund Jephcott. Ed. Eric Dunning, Johan Goudsblom and Stephen Mennell. Oxford: Blackwell.

Emerson, Ralph Waldo. 2000. Self-reliance. In *The Essential Writings of Ralph Waldo Emerson*, ed. Brooks Atkinson, pp. 132–153. New York: The Modern Library.

Evans, T. M. S. 1999. Bourdieu and the logic of practice: Is all giving "Indian-giving" or is "generalized materialism" not enough? *Sociological Theory* **17**:1: 3–31.

Faubion, James D. 1993. *Modern Greek Lessons: A Primer in Historical Constructivism*. Princeton University Press.

1999a. Deus absconditus: Conspiracy (theory), millennialism, and the (end of the) twentieth century. In *Late Editions*. Volume VI: *Conspiracy/Theories*, ed. George E. Marcus, pp. 375–404. University of Chicago Press.

1999b. Figuring David Koresh. In *Critical Anthropology Now*, ed. George E. Marcus, pp. 89–122. Santa Fe: Seminar for American Research Press.

2001a. Introduction: Toward an anthropology of the ethics of kinship. In *The Ethics of Kinship: Ethnographic Inquiries*, ed. James D. Faubion, pp. 1–28. Lanham, Md.: Rowman and Littlefield.

2001b. *The Shadows and Lights of Waco: Millennialism Today*. Princeton University Press.

2001c. Toward an anthropology of ethics: Foucault and the pedagogies of autopoiesis. *Representations* **74** (Special Issue: Philosophies in Time): 83–104.

2003. Religion, violence, and the economy of the vital. *Anthropological Quarterly* **76**:1: 71–85.

2005. Spiritual biopolitics. Paper presented at the 104th meetings of the American Anthropological Association, Washington, D.C., December 1.

2006. Paranomics: On the semiotics of sacral action. In *Christian Ritual and the Limits of Meaning*, ed. Matthew Engelke and Matthew Tomlinson, pp. 189–209. Oxford: Berghahn.

2008a. Heterotopia: An ecology. In *Heterotopia and the City: Public Space in a Postcivil Society*, ed. M. Dehaene and L. De Cauter, pp. 31–39. London: Routledge.

2008b. Homo absconditus: Lévi-Strauss und Foucault. *Wirkungen des wilden Denkens: zur strukturalen Anthropologie von Claude Lévi-Strauss*, ed. Michael Kauppert and Dorett Funcke, pp. 81–97. Frankfurt am Main: Suhrkamp Taschenbuch Wissenschaft.

2009. The ethics of fieldwork as an ethics of connectivity, or the Good anthropologist (isn't what she used to be). In *Fieldwork Is Not What It Used to Be: Learning Anthropology's Method in a Time of Transition*, ed. James D. Faubion and George E. Marcus, pp. 145–164. Ithaca: Cornell University Press.

Faubion, James D., and Jennifer A. Hamilton. 2007. Sumptuary kinship. *Anthropological Quarterly* **80**: 533–559.

Faubion, James D., and George E. Marcus. 2007. Constructionism in anthropology. In *Handbook of Constructionism*, ed. James Holstein and Jay Graber, pp. 67–84. New York: Guilford.

Feld, Stephen, and Keith Basso, eds. 1996. *Senses of Place*. Santa Fe: School for American Research.

Finley, Moses I. 1954. *The World of Odysseus*. New York: Viking Press.

Fischer, Michael M. J. 2003. *Emergent Forms of Life and the Anthropological Voice*. Durham, N.C.: Duke University Press.

References

Foerster, Heinz von. 1974. *Cybernetics of Cybernetics*. Urbana, Ill.: University of Illinois Press.

Foucault, Michel. 1970. *The Order of Things: An Archaeology of the Human Sciences*. A translation of *Les mots et les choses*. New York: Random House.

——— 1972. *The Archeology of Knowledge and the Discourse on Language*. Trans. A. M. Sheridan Smith. New York: Pantheon.

——— 1977. *Discipline and Punish: The Birth of the Prison*. Trans. Alan Sheridan. New York: Vintage Books.

——— 1978. *The History of Sexuality*. Volume I: *An Introduction*. Trans. Robert Hurley. New York: Pantheon.

——— 1985. *The History of Sexuality*. Volume II: *The Use of Pleasure*. Trans. Robert Hurley. New York: Pantheon.

——— 1986. *The History of Sexuality*. Volume III: *The Care of the Self*. Trans. Robert Hurley. New York: Vintage Books.

——— 1994. *The Birth of the Clinic: An Archaeology of Medical Perception*. Trans. A. M. Sheridan Smith. New York: Vintage Books.

——— 1997a. The ethics of the concern of the self as a practice of freedom. In *Essential Works of Michel Foucault*. Volume I: *Ethics: Subjectivity and Truth*, series ed. Paul Rabinow, ed. Paul Rabinow, pp. 281–302. New York: The New Press.

——— 1997b. On the genealogy of ethics: Overview of a work in progress. In *Essential Works of Michel Foucault*. Volume I: *Ethics: Subjectivity and Truth*, series ed. Paul Rabinow, ed. Paul Rabinow, pp. 253–280. New York: The New Press.

——— 1997c. Self-writing. In *Essential Works of Michel Foucault*. Volume I: *Ethics: Subjectivity and Truth*, series ed. Paul Rabinow, ed. Paul Rabinow, pp. 207–222. New York: The New Press.

——— 1997d. Technologies of the self. In *Essential Works of Michel Foucault*. Volume I: *Ethics: Subjectivity and Truth*, series ed. Paul Rabinow, ed. Paul Rabinow pp. 223–252. New York: The New Press.

——— 1998. Life: Experience and science. In *Essential Works of Michel Foucault*. Volume II: *Aesthetics, Method, Epistemology*, series ed. Paul Rabinow, ed. James D. Faubion, pp. 465–478. New York: The New Press.

——— 2000a. Questions of method. In *Essential Works of Michel Foucault*. Volume III: *Power*, series ed. Paul Rabinow, ed. James D. Faubion, pp. 223–238. New York: The New Press.

——— 2000b. The subject and power. In *Essential Works of Michel Foucault*. Volume III: *Power*. Series ed. Paul Rabinow, ed. James D. Faubion, pp. 326–348. New York: The New Press.

2005. *The Hermeneutics of the Subject.* Gen eds. François Ewald and Alessandro Fontana. Ed. Frédéric Gros. English Series ed. Arnold I. Davidson. Trans. Graham Burchell. New York: Macmillan Palgrave.

2006 (1961). *History of Madness.* Ed. Jean Khalfa. Trans. Jonathon Murphy and Jean Khalfa. New York: Routledge.

2008. *Le gouvernement de soi et des autres.* Paris: Seuil/Gallimard.

2009. *Le courage de la vérité. Le gouvernement de soi et des autres II.* Paris: Gallimard.

Freyre, Gilberto. 1956 (1933). *The Masters and the Slaves: A Study in the Development of Brazilian Civilization.* Trans. Samuel Putnam. New York: Alfred A. Knopf.

Fustel de Coulanges, Numa Denis. 1980. *The Ancient City: A Study on the Religion, Laws, and Institutions of Greece and Rome.* A Translation of *La cité antique.* Baltimore: Johns Hopkins University Press.

Gallagher, Tom. 1981. The 1979 Portuguese general election. *Luso-Brazilian Review* **18**: 253–262.

Geertz, Clifford. 1960. *The Religion of Java.* University of Chicago Press.

1963. *Peddlers and Princes: Social Development and Economic Change in Two Indonesian Towns.* University of Chicago Press.

1968. *Islam Observed: Religious Development in Morocco and Indonesia.* New Haven: Yale University Press.

1973. *The Interpretation of Cultures.* New York: Basic Books.

1983. *Local Knowledge: Further Essays in Interpretive Anthropology.* New York: Basic Books.

Gellner, Ernest. 1970. Concepts and society. In *Rationality,* ed. Bryan Wilson, pp. 18–49. Evanston, Ill.: Harper and Row.

Genet, Jean. 2008 (1943). *Our Lady of the Flowers.* Trans. Bernard Fechtman. New York: Grove Press.

George, Frederico H., and Jorge N. Bastos. 1993. *The Palácio Fronteira North Loggia Restoration Process.* Report for the International Association for Bridge and Structural Engineering Symposium, Rome, Italy. Zurich:/ABSE.

Giddens, Anthony. 1986. *The Constitution of Society: Outline of the Theory of Structuration.* Berkeley: University of California Press.

1991. *Modernity and Self-identity: Self and Society in the Late Modern Age.* Cambridge: Polity Press.

1993. *The Transformation of Intimacy: Love, Sexuality and Eroticism in Modern Societies.* Stanford University Press.

Goffman, Erving. 1959. *The Presentation of the Self in Everyday Life.* New York: Doubleday.

References

1963. *Stigma: Notes on the Management of Spoiled Identity.* Englewood Cliffs, N.J.: Prentice-Hall.

Goody, Jack. 1983. *The Development of the Family and Marriage in Europe.* Cambridge University Press.

Graeber, David. 2001. *Toward an Anthropological Theory of Value: The False Coin of Our Own Dreams.* New York: Palgrave.

Greenway, Christine. 1998. Hungry earth and vengeful stars: soul loss and identity in the Peruvian Andes. *Social Sciences and Medicine* **47**: 993–1004.

Griaule, Marcel. 1965. *Conversations with Ogotemmêli: An Introduction to Dogon Religious Ideas.* Translation of *Dieu d'eau: entretiens avec Ogotemmêli.* London: Oxford University Press.

Griffiths, Paul E. 1997. *What Emotions Really Are: The Problem of Psychological Categories.* University of Chicago Press.

Gutmann, Matthew. 1996. *The Meaning of Macho: Being a Man in Mexico City.* Berkeley: University of California Press.

Habermas, Jürgen. 1984. *The Theory of Communicative Action.* Trans. Thomas McCarthy. Boston: Beacon Press.

Hallowell, I. A. 1960. Ojibwa ontology, behavior and worldview. In *Culture in History: Essays in Honor of Paul Radin*, ed. Stanley Diamond, pp. 19–52. New York: Columbia University Press.

Halperin, David M. 1990. *One Hundred Years of Homosexuality and Other Essays on Greek Love.* New York: Routledge.

Harding, Susan Friend. 2000. *The Book of Jerry Falwell: Fundamentalist Language and Politics.* Princeton University Press.

Hardt, Michael, and Antonio Negri. 2000. *Empire.* Cambridge, Mass.: Harvard University Press.

Hare, R. M. 1967. The promising game. In *Theories of Ethics*, ed. Philippa Foot, pp. 115–127. Oxford University Press.

Harvey, David. 1990. *The Condition of Postmodernity: An Enquiry into the Origins of Cultural Change.* Cambridge, Mass.: Blackwell.

Hatch, Elvin. 1983. *Culture and Morality: The Relativity of Values in Anthropology.* New York: Columbia University Press.

Havelock, Eric A. 1963. *A History of the Greek Mind.* Volume 1: *Preface to Plato.* Cambridge, Mass.: Harvard University Press.

1982. *The Literate Revolution in Greece and its Cultural Consequences.* Princeton University Press.

Hegel, G. W. F. 1952. *The Philosophy of Right.* Trans. T. M. Knox. In *Hegel.* Great Books of the Western World **46**. Ed. Mortimer J. Adler. University of Chicago Press.

Heidegger, Martin. 1962. *Being and Time*. Trans. John Macquarrie and Edward Robinson. San Francisco: Harper San Francisco.

Herodotus. 1987. *The History*. Trans. David Grene. University of Chicago Press.

Herzfeld, Michael. 1985. *The Poetics of Manhood: Contest and Identity in a Cretan Mountain Village*. Princeton University Press.

——— 1997. *Portrait of a Greek Imagination: An Ethnographic Biography of Andreas Nenedakis*. University of Chicago Press.

Hesiod. 1983. *Theogony, Works and Days, Shield*. Trans. Apostolos N. Athanassakis. Baltimore: Johns Hopkins University Press.

Hobsbawm, Eric J. 1963. *Primitive Rebels: Studies in Archaic Forms of Social Movements in the 19th and 20th Centuries*. New York: Praeger.

Holmes, Douglas R. 2000. *Integral Europe: Fast-Capitalism, Multiculturalism, Neofascism*. Princeton University Press.

Holmes, Douglas, and George E. Marcus. 2005. Cultures of expertise and the management of globalization: toward a re-functioning of ethnography. In *Global Assemblages: Technology, Politics, and Ethics as Anthropological Problems*, ed. Aihwa Ong and Stephen Collier, pp. 235–252. Malden, Mass.: Blackwell.

——— 2006. Fast capitalism: paraethnography and the rise of the symbolic analyst. In *Frontiers of Capital: Ethnographic Perspectives on the New Economy*, ed. Melissa Fisher and Gary Downey, pp. 33–57. Durham, N.C.: Duke University Press.

Holston, James, ed. 1999. *Cities and Citizenship*. Durham, N.C.: Duke University Press.

——— 2008. *Insurgent Citizenship: Disjunctions of Democracy and Modernity in Brazil*. Princeton University Press.

Holton, Kimberley DaCosta. 2002. Bearing material witness to musical sound: Fado's L94 museum project. *Luso-Brazilian Review* **39**:2: 107–123.

Homer. 1951. *The Iliad of Homer*. Trans. Richmond Lattimore. University of Chicago Press.

Howell, Signe. 1997. Introduction. In *The Ethnography of Moralities*, ed. Signe Howell, pp. 1–24. London: Routledge.

Humphrey, Caroline. 1997. Exemplars and rules: Aspects of the discourse of moralities in Mongolia. In *The Ethnography of Moralities*, ed. Signe Howell, pp. 25–48. London: Routledge.

Hunter, Virginia. 1994. *Policing Athens: Social Control in the Attic Lawsuits, 420–320 BC*. Princeton University Press.

Jakobson, Roman, and John Lotz. 1949. Notes on the French phonemic pattern. *Word* **5**: 151–185.

Kant, Immanuel. 1933. *Immanuel Kant's Critique of Pure Reason*. Trans. Norman Kemp Smith. London: Macmillan.

References

1952. *The Critique of Judgement.* Trans. James Creed Meredith. In *Kant.* Great Books of the Western World **42**. Ed. Mortimer J. Adler. University of Chicago Press.

2002. *Critique of Practical Reason.* Trans. Werner S. Pluhar. Indianapolis: Hackett.

Keane, Webb. 2007. *Christian Moderns: Freedom and Fetish in the Mission Encounter.* Berkeley: University of California Press.

Kelty, Christopher, with Hannah Landecker, Ebru Kayaalp, Anthony Potoczniak *et al.* 2008. Collaboration, coordination, and composition: fieldwork after the Internet. In *Fieldwork Is Not What It Used to Be: Learning Anthropology's Method in a Time of Transition,* ed. James D. Faubion and George E. Marcus, pp. 184–106. Ithaca: Cornell University Press.

Keuls, Eva. 1985. *The Reign of the Phallus: Sexual Politics in Ancient Athens.* Berkeley: University of California Press.

Kirtsoglou, Elizabeth. 2004. *For the Love of Women: Gender, Identity and Same-sex Relations in a Greek Provincial Town.* New York: Routledge.

Konner, Melvin. 1988. *Becoming a Doctor: A Journey of Initiation into Medical School.* New York: Penguin.

Koselleck, Reinhart. 1985. *Futures Past: On the Semantics of Historical Time.* Trans. Keith Tribe. Cambridge, Mass.: MIT Press.

Kripal, Jeffrey J. 2001. *Roads of Excess, Palaces of Wisdom: Eroticism and Reflexivity in the Study of Mysticism.* University of Chicago Press.

Kuper, Adam. 1988. *The Invention of the Primitive: Transformations of an Illusion.* London: Routledge.

Kurke, Leslie. 1999. *Coins, Bodies, Games, and Gold: The Politics of Meaning in Archaic Greece.* Princeton University Press.

Laidlaw, James. 2002. For an anthropology of ethics and freedom. *Journal of the Royal Anthropological Institute (n.s.)* **8**: 311–332.

2007. The intension and extension of wellbeing: transformation in Jain understandings of non-violence. In *Culture and Well-being: Anthropological Approaches to Freedom and Political Ethics,* ed. Alberto Corsin Jimenez, pp. 156–179. London: Pluto Press.

Lambek, Michael. 2003. *The Weight of the Past: Living with History in Mahajanga, Madagascar.* London: Palgrave Macmillan.

2008. Value and virtue. *Anthropological Theory* **8**: 133–157.

Latour, Bruno. 1993. *We Have Never Been Modern.* Trans. Catherine Porter. Cambridge, Mass.: Harvard University Press.

Leach, Edmund. 1956. *Political Systems of Highland Burma: An Account of Kachin Social Structure.* Cambridge, Mass.: Harvard University Press.

1969. *Genesis as Myth, and Other Essays.* London: Cape.

Le Goff, Jacques. 1980. *Work, Time and Culture in the Middle Ages.* Trans. Arthur Goldhammer. University of Chicago Press.

Levinas, Emmanuel. 2003. *The Humanism of the Other.* Trans. Nidra Poller. Urbana: Illinois University Press.

Lévi-Strauss, Claude. 1950. Introduction à l'oeuvre de Marcel Mauss. In Marcel Mauss, *Sociologie et anthropologie*, pp. ix–lii. Paris: Presses Universitaires de France.

1966. *The Savage Mind.* Translation of *La Pensée sauvage.* University of Chicago Press.

1969. *The Elementary Structures of Kinship.* Ed. Rodney Needham. Trans. James Harle Bell, Richard von Sturmer and Rodney Needham. Boston: Beacon Press.

1973. Social structure. In *High Points in Anthropology*, ed. Paul Bohannon and Mark Glazer, pp. 373–409. New York: Alfred A. Knopf.

Lindstrom, Lamont. 1993. *Cargo Cult: Strange Stories of Desire from Melanesia and Beyond.* Honolulu: University of Hawai'i Press.

Lingis, Alphonso. 2000. *Dangerous Emotions.* Berkeley: University of California Press.

Littlewood, Roland. 1992. *Pathology and Identity: The Work of Mother Earth in Trinidad.* Cambridge University Press.

Løgstrup, Knut Ejler. 1997. *The Ethical Demand.* Notre Dame, Ind.: Notre Dame University Press.

Lomax, Bill. 1983. Ideology and illusion in the Portuguese revolution: the role of the left. In *In Search of Modern Portugal: The Revolution and its Consequences*, ed. Lawrence S. Graham and Douglas L. Wheeler, pp. 105–133. Madison: The University of Wisconsin Press.

Luhmann, Niklas. 1989. *Ecological Communication.* Trans. John Bednarz, Jr. University of Chicago Press.

1990. *Essays on Self-reference.* New York: Columbia University Press.

1996. The sociology of the moral and ethics. *International Sociology* 11:1: 27–36.

1998. *Observations on Modernity.* Trans. William Whobrey. Stanford University Press.

2000. *Art as a Social System.* Trans. Eva M. Knodt. Stanford University Press.

Lyotard, Jean-François. 1988. *The Inhuman.* Trans. Geoff Bennington and Rachel Bowlby. Stanford University Press.

Macbeath, Alexander. 1952. *Experiments in Living: A Study of the Nature and Foundation of Ethics or Morals in the Light of Recent Work in Social Anthropology.* London: Macmillan.

McGovern, Timothy. 2006. Narrating homophobia and the closet in Portugal: Guilherme de Melo and the emergence of queer canons. *Luso-Brazilian Quarterly* 43:1: 94–109.

References

MacIntyre, Alasdair. 1984. *After Virtue: A Study in Moral Theory.* Notre Dame, Ind.: University of Notre Dame Press.

Mackie, John L. 1977. *Ethics: Inventing Right and Wrong.* New York: Penguin.

Mahmood, Saba. 2005. *Politics of Piety: The Islamic Revival and the Feminist Subject.* Princeton University Press.

Malinowski, Bronislaw. 1922. *Argonauts of the Western Pacific: An Account of Native Enterprise and Adventure in the Archipelagoes of Western Melanesia.* New York: E. P. Dutton and Sons.

——— 1939. Group and individual in functional analysis. *American Journal of Sociology* **44**: 938–64.

Marcus, George E. 1992. *Lives in Trust: The Fortunes of Dynastic Families in Late Twentieth-century America.* With Peter Dobkin Hall. Boulder, Colo.: Westview Press.

——— 1998. *Ethnography through Thick and Thin.* Princeton University Press.

Marcus, George E., and Diana L. L. Hill. 2005. Appendix C: The Portuguese nobility today: A preliminary report. In George E. Marcus and Fernando Mascarenhas, *Ocasião: The Marquis and the Anthropologist, a Collaboration,* pp. 335–393. Walnut Creek, Calif.: Rowman and Littlefield.

Marcus, George E., and Fernando Mascarenhas. 2005. *Ocasião: The Marquis and the Anthropologist, a Collaboration.* Walnut Creek, Calif.: Rowman and Littlefield.

Marrou, Henri. 1956. *A History of Education in Antiquity.* Trans. George Lamb. New York: Sheed and Ward.

Maturana, Humberto, and Francisco Varela. 1980. *Autopoiesis and Cognition.* Dordrecht: D. Reidel.

——— 1992. *The Tree of Knowledge: The Biological Roots of Human Understanding.* Revised edition. Trans. Robert Paolucci. Boston: Shambhala.

Mintz, Sidney. 1960. *Worker in the Cane: A Puerto Rican Life History.* New Haven: Yale University Press.

Moeller, Hans-Georg. 2006. *Luhmann Explained: From Souls to Systems.* Chicago: Open Court.

Monteiro, Nuno Gonçalo. 1998. *O Crepúsculo dos Grandes: A Casa e O Patrimonio da Aristocracia em Portugal (1750–1832).* Lisbon: Imprensa Nacional Casa da Moeda.

——— 2000. Aristocratic succession in Portugal (from the sixteenth to the nineteenth centuries). In *Elites: Choice, Leadership, Succession,* ed. João de Pina-Cabral and Antónia Pedroso de Lima, pp. 133–148. Oxford: Berg.

Mooney, James. 1965 (1896). *The Ghost-Dance Religion and the Sioux Outbreak of 1890.* University of Chicago Press.

Moore, G. E. 1903. *Principia Ethica.* Cambridge University Press.

Morgan, Christopher. 1997. Waiting for God: Ecocosmological transformations among the Oksapmin (Saudan Province–PNG). In *Millennial Markers*, ed. Andrew Strathern and Pamela Stewart, pp. 59–86. Townsville, Aus.: JCU – Center for Pacific Studies.

Nadel, S. F. 1951. *The Foundations of Social Anthropology*. Glencoe, Ill.: The Free Press.

Neves, José Cassiano. 1995. *The Palace and Gardens of Fronteira: Seventeenth and Eighteenth Century Portuguese Style*. 3rd edition. Ed. Vera Mendes and Fernando Mascarenhas. Lisbon: Quetzal Editores.

Nietzsche, Frederick. 1954. *The Portable Nietzsche*. Trans. Walter Kaufmann. New York: Viking Press.

———. 1956. *The Birth of Tragedy and the Genealogy of Morals*. Trans. Francis Golffing. Garden City, N.Y.: Doubleday Anchor Books.

———. 2002. *Beyond Good and Evil: Prelude to a Philosophy of the Future*. Ed. Rolf-Peter Horstmann and Judith Norman. Trans. Judith Norman. Cambridge University Press.

———. 2003. *Thus Spake Zarathustra: A Book for All and None*. Trans. Thomas Wayne. New York: Algora.

Nissenbaum, Stephen. 1980. *Sex, Diet and Debility in Jacksonian America: Sylvester Graham and Health Reform*. Westport, Conn.: Greenwood Press.

Nussbaum, Martha. 1992. *Love's Knowledge: Essays on Philosophy and Literature*. Oxford University Press.

Ober, Josiah. 1989. *Mass and Elite in Democratic Athens: Rhetoric, Ideology, and the Power of the People*. Princeton University Press.

Pandian, Jacob. 1991. *Culture, Religion, and the Sacred Self*. Englewood Cliffs, N.J.: Prentice-Hall.

Pandolfo, Stefania. 1997. *Impasse of Angels: Scenes from a Moroccan Space of Memory*. University of Chicago Press.

Paxson, Heather. 2004. *Making Modern Mothers: Ethics and Family Planning in Urban Greece*. Berkeley: University of California Press.

Pedroso de Lima, Antónia. 2000. 'How did I become a leader in my family firm?' Assets for succession in contemporary Lisbon financial elites. In *Elites: Choice, Leadership, Succession*, ed. João de Pina-Cabral and Antónia Pedroso de Lima, pp. 31–51. Oxford: Berg.

Pessar, Patricia. 2004. *From Fanatics to Folk: Brazilian Millenarianism and Popular Culture*. Durham, N.C.: Duke University Press.

Petryna, Adriana. 2002. *Life Exposed: Biological Citizenship after Chernobyl*. Princeton University Press.

Philostratus. 2005a. *Apollonius of Tyana*. Books I–IV. Loeb Classical Library 16. Ed. and trans. Christopher P. Jones. Cambridge, Mass.: Harvard University Press.

References

2005b. *Apollonius of Tyana.* Loeb Classical Library 17. Books v–viii. Ed. and trans. Christopher P. Jones. Cambridge, Mass.: Harvard University Press.

Pina-Cabral, João de. 1986. *Sons of Adam, Daughters of Eve: The Peasant Worldview of the Alto Minho.* Oxford: Clarendon Press.

Pitt-Rivers, Julian. 1977. The law of hospitality. In *The Fate of Shechem; or, The Politics of Sex: Essays in the Anthropology of the Mediterranean,* pp. 94–110. Cambridge University Press.

Plato. 1961. Symposium. In *Plato: The Collected Dialogues,* ed. Edith Hamilton and Huntington Cairns, trans. Michael Joyce. Princeton University Press.

    1992. *Republic.* 2nd edition. Trans. G. M. A. Grube. Revised by C. D. C. Reeve. Indianapolis: Hackett.

Plutarch. 2001. *Plutarch's Lives.* Ed. Arthur Hugh Clough. Trans. John Dryden. Intro. James Atlas. New York: Random House.

Pohlenz, Max. 1966. *Freedom in Greek Life and Thought: The History of an Ideal.* Trans. Carl Lofmark. New York: Humanities Press.

Rabinow, Paul. 1975. *Symbolic Domination: Cultural Form and Historical Change in Morocco.* University of Chicago Press.

    1984. Introduction. In *The Foucault Reader,* ed. Paul Rabinow, pp. 3–29. New York: Pantheon Books.

    1989. *French Modern: Norms and Forms of the Social Environment.* Cambridge, Mass.: MIT Press.

    1994. A vital rationalist. In *A Vital Rationalist: Selected Writings from Georges Canguilhem,* ed. François Delaporte, trans. Arthur Goldhammer, pp. 11–22. New York: Zone Books.

    2008. *Marking Time: On the Anthropology of the Contemporary.* Princeton University Press.

Rabinow, Paul, George Marcus, James D. Faubion and Tobias Rees. 2008. *Designs for an Anthropology of the Contemporary.* Durham, N.C.: Duke University Press.

Rappaport, Roy. 1999. *Ritual and Religion in the Making of Humanity.* Cambridge University Press.

Rasch, William. 2000. *Niklas Luhmann's Modernity: The Paradoxes of Differentiation.* Stanford University Press.

Rawls, John. 1971. *A Theory of Justice.* Cambridge, Mass.: Harvard University Press.

Robb, Kevin. 1994. *Literacy and Paideia in Ancient Greece.* Oxford University Press.

Robbins, Joel. 2004. *Becoming Sinners: Christianity and Moral Torment in a Papua New Guinea Society.* Berkeley: University of California Press.

    2006. Afterword: On limits, ruptures, meaning, and meaninglessness. In *Christian Ritual and the Limits of Meaning,* ed. Matthew Engelke and Matthew Tomlinson, pp. 211–224. Oxford: Berghahn.

Rosaldo, Renato. 1980. *Ilongot Headhunting, 1883–1974: A Study in Society and History.* Stanford University Press.

Rose, Nikolas. 2006. *The Politics of Life Itself: Biomedicine, Power and Subjectivity in the Twenty-first Century.* Princeton University Press.

Rousseau, Jean-Jacques. 1953 (1781). *The Confessions.* Trans. J. M. Cohen. New York: Penguin.

Rumsey, Alan, and James F. Weiner, eds. 2000. *Emplaced Myth: Space, Narrative, and Knowledge in Aboriginal Australia and Papua New Guinea.* Honolulu: University of Hawai'i Press.

Santos, Boaventura de Sousa. 2002. Prospero and Caliban: colonialism, postcolonialism, and inter-identity. *Luso-Brazilian Review* **39**: 9–43.

Sapir, Edward. 1949. The emergence of a concept of personality in the study of cultures. In *Culture, Language, Society: Selected Essays*, ed. G. E. Mandelbaum, pp. 194–207. Berkeley: University of California Press.

Sartre, Jean-Paul. 1963. *Saint Genet: Actor and Martyr.* Trans. Bernard Frechtman. New York: George Brazziler.

1981. *The Family Idiot: Gustave Flaubert, 1821–1857.* Volume I. Trans. Carol Cosman. University of Chicago Press.

Scholem, Gershom. 1971. *The Messianic Idea in Judaism and Other Essays on Jewish Spirituality.* New York: Schocken.

Scott, Bernard. 2003. Second-order cybernetics: An historical introduction. Fourth International Conference of Sociocybernetics. Corfu, Greece. www.unizar.es/sociocybernetics/congresos/CORFU/papers/scot.html. Accessed November 2, 2010.

Searle, John. 1967. How to derive 'ought' from 'is.' In *Theories of Ethics*, ed. Philippa Foot, pp. 101–114. Oxford University Press.

Shostak, Marjorie. 1981. *Nisa, Portrait of the Life and Words of an !Kung Woman.* Cambridge, Mass.: Harvard University Press.

Situacão Portuguesa. 2002. International Lesbian and Gay Association–Portugal. http://ilga-portugal.oninet.pt/glbt.

Sloterdijk, Peter. 1987. *Critique of Cynical Reason.* Trans. Michael Eldred. Minneapolis: University of Minnesota Press.

Snodgrass, Anthony. 1980. *Archaic Greece: The Age of Experiment.* Berkeley: University of California Press.

Sohm, Rudolph. 1892. *Kirchenrecht.* Volume I. Leipzig: Duncker and Humblot.

Sokolow, Jayme. 1983. *Eros and Modernization: Sylvester Graham, Health Reform and the Origins of Victorian Sexuality in America.* London: Associated University Press.

Sourvino-Inwood, Christiane. 2003. *Tragedy and Greek Religion.* Lanham, Md.: Lexington.

References

Strathern, Marilyn. 1988. *The Gender of the Gift: Problems with Women and Problems with Society in Melanesia.* Berkeley: University of California Press.

——— 1992. *After Nature: English Kinship in the Late Twentieth Century.* Cambridge University Press.

——— 2004. *Partial Connections.* Updated edition. Walnut Creek, Calif.: AltaMira Press.

Tabor, James, and Eugene Gallagher. 1995. *Why Waco? Cults and the Battle for Religious Freedom in America.* Berkeley: University of California Press.

Tacitus, Cornelius. 2009. *Annals.* Ed. Bill Thayer. http://penelope.uchicago.edu/Thayer/E/Roman/Texts/Tacitus/home.html. Accessed November 2, 2010.

Tinhorão, José Ramos. 1994. *Fado: Dança do Brazil, Cantar de Lisboa.* Lisbon: Caminho.

Tocqueville, Alexis de. 2004 (1835–40). *Democracy in America.* Trans. Arthur Goldhammer. New York: Library of America.

Tomlinson, Matthew. 2006. Retheorizing mana: Bible translation and discourse of loss in Fiji. *Oceania* **76**: 150–172.

Touraine, Alain. 1971. *The Post-industrial Society.* Trans. L. F. X. Mayhew. New York: Random House.

Turner, Victor. 1969. *The Ritual Process: Structure and Anti-structure.* Ithaca: Cornell University Press.

Tyler, Stephen. 1998. Them others – voices without mirrors. *Paideuma* **44**: 31–50.

Vale de Almeida, Miguel. 1996. *The Hegemonic Male: Masculinity in a Portuguese Town.* Providence, R.I.: Berghahn.

——— 2004. *An Earth-colored Sea: "Race," Culture, and the Politics of Identity in the Postcolonial Portuguese-speaking World.* New York: Berghahn.

Varela, Francisco, Evan Thompson and Eleanor Rosch. 1993. *The Embodied Mind: Cognitive Science and Human Experience.* Cambridge, Mass.: MIT Press.

Vernant, Jean Paul. 1982. *The Origins of Greek Thought.* Translation of *Les origines de la pensée grecque.* Ithaca: Cornell University Press.

Vernon, Paul. 1998. *A History of the Portuguese Fado.* London: Ashgate.

Von Neumann, John, and Oskar Morgenstern. 2004 (1944). *Theory of Games and Economic Behavior.* 60th anniversary edition. Princeton University Press.

Wallace, Anthony. 1956. Revitalization movements. *American Anthropologist* **58**: 246–286.

Warner, Michael. 2002. *Publics and Counterpublics.* New York: Zone.

Weber, Max. 1946a. Class, status, party. In *From Max Weber: Essays in Sociology*, ed. Hans H. Gerth and C. Wright Mills, pp. 180–195. Oxford University Press.

——— 1946b. Religious rejections of the world and their directions. In *From Max Weber: Essays in Sociology*, ed. Hans H. Gerth and C. Wright Mills, pp. 323–359. Oxford University Press.

1946c. The social psychology of the world religions. In *From Max Weber: Essays in Sociology*, ed. Hans H. Gerth and C. Wright Mills, pp. 267–322. Oxford University Press.

1946d. The sociology of charismatic authority. In *From Max Weber: Essays in Sociology*, ed. Hans H. Gerth and C. Wright Mills, 245–252. Oxford University Press.

1958a. *The Protestant Ethic and the Spirit of Capitalism*. Trans. Talcott Parsons. New York: Charles Scribner's Sons.

1958b. *The Religion of India: The Sociology of Hinduism and Buddhism*. Ed. and trans. Hans H. Gerth and Don Martindale. New York: The Free Press.

Weiner, Annette. 1992. *Inalienable Possessions: The Paradox of Keeping-while-giving*. Berkeley: University of California Press.

Wheeler, Douglas L. 2002. *Historical Dictionary of Portugal*. 2nd edition. Lanham, Md.: The Scarecrow Press.

Whitehead, Neil L. 2003. *History and Historicities in Amazonia*. Lincoln: University of Nebraska Press.

Wilson, Bryan. 1973. *Magic and the Millennium: A Sociological Study of Religious Movements of Protest among Tribal and Third-world Peoples*. New York: Harper and Row.

Winkler, John. 1990. *The Constraints of Desire: The Anthropology of Sex and Gender in Ancient Greece*. New York: Routledge.

Wittgenstein, Ludwig. 1958 *Philosophical Investigations*. Trans. G. E. M. Anscombe. New York: Macmillan.

Wolfe, Cary. 1995. In search of post-humanist theory: The second-order cybernetics of Maturana and Varela. *Cultural Critique* **30**: 33–70.

Worsley, Peter. 1968. *The Trumpet Shall Sound: A Study of "Cargo Cults" in Melanesia*. 2nd edition. New York: Schocken.

Xenophon. 1923. *Memorabilia, Oeconomicus, Symposium, Apology*. Loeb Classical Library 168. Trans. E. C. Merchant and O. J. Todd. Cambridge, Mass.: Harvard University Press.

Zigon, Jarrett. 2007. Moral breakdown and the ethical demand: A theoretical framework for an anthropology of moralities. *Anthropological Theory* **7**: 131–150.

Index

Index

Aristotle
  and the anthropology of ethics, 12
  on barbarians, 76
  and biological analysis, 6
  and boulêsis, 34
  and gender roles, 30
  Luhmann on, 110
  and pedagogy, 55
  on the plurality of good, 100
  on politikê, 22–24
  on practice, 23, 102
Asad, Talal, 11, 127, 214
asceticism
  and askêsis, 45, 47
  Foucault on, 34
  genealogy of, 211
  vs. mysticism, 10
  and sôfrosunê, 35, 44
ascription and achievement of a
      subject position, 60, 142
  and the valence of moral
      ascription, 62
askêsis, 78, 116
  and asceticism, 45, 46
  conversation as, 265
  definition of, 4
  and the other, 75
  and taste, 137
  and technologies of the self, 47–49
assemblage, 119, 206, 253, 263
Athens, 41, 76, 77
  Adkins on, 41
  classical as inspiration for
      Foucault, 15
  fieldwork and classical, 17
Aurelius, Marcus, 51, 55
autopoiesis, 92, 93, 94
  of the anthropologist–
      anthropologized dyad, 207

  and arbitrariness, 107
  and communication, 106
  definition of, 5
  pedagogies of, 86
  and reflection, 48
  social, 92
  and voice, 258–259

barbarian, the, 75–76
Basto, José Maria Pinto, 123, 157,
    168, 195
Beck, Ulrich, 11
Bellah, Robert, 10, 99
Bemfica, 123, 181
Bharati, Agehananda, 96
bioethnographic, the. See life history
biopolitics, 224–225
Bli. See Isabel
Boltanski, Luc, 11
Bourdieu, Pierre, 45, 87–89, 93, 273
  on misrecognition, 125
  and taste, 137
bourgeoisie, 132
  and biopolitics, 225
  and the casa, 153
  and the New Denominations, 229
  vs. nobility, 132–133
Bragança dynasty, 129, 130, 131
Bragança, Duke of (Duarte), 129, 141
Branch Davidian church, 225, 238
  and Araucaria, 233
  and biopolitics, 224
  Solemn Assembly of, 233
Branch Davidian compound.
    See Mount Carmel
bravery, 72–73, 78, 80
Brown, Peter, 10
Buddhists, 98, 171

Index

embodiment, 21, 38, 43, 144
Emerson, Ralph Waldo, 226
emotions, 136–137
emplacement, 144, 150, 158
energeia, 29, 32
environment, 70
  and autopoietic systems, 5
  and communication, 58–59
  and history of biology, 5
  and open and closed systems, 6, 89
  and systemic irritants, 107
  and the themitical, 105
ethical complexity, 14, 17, 85, 141
  and the themitical, 115
ethical discourse, 9, 10, 69–70, 85
  classical, 27
  as intersubjective, 71
ethical domain, 36, 38, 276
  anthropological schematic
    of the, 115
  in anthropology, 11
  as an ecological domain, 74, 91
  four parameters of, 3
  limit of the, 37
  method of investigation of, 9
  open-system-theoretic approach
    to, 105
  praxis, poiesis, einai and the, 102
  timeliness of the study of the, 13
ethical exemplar, 51–53, 156
ethical judgment, 69
  and Araucaria, 242
  universalistic criteria of, 106
ethical justification, 69, 70, 83
  criteria of, 91
  and the programming of ethical
    discourse, 85
ethical moment, 85
ethical other, the, 53, 90

  as an addressee of justness, 71
  and care of the self, 75
  and charisma, 84
  chrism of, 87
  and ethical regard, 90
  and Jesus of Nazareth, 89
  the pedagogue as, 71
  transcendental, 90
ethical regard, 90, 103, 115
ethical substance, 38, 116
  carnal pleasures as, 39
  definition of, 3
  embodiment as, 42
  and liminality, 97
  and voice, 257
ethical training. *See* askêsis
ethical valuation, 91
  See also mode of ethical valuation
ethical value, 91, 95, 114
ethics
  and adaptation, 111
  and the aesthetics of existence, 51
  etymology, 21
  intersubjective, 56, 68, 91
êthos, 21, 38, 74, 83
  See also triangle of alêtheia, politeia,
    and êthos

Fadistas, 135
Fado, 134–136
farm, the. *See* Condado de Torre
Faubion, James D., 204
  as an anthropologist, 240
  and chrism, 237
  on gender conformity, 216
  in Greece, 246, 252
  on religious commitment, 216–217
  religious upbringing of, 215
  subjectivity of, 239

Index

Index

mode of subjectivation, 49–50, 52, 115
  See also subjectivation
  definition of, 4
  mode of determination of, 60,
    62, 115
  scope, structure and priority of,
    66, 116
  and the themitical, 104
Monteiro, Nuno Gonçalo, 128–131
Moore, G. E., 8
moral breakdown, 20
moral philosophy, 20, 56, 72
  and analytics, 44
  vs. anthropology of ethics, 8
  as directives of judgment and
    conduct, 8
morality, 21, 85
  ancient Greek, 110
  vs. ethics, 22
  and ethics in Luhmann, 108–111
  etymology, 22
Mormonism, 84, 99
Mount Carmel, 203, 204, 205,
    217–218
Ms. Roden. *See* Roden, Amo Paul
  Bishop

naked life, 172
naturalistic fallacy, 8
  and Alexander Macbeath, 11
  and criteria of ethical judgment, 106
  and ethical valuation, 91
  and the normativity of the
    autopoietic system, 114
  and the pedagogy of virtue, 56
New Denominations, 228, 229, 267
New or Higher Criticism.
  See hermeneutics
New Social Movements, 229

Nietzsche, Frederick, 10, 174, 187
  and asceticism, 44–45, 46–47
  Genealogy of Morals, 10, 44, 46, 84
nobility, 178
  and ascription vs. achievement,
    126–127
  and bourgeois respectability, 133, 190
  and bourgeoisie, 131
  and class and status, 128, 140
  European, 16, 131, 185
  Portuguese, 16, 128, 131, 152, 180
  and service, 179–180
  as subject position, 126
nobreza. *See* nobility, Portuguese
normativity, 24, 113, 114
  See also themitical, the
  and the chrism of the ethical
    other, 87
  and ethical value, 85
  of functional differentiation, 109
  Luhmann on, 108
  and the principles of autopoiesis, 114
  and social system adjustment, 105

objective possibilities, 120, 159, 209, 241
Ocasião, 16, 25, 26, 27, 28, 29, 30
oikonomikê, 23
oikoumenê, 75
Opportunity. *See* Ocasião
other, the. *See* ethical other, the

palace. *See* Fronteira
Palácio Fronteira. *See* Fronteira
parrhêsia, 78
  and the artist, 19
  and care of the self, 27
  definition, 14
  and the supression of voice, 259
Parsons, Talcott, 6, 94

Index

Index

Printed in Great Britain
by Amazon